Detroit: I Do Mind Dying
A Study in Urban Revolution

Detroit: I Do Mind Dying
A Study in Urban Revolution

Dan Georgakas and Marvin Surkin

Haymarket Books
Chicago, IL

First edition published by St. Martin's Press, New York City, NY, 1975.
Second edition published by South End Press, Cambridge, MA, 1998.

This edition published in 2012 by
Haymarket Books
PO Box 180165
Chicago, IL 60626
773-583-7884
info@haymarketbooks.org
www.haymarketbooks.org

ISBN: 978-1-60846-221-6

Trade distribution:
In the US, Consortium Book Sales and Distribution, www.cbsd.com
In Canada, Publishers Group Canada, www.pgcbooks.ca
In the UK, Turnaround Publisher Services, www.turnaround-uk.com
In Australia, Palgrave Macmillan, www.palgravemacmillan.com.au
All other countries, Publishers Group Worldwide, www.pgw.com

Cover design by Eric Ruder.
Cover photo of The DRUM Slate: (left to right) Ron March, President; Don Jackson,
Vice President; Charles Roberts, Trustee; Charles Williams, Trustee; Raymond Johnson,
Financial Secretary; Don Gaitor, Sergeant at Arms; Betty Griffith, Trustee; Grover
Douglas, Trustee; Lafayette Philyaw, Guide; and Gerald Wooten, Recording Secretary.

Published with the generous support of Lannan Foundation
and the Wallace Global Fund.

Printed in the United States by union labor.

Library of Congress cataloging-in-publication data is available.

10 9 8 7 6 5 4 3 2 1

Material quoted from the film *Finally Got the News* is printed by permission of the film's
present distributor: The Cinema Guild, 1967 Broadway, New York, NY 10019-5904. Excerpts
from the lyrics of "Please, Mr. Foreman" by Joe L. Carter reprinted by permission of Joe L.
Carter. Excerpt from "Father" by Abdeen Jabara from the book *Z: An Anthology of Revolutionary Poetry* (New York: Smyrna, 1968) reprinted by permission of the author. Excerpt
of the poem "Coming Home: Detroit, 1968" from the book *They Feed They Lion* by Philip
Levine, (New York: Atheneum, 1968, 1972) reprinted by permission of the publisher and the
author. Excerpt from "Booker T. and W.E.B." by Dudley Randall reprinted by permission of
the author. Excerpt from the untitled poem by C.G. Johnson from the book *Only Humans
With Songs to Sing* (New York: Smyrna/Ikon, 1969) reprinted by permission of the author.
"The Ceremony" and excerpt from "Freeway Series/1" by B. P. Flanigan reprinted by permission of the author. The authors are deeply grateful for a research grant from the Louis M.
Rabinowitz Foundation, Inc., which allowed them to begin the study that ultimately resulted
in this book.

To our fathers and mothers—

Xenophon   *Abraham Jack*
Sophia   *Betty*

Contents

Acknowledgments

We extend our thanks to the many Detroiters who had kindly fed us a steady stream of data, news clippings, and gossip for more than three decades. We also wish to thank Herb Boyd, Sheila Murphy Cockrel, Edna Watson, and Mike Hamlin for their invaluable contributions to this edition and their earlier assistance when we first projected such a book in the 1970s. And we especially want to thank Anthony Arnove of Haymarket Books who worked so dilligently and imaginatively to make the present edition possible.

Foreword

Manning Marable

Detroit: I Do Mind Dying presents the extraordinary history of the League of Revolutionary Black Workers. Although most histories of the Civil Rights and Black Power movements give greater attention to formations such as the Student Nonviolent Coordinating Committee (SNCC) and the Black Panther Party, the League was in many respects the most significant expression of black radical thought and activism in the 1960s. At a time when even reactionary politicians such as Richard Nixon were embracing the slogan "Black Power," the League represented a militant black perspective calling for the fundamental socialist transformation of U.S. society. The League took the impetus for Black Power and translated it into a fighting program focusing on industrial workers.

The League itself was a product of the growing radicalization of the Black Freedom Movement. With the achievement of the destruction of legal segregation and the passage of the Voting Rights Act in 1965, the focus of the black struggle shifted from the largely rural South to the urban ghettos of the Northeast, Midwest, and West Coast. Greater emphasis was placed on issues such as economic justice and police brutality. Martin Luther King, Jr., for example, increasingly called for more radical economic measures and was assassinated in Memphis during his involvement in a strike of black sanitation workers. Several months after King's death, King lieutenants Andrew Young, Ralph Abernathy, and Hosea Williams were arrested for leading a protest of black sanitation workers in Atlanta.

By 1968, more than 2.5 million African Americans belonged to the AFL-CIO. Yet the vast majority of black workers were marginalized and alienated from labor's predominantly white conservative leadership. In 1967, black militant workers at Ford Motor Company's automobile plant in Mahwah, New Jersey, initiated the United Black Brothers. In 1968, African-American steelworkers in Maryland established the Shipyard Workers for Job Equality to oppose the discriminatory policies and practices of both their union and management. Similar black workers' groups, both inside and outside trade unions, began to develop throughout the country. The more moderate liberal to progressive tendency of this upsurge of black workers was expressed organizationally in 1972 with the establishment of the Coalition of Black Trade Unionists.

A much more radical current of black working-class activism developed in Detroit. Only weeks following King's assassination, black workers at the Detroit Dodge Main plant of Chrysler Corporation staged a wildcat strike, protesting oppressive working conditions they called "niggermation." The most militant workers established DRUM, the Dodge Revolutionary Union Movement. DRUM soon inspired the initiation of other independent black workers' groups in metro Detroit, such as FRUM, at Ford's massive River Rouge plant, and ELRUM, at Chrysler's Eldon Avenue Gear and Axle plant. Other RUMs were developed in other cities, from the steel-mills of Birmingham to the automobile plants of Fremont, California, and Baltimore, Maryland. The Detroit-based RUMs coalesced in the League of Revolutionary Black Workers, which espoused a Marxian analysis of black working people's conditions, calling for a socialist revolution against the oppression of corporate capitalism.

The League possessed an incredibly talented and dedicated core of activists, each of whom brought their own experiences and perspectives into the process of building this movement: General Baker, Mike Hamlin, Kenneth Cockrel, Chuck Wooten, Luke Tripp, John Williams, and John Watson. James Forman, a veteran SNCC organizer, joined the League and developed a reparations project that funneled resources from religious groups into black radical formations. However, tensions within the League over the appropriate strategies for consolidating and expanding black workers' movements by 1970 culminated in a split. A number of key leaders aligned with Forman, including Cockrel and Hamlin, supported the establishment of the Black Workers Congress, which continued to promote the development of RUM-like workers' groups, especially among radicalized ethnic minorities. Other leaders opposed to this move, such as Baker, Tripp, and Wooten, maintained the League and focused mostly on local struggles. As the revolutionary upheavals inside black America began to subside, the political space for both the League and the Black Workers Congress declined, as well.

Dan Georgakas and Marvin Surkin have documented the oppressive social conditions leading to the formation of DRUM, and the subsequent rise and disintegration of the League. *Detroit: I Do Mind Dying* is a study in urban rebellion. Its power as a text of political economy and historical sociology is only surpassed by its passionate commitment to the struggles which were waged by its central actors. That struggle for justice still continues, and this wonderful book will inspire new generations to join that fight.

Manning Marable
Director
Institute for Research in African-American Studies
Columbia University

Preface to the Second Edition

When the opportunity arose to publish a second edition of *Detroit: I Do Mind Dying*, our immediate reaction was that we did not wish to revise the text beyond typographical and technical errors. This stemmed from our belief that the tenor of the book is expressive of its era. Tampering with its words and tempo would detract significantly from what it has to say about those times that might be relevant for these times. Providing biographical updates and an account of the city's history in new chapters was relevant, but much of that work has already been done by others. We particularly recommend Bob Mast's *Detroit Lives*, published in 1994, whose scores of oral histories include numerous individuals who figure both prominently and marginally in our own book.

The new chapters we have added fulfill a different mandate. They seek to reanimate the past to better comprehend the present. For all its faults, we believe the League of Revolutionary Black Workers was a victory in the long march Americans have made toward economic and social justice. Although not quite a full dress rehearsal for the struggles now taking shape, the League experience offers precious insights regarding pitfalls to avoid, strategies to deploy, and risks that must indeed be taken. To assist us in examining the League's legacy, especially its electoral, gender, and workplace history, we have called on four Detroiters: Sheila Murphy Cockrel, Edna Ewell Watson, Michael Hamlin, and Herb Boyd.

As readers of this book will discover in the final chapter, Sheila Murphy Cockrel was raised in an anarcho-Catholic environment and has never ceased being a political activist. Following the untimely death of her husband, Ken Cockrel, she worked for the Coleman Young administration before being elected to the Detroit Common Council, the city's legislative body. In her essay, Sheila Murphy Cockrel focuses on electoral politics.

Edna Ewell Watson was a militant student and medical activist before the foundation of the League, and during the height of the League, she was one of the many women who worked largely behind the scenes and outside the media limelight. She reflects on the sexual issues that troubled the movements of the 1960s. The form of her essay, as well as its content, makes real the observation championed by the feminist movement that the personal is political and the political is personal.

Michael Hamlin, more than any other League leader, was completely comfortable with all aspects of the League's constituency: its manufacturing base, its white allies, and its community and intellectual initiatives. For more than 30 years, he has been engaged in labor education, health and safety issues, and conflict resolution. Heartened by the new currents in the AFL-CIO, Hamlin offers advice to union leaders and black workers on how to make the new century one to celebrate rather than fear.

Herb Boyd was a young man during the heyday of the League. Like many other ambitious Detroiters, he eventually left the city to pursue a career in New York. He has written extensively in the popular press, most notably in the *Amsterdam News,* is author of *African History for Beginners,* and is co-editor with Robert Allen of *Brother Man.* He relates the Detroit experience to the struggles he sees developing in contemporary America.

Our own contribution, "Thirty Years Later," considers the ways the League foresaw many of the problems now troubling Americans at a time when those problems were still in embryonic form. The League's solutions were also embryonic. Now, our collective task is to hone them into mature forms which shatter the illusion of inevitable gender, ethnic, and generational conflict. Our times demand bold vision and a leadership brave enough to make real our best aspirations. Working America needs to shed a casino mentality in which an individual presumes to beat the odds that does in his or her neighbors. Instead, we need to join together to guarantee jobs, genuine equality of opportunity, and healthy work and living environments. Rather than squabble over allocation of resources, we need to declare that universal quality education and quality health care are basic human rights. If that perspective leads some to suggest we wish to fan the flames of discontent, we plead guilty.

Preface to the Third Edition

This new edition of *Detroit: I Do Mind Dying* comes out in an era when the problems facing Detroit in the late 1960s now have troubling national parallels. When we chose the title for our book, we did not intend to be prophetic. We did not foresee that in the next five decades the city's population would decline from nearly two million at its height in the 1970s to 713,000 in 2012, with no stabilization in sight.

We did not contemplate that what had been one of America's five largest cities, once touted as the Paris of the Midwest, would become so dilapidated that its ruins would be compared to those of ancient Pompeii. We certainly did not imagine that mighty General Motors, whose president Charles Erwin Wilson boasted in 1953 that for years he had thought that "what was good for the country was good for General Motors and vice versa" would go bankrupt and be saved from extinction only by a taxpayer bailout. Nor did we foresee that Chrysler, the major employer in Detroit, would not only go bankrupt but would be bought by a German rival and then resold to Fiat of Italy.

What we did see was that the famed arsenal of democracy was in crisis. The automobile industry that had generated the city's prosperity had already decided to ship out as many jobs as possible, to use automation as a means of lowering the quality of its products, and to worsen the working conditions, pay, and benefits of ever-fewer workers. We saw the cracks in the city's infrastructure and in its vibrant school system. We saw how the city's growing African American community faced patterns of discrimination that were less blatant but as unjust as those in the segregated South.

The Great Rebellion of 1967, which was not a riot against whites but against the local power structure, was a wake-up call for the establishment. The power elite, however, responded with crisis management techniques rather than viable change. Urban decay and inner city rot would somehow be remedied by luxurious housing, advancing like stealth aircraft from the riverside. A state-of-the-art hotel and office complex dubbed the Renaissance Center and an expanded sports arena would supposedly attract conventions and make the city a tourist destination. Missing from the agenda were serious efforts to address the problems in city services and civic infrastructure. More African Americans would become visible in the circles of established power, but there was not even a whisper of bringing the city new enterprises. Auto executives would continue to set the political agenda.

The most powerful progressive force in the city since the 1930s had been the United Auto Workers (UAW). Always militant, sometimes visionary, the union's victories had resulted in the establishment of a decent standard of living for workers in the auto industry and that industry's multitude of related institutions. As the 1960s progressed, however, the UAW became increasingly defensive, more concerned about protecting existing and retired members than in organizing the new auto factories being constructed in states with rigid anti-union policies (often coded in right-to-work legislation). The UAW advocated civil rights in its public statements, but as we demonstrate in the following pages, that commitment was shallow within the UAW's own structure. Control of conditions on the shop floor waned and radical demands such as forty hours' pay for thirty hours' work were squelched as fantasies. As a consequence of these policies, UAW membership has since fallen to 373,000 in 2012 after peaking at 1.5 million in 1970s. Moreover, many of its present members are not auto workers, but work in non-manufacturing jobs such as college adjunct lecturers. Some of this membership decline must be attributed to the decline in auto production and automation, but it is also due to the fact that the UAW has been unable to organize even one of the many new foreign-owned factories that now produce half of the cars in America. UAW officials offer no vision for the future beyond preserving as much as possible of what is already in hand.

The long-term consequence of this complex of factors is visible in twenty-first-century Detroit. The city scores very low on positive statistics such as property values, median income, and educational achievement scores, and it scores very high in negative civic statistics such as those related to crime. The massive housing bubble that burst in 2008 and engulfed the entire nation reduced Detroit housing values to new lows. Long before that collapse, however, high-stakes properties such as the Renaissance Center proved to be financial disasters. The Center was not profitable as a hotel or as a convention center; rather than creating new jobs, its office space mainly served to scoop up existing downtown jobs like a vacuum cleaner. The downtown sports complex also failed to revitalize the center. Then came gambling casinos and a new baseball stadium that also failed to be the elusive revitalization formula for a new Detroit. Suburbanites might indeed come into the city for a special event, but they rarely ventured beyond the confines of the gambling or sports venues.

What became an overwhelmingly black city elected a series of black mayors and representatives, mostly allied with the old establishment. Many soon became infamous and a number were criminally prosecuted for their pork-barrel corruption. Others, although elected as reformers, thought the way forward was to continue to cut social services, weaken the public sector unions, and raise nuisance taxes. With no new strategies to establish a viable economy, stagnation and decline came to dominate the Detroit horizon.

Despite adversity, numerous civic activists are indefatigable in their commitment to the city and their visions of change and progress. Some new artistic hubs have revived a few neighborhoods, and a vibrant urban gardening movement has taken hold. Nonetheless, Detroit is moribund and its elected government faces suspension in favor of a state-appointed administrator. It is no wonder that Detroit has experienced a level of massive depopulation and devastations unknown in the modern world outside of war zones.

If the perspectives of redevelopment and renewal in Detroit had been different, the energy unleashed by the Great Rebellion of 1967 could have resulted in a far different Detroit than the one that has evolved. The most promising vision for a post-Rebellion Detroit was offered by the League of Revolutionary Black Workers. In the following pages, we chronicle the rise and fall of that movement. Our objective in publishing a new edition of our book is not simply to retain a portrait of another time and political space, but to highlight the extraordinary foresight and relevance of the League's analysis to the current morass in American political and economic life. Except for correcting spelling, grammar, and one misquote, we have not made any changes in the text.

The radical consciousness the League projected was not a product of the Great Rebellion, as some scholars have believed. The individuals involved were active well before the Great Rebellion. They were well versed in African American history; many of them had studied Marx and other revolutionary thinkers. Education for them, however, did not mean mere mastery of facts and theory; it meant forging a new mass consciousness and learning how to set the agenda for political discourse.

The League radicals argued that the priority for Detroit auto workers was how to better working conditions, wages, and benefits, not to settle for fighting against givebacks or commiserating with corporations when their profits were temporarily down. The corporations had to give back, not the workers. The workers needed to control automation rather than be controlled by it. Automation should serve to increase the quality of cars, not profit margins. Winning support for such a perspective required extensive public education. We write at length on how the League struggled to accomplish that intellectual agenda and how it tried to set the rhetoric for discussions of race, class, finance, housing, education, and health.

The organizational focus of the League was the African American worker. But the leadership was not narrowly nationalist or separatist; it understood that fundamental change went beyond race issues. The League understood that interest rates and regulation of commerce were determined by government, but unlike entrepreneurs and bankers, the League thought economic planning should be directed to benefit the average American rather than executives, financiers, and the economic elite. Perhaps the League's most brilliant demonstration of how public resources could be used immediately was its transformation of Wayne State University's daily student newspaper from a socially marginal student organ into a dynamic community voice seeking to influence public policy. The League and its allies gained control of the paper by following the rules of the system. Moreover, their editorial work hewed to the spirit of the First Amendment's guarantee of the rights of freedom of speech, discourse, and assembly.

Unlike the movement identified with Martin Luther King Jr., the League was secular and urban. Unlike the urban movement identified with Malcolm X, the League initiated direct action to achieve racial equality whenever it thought the conditions were favorable. Unlike the Black Panthers who based themselves on youth and spoke repeatedly of white guilt, the League focused on workers and spoke repeatedly of capitalist guilt. In *Finally Got the News*, a film produced by the League, John Watson, one of the League's founders stated a major organizational premise: workers, unlike students or street people, had the power to shut down society in a general strike. Students and street people were not to be ignored, but they were not structurally situated to be the engine of social change.

In calling for direct action, the League did not mean symbolic events, but actions at factories and in the community where workers and activists had their greatest power. The League was not afraid to confront the police, but its leader thought it foolish to provoke them and did not want to be forced into spending its resources on perpetual legal defense efforts. Conventional democratic means were employed to gain influence in the UAW, but the League refused to desist when union leaders resorted to various forms of intimidation and force to thwart their efforts. The League was prepared to go to court to advance or defend its initiatives, but it understood that the court system, like the mass media, was not especially favorable terrain due to the legal system's confluence with established power. What weight elections and media should carry in the League's efforts remained problematic, and eventually created fatal disagreements about just how much energy should go into electoral efforts and creating media versus point-of-production and direct community organizing. What we wish to underscore here is that the objective was to create a mass consciousness for social change that was not bound by race or gender. Socialism would not come about in a spectacular leap forward, but as a demand by rank-and-file Americans who had, as one of the League organizers chanted, "Finally got the news about how your dues are being used."

The crisis that Detroit confronted in the 1960s is now painfully evident on a national scale. The racial temperament of America is certainly not what it was four decades ago. A considerable number of African Americans now have opportunities that were denied their parents and grandparents. African American political power is a reality, and we have seen the election of an African American as president of the United States. Nonetheless, the income gap with other ethnic groups, the average life span, the poverty rate, the incarceration rate, and other indicators of well-being for African Americans are now no better—and often worse—than they were forty years ago.

More generally, all working Americans now face a future in which their standard of living is in gradual but steady decline. Countless commentaries have forecast the death of the American middle class. Mass media speak openly about a permanent army of the unemployed, even though they do not use that term. The American public school system, once the pride of the nation, crumbles while the power elite would have the public believe that the solution is cutting the pay and number of teachers and possibly privatizing education altogether. The money required to maintain a thousand overseas military bases is always available, but funds are always lacking to address the decaying American infrastructure, whose deterioration is only fleetingly visible when a bridge collapses or faulty tracks derail trains that are at least two generations behind global standards. The costs of health care and higher education skyrocket, and the proposed solution of the elites is to strengthen the hand of the insurance companies and drug companies that have created the current malaise. National, state, and civic budgets are to be balanced by pushing back the retirement age, cutting benefits, ignoring environmental degradation, and weakening safety standards. Corporate leaders demand that all restraints on their behavior be dropped and their taxes lowered even as they build their new factories overseas and take an ever-increasing share of the national wealth.

As we observed in the preface to the second edition of this book, surely the time has come to say, as the League said: Enough! America, we don't mind working, but we do mind dying.

Dan Georgakas

Marvin Surkin

Introduction to the First Edition

Detroit is the fifth-largest city in the United States, the major industrial center of the nation's heartland, the headquarters of the automobile industry, which directly or indirectly employs one out of every six Americans. In 1972, Lawrence M. Carino, chair of the Greater Detroit Chamber of Commerce, made the observation that "Detroit is *the* city of problems. If they exist, we've probably got them. We may not have them exclusively, that's for sure. But we probably had them first. . . . The city has become a living laboratory for the most comprehensive study possible of the American urban condition." When Detroit burned in July 1967, in the most widespread and costly of hundreds of urban rebellions throughout the United States, the men who rule America knew they had to take immediate action to end the general crisis. In Detroit, they formed a self-appointed blue ribbon New Detroit Committee. This organization of the city's ruling elite intended to put an end to urban unrest with a vast building program designed to replace inner-city squalor with the sleek new architecture of modern office buildings, banks, condominiums, hotels, convention attractions, and a host of related enterprises. The program was meant to stimulate economic development, create jobs, and provide social stability and confidence for a troubled city.

The New Detroit Committee was not operating in a social vacuum. Already embodied within the process of destructive violence represented by the Great Rebellion of July 1967 was a fresh surge of positive revolutionary energy. An attempt to organize the power of the Great

Rebellion into a political force capable of restructuring American society began as soon as minimal order had been restored by the National Guard and police. Black-owned newspapers and organizations of black industrial workers began to present a series of programs and revolutionary visions in sharp contrast to the ideas put forward by the New Detroit Committee. The revolutionaries combined the experience of the black liberation struggle with the radical tradition within the labor movement to speak of a society in which the interests of workers and their families would become the new foundation of all social organization. Even as the New Detroit Committee began to put its plans into action, black workers unleashed a social movement of their own which soon forced a series of organizational, ideological, cultural, political, and economic confrontations with established wealth and power.

The New Detroit Committee represented forces that were the social antithesis of the movement led by black revolutionaries. Its personnel was headed by Henry Ford II, chairman of the Ford Motor Company; James Roche, chairman of the General Motors Corporation; Lynn Townsend, chairman of Chrysler Corporation; Walker Cisler, chairman of Detroit Edison (Detroit's power and light utility); Joseph L. Hudson, chairman of the J.L. Hudson Company (Detroit's largest department store chain); Stanley J. Winkelman, president of Winkelman Stores, Inc. (another major retail chain); William G. McClintock, vice-president of the National Bank of Detroit; William M. Day, vice-president of Michigan Bell; and Ralph McElvenny, president of Michigan Consolidated Gas Company. Other members included Max Fisher, chairman of Marathon Oil and chairman of the United Foundation (Detroit's united charities fund); Dr. William Keast, president of Wayne State University; Dr. Norman Drachler, a retired superintendent of the Detroit Public Schools; Walter Reuther, president of the United Auto Workers; Robert Holmes, vice-president of the Teamsters union; and a number of local political figures. The committee was organized in such a way that it was able to bypass openly the elected government and to finance its projects directly from corporate and foundation coffers. More than $50 million was immediately earmarked by some 50 Detroit firms for a massive waterfront rebuilding plan which led to the formation of a separate organization called Detroit Renaissance. $200 million in short-term mortgage loans were arranged for Detroit Renaissance by a group of 38 banks led by the National

Bank of Detroit. This loan was designed to have a second phase beginning in 1977 when the financing would shift to the Ford Motor Credit Company and four insurance companies (Aetna Life and Casualty, Equitable Life Assurance Society of the United States, John Hancock Mutual Life Insurance Co., and Travelers Insurance Co.), An enthusiastic Governor Milliken described Detroit Renaissance as "a monument to the vision of a few men and the faith of many."

The rebuilding of the center of Detroit proposed by the New Detroit Committee would mean that eventually the blacks, Appalachians, and students who inhabited the area between the riverfront commercial center and the Wayne State University area would be removed to make room for a revitalized core city repopulated by middle- and upper-class representatives of the city's various racial and ethnic groups. Stopgap anti-poverty programs were to be used as a short-term solution to street violence as a new class of black politicians and businessmen were given a wider role in running the city. These individuals would take places in corporate boardrooms, on union executive boards, and in whatever elective offices their "bloc" vote could carry them to. The police, desegregated and strengthened, were to be a front-line force against "extremists of the Right and Left" who sought to upset the new dynamism.

The New Detroit Committee, for all its financial and political clout, represented little more than a recycling of pre-1967 Detroit. It sought to deal with the basic contradictions and problems which had produced the Great Rebellion with what amounted to a showcase public relations program. In the first six years of the New Detroit Committee's existence, the quality of life in the city deteriorated to a new low. The industrial workers who made up more than 35 percent of the population were the hardest hit. They found that the New Detroit meant working longer and faster and paying higher taxes in exchange for diminishing city services and for wage gains more than outpaced by inflation. "Runaway" factories, new managerial demands, and a declining automotive industry made the very existence of many of their jobs a real issue. Union leaders, humiliated time and again by corporate managers pursuing higher productivity and higher profits, found themselves fighting their own membership as vigorously and as often as they fought the company. Black workers continued to hold the most arduous, dangerous, and unhealthy jobs. Their moves toward job improvement, union office, and shop floor reform were resisted by the company, the union, and even their fellow workers. The black population also bore much of the burden of curtailed public services, especially the nearly nonexistent public transit and a school system on the verge of bankruptcy. Thousands of homes in the city proper were deserted as a result of corruption in public and private lending institutions, making a mockery of the multimillion dollar towers of Detroit Renaissance. The grievances of "invisible" minorities such as white Appalachians and the city's growing Arab population remained largely unheard and unresolved. Established ethnic groups such as the Polish Americans and Italian Americans worried increasingly about jobs, property values, and personal safety. The police department resisted desegregation of its ranks, created secret elite units, and organized to win direct political power in city government. The organized state violence and the unorganized street violence of 1967 became more and more institutionalized. Motor City became Murder City, leading the nation and perhaps the world in homicides and crimes of violence. In 1973, the number of homicide victims in Detroit was triple the death toll on all sides in the civil disturbances that took place in Northern Ireland during the same year. Head-in-the-sand reformers talked glibly of gun control while literally millions of guns were sold to Detroiters of every race and class who sought protection from social chaos.

In the pages that follow, we have attempted to relate the history of the Detroit struggle from 1967-1974, taking the activities of urban revolutionaries as our point of departure. We begin with a small core of black revolutionaries who began their political work in this period by publishing a newspaper and organizing in the factories and then led a series of activities which inspired other insurgent forces within the city and beyond. More than anywhere else in the United States, the movement led by black workers defined its goal in terms of real power—the power to control the economy, which meant trying to control the shop floor at the point of production. The Detroit revolutionaries did not get sidetracked into a narrow struggle against the police per se or with one aspect of power such as control of education. The movement attempted to integrate within itself all the dissident threads of the rebellious 1960s in order to create a network of insurgent power comparable to the network of established power. This movement, clearly in conflict with the wealth, power, and interests represented by the New Detroit Committee, generated an amazing sequence of separate but interlocked confrontations in the factories, in the polling booths, in the courts, in the streets, in the media, in the schools, and in the union halls.

What clearly differentiated the Detroit experience from other major social movements of the 1960s and early 1970s was its thoroughly working-class character. We have tried to ascertain exactly what this movement by working people meant in terms of the mass culture and the quality of life found in the factories, schools, and neighborhoods of the city of Detroit. Without minimizing the enormous tensions within the working class, tensions between blacks and whites, between men and women, and between competing ideologies and strategies, we have attempted to determine, from primary sources, what those involved in the struggle accomplished and what they had to say about their ultimate goals. At various moments in this effort by working people to gain control of their own lives, different individuals and organizations became more important than others. Our purpose has been to follow the motion of the class which supported them rather than to trace particular destinies or to speculate on the possible future importance of specific individuals, ideologies, or organizations.

We have used original interview material extensively. Most of these interviews were conducted in the summer of 1972. All of them were recorded on tape, and the majority were recorded in the privacy of the homes of the people being interviewed. Usually, the person interviewed responded at length to a few introductory questions and then answered in more detail specific questions arising from the general discussion. We also had access to the personal papers of several important participants and to numerous plant bulletins, organizational memos, newspapers, and similar documents. In the pages which follow, when reproducing those materials, we have not tampered with the original in any way; this means that some typographical errors, unusual spellings, and grammatical mistakes have been reproduced. We believe this approach is necessary to preserve the unique flavor and tone of the language. Likewise, when quoting speeches, we have retained slang expressions and awkward constructions in the original without using brackets and other devices to make the speech patterns conform to more standard conventions.

Our account concludes on what may seem to be a pessimistic note. That is not our intent and our conclusion is not a pessimistic one. Nothing fundamental has changed in Detroit because the forces that controlled the city prior to 1967 still control the city and the nation. The strategies and tactics that guided their actions prior to 1967 remain more or less unaltered. Neither the ruling elite nor the workers have been able to revive the Motor City. But hundreds of thousands of people have begun to question basic assumptions about the organization and purpose of their lives and about the institutions that control them. They have begun to accumulate valuable skills and experiences necessary to challenge those institutions and to create substitute or parallel structures of power.

Increasingly, groups of white workers have begun to voice the complaints and pursue the objectives that black workers began to voice and pursue in the late 1960s. Ideas once limited to Marxists, youth counter-culturalists, and women's liberation groups can now be found on the shop floor in myriad demands and actions for a humane way of life. The capitalist work ethic has been discredited. Men and women no longer wish to spend 40 to 50 years performing dull, monotonous, and uncreative work. They see that the productive system which deforms their lives for a profit of which they have less and less of a share is also one that destroys the air they breathe, wastes the natural resources of the planet, and literally injures or disables one out of ten workers each year. Their rebellion is expressed in extraordinary absenteeism, particularly on Mondays and Fridays, in chronic lateness, in the open use of drugs, in poor workmanship, in repeated demands for earlier retirement, in sabotage, and in the wildcat strike. At the same time, many members of the working class, especially young whites unable to find well-paying jobs, have found a solution to their employment woes by volunteering for the police and armed forces. White workers who can accept racial cooperation on the shop floor often remain hostile to similar cooperation in matters of housing, schooling, health care, and a whole range of social issues. Whether internal divisions will thwart the development of united class action is a question that remains to be answered.

The decade of the 1960s with its assassinations, protests, riots, war, and violence has given birth to a decade that is deceptively quiet on the surface, while the forces of change move even more certainly toward the taproots of American society. Popular doubt about the ability of the dominant class to govern effectively has become increasingly widespread in the wake of the energy crisis, corruption in the highest elective office, and malicious corporate intrigues. The system no longer produces what was once touted as the "highest standard of living on earth." The people of the city of Detroit have been dealing with the crisis of power in a dramatic fashion, sometimes emphasizing race and sometimes emphasizing class, sometimes seized by fear and sometimes with vision. This book is about their experiences, a history of the contemporary United States in microcosm, an exemplary case of a social condition and conflicting social visions which stretch from one end of America to the other.

James Johnson:
A Prologue

On July 15, 1970, one of those midsummer days when the most important thing in town is the baseball game, a black auto worker named James Johnson entered the Eldon Avenue Gear and Axle plant of Chrysler Corporation with an M-1 carbine hidden in the pant leg of his overalls. The factory had been the scene of a series of bitter wildcat strikes for most of the year, and during a two-week period one female and one male worker had been killed from on-the-job accidents. The noise, oil pools, and defective machinery that characterized the plant were all around Johnson when he spotted one of the foremen who had been involved in his dismissal earlier that day. He took out his carbine, and before he was finished shooting, one black foreman, one white foreman, and one white job setter lay dead on the factory floor.

Few of the Eldon workers knew much about James Johnson. He was not identified with the militants of the Eldon Avenue Revolutionary Union Movement (ELRUM), the Wildcat group, or the Safety Committee. James Johnson didn't even go to union meetings. He was one of those thousands of anonymous workers who spoke little and laughed less. He did not drink in the bars near the factory, and he was not a ladies' man. James Johnson was a Bible reader, and his biggest source of pride was the small house he was buying for himself and his sister.

Some days later, word got around the factory that Johnson's attorney would be Kenneth Cockrel. A few of the workers knew that Cockrel was on the seven-man Executive Committee of the League of Revolutionary Black Workers; more had heard of him because of the

New Bethel case, in which he had successfully defended members of the Republic of New Africa accused of shooting two policemen. Sympathy for James Johnson grew at the plant when workers learned that he had received a suspension the morning of the shooting after he had refused to participate in a work speed-up. Later, Eldon workers learned of other disputes involving lost pay and lost vacation time in which Johnson had been treated unfairly.

A few days after the shooting, ELRUM published a leaflet with the headline "Hail James Johnson." The leaflet gave a brief biography of Johnson and went into detail about the various incidents leading to the fatal events of July 15. ELRUM blamed the deaths squarely on working conditions at Chrysler and on Johnson's lifetime experience as a victim of racism. ELRUM argued that Chrysler had pulled the trigger and the United Auto Workers (UAW) was an accessory after the fact. Similar leaflets favorable to Johnson appeared as far away as the General Motors plant in Fremont, California, and the Ford plant at Mahwah, New Jersey.

The judge for the James Johnson murder trial was Robert Colombo, formerly an attorney for the Detroit Police Officers Association. The preceding year, Ken Cockrel, assisted by Justin Ravitz, one of his law partners, had challenged the jury selection which had resulted in an all-white jury for the New Bethel case. Cockrel and Ravitz had argued that, given that the New Bethel case involved racial violence in a city with a black majority, the defendants, who were all black, were being denied a jury of their peers as guaranteed in the constitution. In the Johnson case, Cockrel, again assisted by Ravitz, argued that the criteria for a jury of Johnson's peers involved class as well as color. The final jury was just what Cockrel wanted. It was sexually and racially integrated. Ten of the 12 jurors had direct work experience in the city of Detroit, two were auto workers themselves, and three were married to auto workers. The defense's presentation was complex. Johnson's relatives and friends came from Mississippi to testify about his boyhood in one of the backwater regions of America. They told all the familiar Southland horror tales. These included an account of how a five-year-old James Johnson had seen the dismembered body of his cousin on a highway following a lynching. The jury learned that Johnson had enlisted in the Army, only to be discharged for psychological problems. They learned the details of a work history in which an inferior education and racism led from one poor job to another in a pattern characterized by emotional outbursts and threats from both Johnson and various employers. They learned, too, that Johnson had finally found a steady job at Eldon, where he had worked for three years, supporting members of his family as well as himself. His attorneys presented evidence that Eldon was one of the most dangerous plants in the United States and that the UAW was unable or unwilling to protect workers on the shop floor. As a climax to the defense, Cockrel took the entire jury to the scene of the crime so they could judge conditions for themselves.

When the jury found James Johnson not responsible for his acts, an irate Judge Colombo called a press conference at which he released a letter he was sending to the Ionia State Hospital. The letter recommended most vehemently that Johnson be kept in custody for the rest of his natural life. Judge Colombo stated that it was his opinion that if Johnson were ever released he would kill again.

On November 2, 1972, Justin Ravitz was elected to a ten-year term as a judge of Recorder's Court, Detroit's criminal court, thus becoming a colleague of Judge Colombo. His election indicated popular support for the legal principles advanced in the New Bethel case, the Johnson case, and other well-publicized judicial battles involving Cockrel and Ravitz.

On May 12, 1973, James Johnson, represented by Ron Glotta, a white lawyer who was a member of the radical Motor City Labor League, was awarded workman's compensation for the injuries done to him by Chrysler. The courts ordered Chrysler to pay Johnson at the rate of $75 a week, retroactive to the day of the killing.

At the end of 1970, the year in which James Johnson had reached his breaking point, the huge Goodyear computer, located where the Chrysler Expressway intersects the Ford Expressway, indicated that car production for the year reached a total of 6,546,817. In Solidarity House, the international headquarters of the UAW, the research department records showed that injuries in the auto factories that year exceeded 15,000 with an unknown number of deaths. The Detroit Tigers had completed their 1970 season with 79 games won and 83 lost to finish fourth in the Eastern Division of the American League.

Chapter One

Inner City Voice

1

In the violent summer of 1967, Detroit became the scene of the bloodiest uprising in a half century and the costliest in terms of property damage in U.S. history. At the weeks' end, there were 41 known dead, 347 injured, 3,800 arrested. Some 5,000 people were homeless . . . while 1,300 buildings had been reduced to mounds of ashes and bricks, and 2,700 businesses sacked. Damage estimates reached $500 million.

—*Time Magazine*, August 4, 1967

Less than 30 days after the Michigan National Guard lifted its occupation of the city of Detroit, H. Rap Brown spoke to an explosive crowd of some 5,000 persons gathered in and around a theater on Dexter Avenue just a mile or so from what had been the center of the Great Rebellion. Brown, who in August of 1967 was near the height of his influence as a revolutionary orator, delivered the kind of angry and militant speech for which he was famous. Later, he would be quoted as saying, "There are people who can relate the struggle of black people better than I can. People in Detroit, for instance." The sponsors of his appearance were some of those people. Their purpose had been to raise interest in their new monthly newspaper, the *Inner City Voice*.

The first issue of the newspaper appeared in October 1967. The headline was "MICHIGAN SLAVERY," and the focus on urban revolt was underscored in one of the first editorials:

In the July Rebellion we administered a beating to the behind of the
white power structure, but apparently our message didn't get over. . . .
We are still working, still working too hard, getting paid too little, living in bad housing, sending our kids to substandard schools, paying
too much for groceries, and treated like dogs by the police. We still
don't own anything and don't control anything. . . . In other words,
we are still being systematically exploited by the system and still have
the responsibility to break the back of that system.

Only a people who are strong, unified, armed, and know the enemy
can carry on the struggles which lay ahead of us. Think about it
brother, things ain't hardly getting better. The Revolution must continue.

ICV (Inner City Voice) carried two descriptive phrases astride its
masthead—"Detroit's Black Community Newspaper" and "the Voice of
Revolution." These reflected a belief that the paper's hard-hitting and
revolutionary viewpoint was an accurate expression of the dominant mood
of Detroit's black population. *ICV* was not like the alternate-culture newspapers of that period. Its editors did not see its function simply as one of a
principled opposition to the dominant culture. Using their own resources,
they tried to build their paper into a vehicle for political organization,
education, and change. *ICV* was to be a positive response to the Great
Rebellion, elaborating, clarifying, and articulating what was already in
the streets. There seemed to be no reason why *ICV* could not supplant
the weekly *Michigan Chronicle*, Detroit's largest-circulating black newspaper, and perhaps one day become a black-owned daily able to com-
pete with the morning *Detroit Free Press* and the evening *Detroit News*.

The people who put out *ICV* were not newcomers to struggle and
they were not underground journalists of the type which produced
hundreds of periodicals during the late 1960s. Their collective experience included every major black revolutionary movement of the previous decade. They had been active in SNCC (the Student Nonviolent
Coordinating Committee), the Freedom Now Party (an all-black party
which gained ballot status in Michigan), UHURU (a Detroit radical action group), RAM (Revolutionary Action Movement), and a number of
additional formal and informal groupings. Some of them had been part
of a group which defied the State Department ban on travel to Cuba in
1964, and some of them had personal conversations with Ernesto
"Che" Guevara.

ICV met its monthly publishing schedule for the next year with an average press run of some 10,000 copies. Each issue coupled a dynamic prose style with explicit revolutionary ideas about local, national, and international events. The first issue set the tone with three front-page stories concerning living and working conditions in the city of Detroit. The lead story was an exposé of substandard conditions at Detroit General Hospital, an institution most poor people in the inner city had personal contact with. International problems were given a sharp local focus by *ICV*'s advocacy of massive black participation in the national anti-war March on Washington scheduled for October 21, 1967. Subsequent issues dealt with self-defense in the event of new fighting, with food and water logistics treated as seriously as overt military problems. Stories covering national events adopted a united front approach. Every figure or group actively engaged in struggle was given space, whether a white Catholic integrationist priest such as Father Groppi in Milwaukee, the emerging Black Panther Party of Oakland, California, or a black nationalist such as Imamu Amiri Baraka (Le Roi Jones) in Newark. Much of the paper dealt with revolutionary events on the national and international levels, but the front-page and feature stories were rooted in Detroit conditions. Over the year, the headlines included:

MICHIGAN SLAVERY
COPS ON RAMPAGE—14 YEAR OLD SHOT
GIRL LOSES EYE RUNNING FROM RATS
WHITE FOREMAN KILLED AFTER RACIST INSULT AT FORD'S
BLACK WORKERS UPRISING

The literary style and sensationalistic photographs of *ICV* were deliberately provocative. The editors of *ICV* wanted to present complicated revolutionary ideas in a popular and exciting format. The influences of Malcolm X and Che Guévara were strong, but there were many other currents. *ICV* regularly reproduced articles from the *Crusader*, a newsletter written by Robert Williams, an ex-marine whose advocacy in 1954 of armed black self-defense while head of the Monroe, North Carolina, NAACP had led to a kidnapping charge and self-exile, first in Cuba and then in China. *ICV* featured a regular column by Detroiter James Boggs, who had published *The American Revolution: Pages from a Negro Worker's Notebook* in 1963. Some of the *ICV* staff had worked with Boggs in political groups, and he was highly respected even when people did not agree with him. *ICV* also reprinted speeches by black Marxist C.L.R. James, best known for his book *Black Jacobins*, a study of the Haitian revolt led by Toussaint L'Ouverture. James had organized political groups in the city, and Martin Glaberman, the chairman of one of those groups, had once conducted a private study class on Marx's *Capital* for some of the individuals most prominent in producing *ICV*. Although a totally black-owned and -operated paper, *ICV* published a few stories by whites which were either written exclusively for the paper or taken from wire services. The unifying ingredient in all *ICV* material was the sharp emphasis on defining the strategy and tactics of the ongoing black liberation struggle and how it might prefigure and trigger a second American revolution.

Virtually all the individuals who later emerged as the leadership of the League of Revolutionary Black Workers worked on *ICV*, but the key person was editor John Watson, a slightly built man then in his early twenties. Watson already had a long political history. As early as 1960, he had been identified as too radical for CORE (Congress of Racial Equality). A few years later, he was expelled from SNCC, along with the entire Detroit chapter, because the group had advocated direct action in the North as well as in the South. During the next few years, he worked with NAC (Negro Action Committee), the Freedom Now Party, and UHURU. In 1963, Watson was part of a group accused of jeering at the American flag and booing the national anthem during a ceremony at City Hall staged to interest the Olympic Committee in selecting Detroit as a site for a future Olympiad. A year later, he was part of a group that threatened a mass insurrection of 50,000 blacks if one of their number should be drafted, a pure bluff which brought about the mobilization of hundreds of troops around the Wayne County Induction Center. Instead of 50,000 demonstrators as promised, there were only eight. Nevertheless, the prospective inductee was found "unsuitable" for service.

Watson had been involved in so much activity and he had such a nonchalant personal manner that his power as an intellectual was sometimes underestimated. Watson had attended the Friday night forums of the Socialist Workers Party in the early 1960s, and he had helped organize the all-black group that studied Marxism with Glaber-man. He was a perennial university student, but most of his learning came from private reading, political activism, and contacts with people involved in political struggle. In contrast to some of the original SNCC and UHURU people who fell away from activism, Watson became increasingly important as an idea man, a public speaker, and a person who could get things started. A relatively poor administrator who was sloppy with details and time schedules, Watson was most effective when he had a colleague to handle day-to-day operations. He had almost unlimited energy when he was working on a project he considered important. At considerable cost to his health, his sheer energy pushed through project after project that others considered too bold for success. Watson had the ability to take an idea, shape it to Detroit reality, and somehow find funds to put it into action. Watson, more than anyone else, was responsible for the existence of *ICV* and for its characteristic ability to present complicated ideological analyses of capitalism in a popular style which made the leap from theory to practice seem almost automatic. An editorial of February 29, 1968, was typical:

> To struggle in our own interest means that the black people of the ghetto must struggle to overthrow white capitalism. The struggle against capitalism is world wide and the revolutionary struggle of the ghetto is crucial and essential in the over all world revolution. If the Koreans and Vietnamese can overthrow imperialism in Asia then Asia will be free. But if the Black Revolution can overthrow capitalism and imperialism in the U.S., then the whole world will be freed. This, then, is our role.
>
> With this understanding, let us praise the Vietnamese and Koreans, but let us pass the ammunition and do our own thing.

The paper's consistent anti-capitalist analysis transformed articles about hospitals, police, and housing from simple expressions of grievances capable of reform to a critique of the entire social order. While emphasizing caution, *ICV* continually evoked the liberating spirit of the Great Rebellion, which it referred to with the phrases "shopping for free" and "the general strike of '67." The *ICV* analysis of what was happening to blacks in the Detroit auto plants followed the same style. Other forces in the city spoke stridently of an abstract black power, but *ICV* raised the specter of an uprising of black workers which not only would strike at the company but would totally bypass the United Auto

Workers as well. A June 1968 front-page story laid out the problems of black workers and spoke of direct action on the shop floor:

> [B]lack workers are tied day in and day out, 8-12 hours a day, to a massive assembly line, an assembly line that one never sees the end or the beginning of but merely fits into a slot and stays there, swearing and bleeding, running and stumbling, trying to maintain a steadily increasing pace. Adding to the severity of working conditions are the white racist and bigoted foremen, harassing, insulting, driving and snapping the whip over the backs of thousands of black workers, who have to work in these plants in order to eke out an existence. These conditions coupled also with the double-faced, back stabbing of the UAW have driven black workers to a near uprising state. The UAW with its bogus bureaucracy is unable, has been unable, and in many cases is unwilling to press forward the demands and aspirations of black workers. In the wildcat strikes the black workers on the lines do not even address themselves to the UAW's Grievance Procedure. They realize that their only method of pressing for their demands is to strike and to negotiate at the gates of industry.

The first steps to stop such messages from reaching the streets of Detroit were taken by the American Legion and other well-organized groups of the Right who tried to use their influence in the state legislature and the mayor's office. They contended that *ICV* was calling for a resumption of the Great Rebellion, but, in fact, the paper stayed within the boundaries of the Bill of Rights and could not be legally suppressed. Breakthrough, a Detroit split-off from the John Birch Society which had terrorized peace marchers with physical assaults, began to attack *ICV* through its spokesman, Donald Lobsinger. Breakthrough eventually attempted to disrupt a public meeting. An *ICV* article carried this terse information on the outcome: "Lobsinger found one of his followers laying in the lavatory floor in a pool of his own blood." *ICV* omitted all details about its self-defense procedures. This was characteristic of those who produced the newspaper. While considering military matters to have a high priority, they always gave their specific apparatus a very low profile in all public pronouncements.

The enemies of *ICV* soon found more effective pressures than violence and open censorship. The FBI made a practice of visiting shops which produced the paper and of inquiring why the owners were supporting subversion. The usual result was an immediate refusal to print any more issues. An even more effective weapon was the typographers' union, which took the position that even if a printer was willing to publish *ICV*, the union would call a strike to prevent it. John Watson recalls with bitterness that one of the officials of the union had been a well-known member of the Communist Party. When personally asked to use his influence within the union, the official replied that nothing could be done. Other established radical groups and individuals associated with them as former or active members were likewise unwilling or unable to aid *ICV*. Their lack of support, rather than apparent ideological differences, was the basis for the generally poor opinion of the Left held by most of the *ICV* staff. As a result of the FBI and union harassment, the *ICV* was never printed in the same shop more than twice. The consequence of the double attack was that copy had to be taken to Chicago, where it was printed by the same firm that printed *Muhammad Speaks*, the newspaper of Elijah Muhammad's Nation of Islam. The printed papers were then trucked back to Detroit for distribution.

2

Senator [Robert] Griffin: Can you tell me what is the significance of General Gordon Baker? Is that really his given name?

Detective Sergeant Paul Chambers: That is his name, sir. . . . It is not a rank.

—U.S. Senate Sub-Committee to Investigate Administration of the Internal Security Act and Other Internal Security Laws, hearings of August 6, 1970

The publishers of *ICV* were the core of a group of some 30 black activists who had organized themselves into an informal study/action group. Most of their time was spent exploring how revolutionary ideas might be implemented in their places of work. One of the most respected members of this group was General Gordon Baker, who was then working at Dodge Main, an assembly plant of Chrysler Corporation. Baker's radical background was extensive. He had been part of RAM, the *Capital* study group, UHURU, and the group that visited Cuba in 1964. In 1966, along with Glanton Dowdell and Rufus Griffin, he had been charged with carrying concealed weapons to a disturbance on the east side of Detroit. He and Dowdell had been convicted and placed on five years probation.

Baker was a powerfully built and amiable man who had often expressed his revolutionary views at work and in the streets, only to find them rejected as too militant. By the spring of 1968, the mood of workers had shifted. Mike Hamlin, another of the key figures at *ICV*, recalled the situation in an interview given to the authors on August 24, 1972: "Gradually he [Baker] began to pull together a group of workers who began to meet in the offices of the *Inner City Voice*. Usually, General and I would meet with them late at night. . . . One of the key persons in the plant was Ron March. It took him a long time to move to understanding that conditions in the plant were related to what was happening in Vietnam. Eventually he came to a sound analysis and with the rest of the group of workers decided to start agitation at Dodge Main."

Hamlin's role as an intermediary between those most concerned with the publication of *ICV* and those who were involved in direct in-plant organizing was one he would repeat many times in the next years. A truck driver and Korean War veteran, Hamlin's special talent was to act as a mediator when serious disagreements arose. A soft-spoken man of great patience, Hamlin spent hours welding together elements that might otherwise have blown up at each other in fits of anger, frustration, and misunderstanding.

Nine months and five days after the Great Rebellion, the work of Baker, Hamlin, and March bore fruit when on May 2, 1968, 4,000 workers shut down Dodge Main in the first wildcat strike to hit that factory in 14 years. The immediate cause of the strike was speed-up and both black and white workers took part, but the driving force was the *ICV* group, which now named itself the Dodge Revolutionary Union Movement—DRUM. The activities and ideas of DRUM were to inspire black workers in factories throughout the United States. No less an authority than the *Wall Street Journal* took them very seriously from the day of the first wildcat, for the *Wall Street Journal* understood something most of the white student radicals did not yet understand: the black revolution of the 1960s had finally arrived at one of the most vulnerable links of the American economic system—the point of mass production, the assembly line. And the DRUM militants were not simply another angry caucus of rank-and-file workers of the type that periodically sprang up in one plant or another. DRUM's anger was the anger of the Great Rebellion and its vision was that of a new society. In one of his rare public writings, General Baker, the soul of DRUM, spoke of being dismissed from his job for leading the wildcat strike. When Baker raised his voice against Chrysler Corporation, his words represented the feelings of many rank-and-file workers, and they reverberated throughout the plants. His views were a mixture of socialism and revolutionary black nationalism, but he was always consistent and forceful in supporting workers' grievances and in pushing confrontation forward. Using the device of an open letter to Chrysler Corporation published in the June 1968 issue of *ICV*, General Baker took the offensive—the DRUM road—against the company and the union:

OPEN LETTER TO CHRYSLER CORPORATION

Dear Sirs:
    In response to my discharge on May 5, 1968 for violation of the 5th section of the agreement between Chrysler Corporation and the UAW, dated Nov. 10, 1967, which reads
        "No Strike or Lockout"
        (1) Strike prohibited (etc.)
    In discharging me you have falsely placed the banner of leadership upon my shoulders. And in so doing you have denied two main things. Number one, you have denied me the right to receive any justice from this corporation. And number two, you have nullified the possibility of the real issues which caused the walkout of ever being aired. Even though you have falsely placed the banner of leadership of a wildcat strike upon my shoulders I shall wear it proudly. For what more nobler banner could a black working man bear. In this day and age under the brutal oppression reaped from the backs of black workers, the leadership of a wildcat strike is a badge of honor and courage. In discharging me you have attempted to belittle the racial overtones in this affair which will prove to be an impossible task on your behalf. Any confrontation between black and white men in this racist decadent society is a racial and therefore a political question. Let it be further understood in the wildcat strike that the harshest discipline was issued against black workers attributing further to your blatant racism. Also, Hamtramck Assembly Plant (old Dodge Main) has a long history of trampling upon the rights of black people. It was as late as 1952 while black men were shedding their blood in the dirty unjust war of aggression against the Korean people that black men were allowed to work

on the assembly lines, in the trim shop, and final assembly. And even then, many white workers stormed off of the line refusing to work next to black men. Some of the same outright white racist policy makers of this corporation are still in control of this racist corporation today. Black people are expected by the Chrysler Corporation to purchase Chrysler finished products, but are brutally oppressed and overworked and harassed on the production lines.

Yes, the struggle between black workers and white racist Corporation owners and operators is the most vicious of all existing struggles in the world today. It is sometimes opened and sometimes closed, it is sometimes hot and sometimes cold. It is, nevertheless, in the final sense a vicious struggle. Let it be further understood that by taking the course of disciplining the strikers you have opened that struggle to a new and higher level and for this I sincerely THANK YOU. You have made the decision to do battle with me and therefore to do battle with the entire black community in this city, this state, this country, and in this world of which I am a part. Black people of the world are united in a common struggle which had its beginning with the exploitation of non-white people on a world wide scale. To quote from W.E.B. DuBois, "The emancipation of man is the emancipation of labor and the emancipation of labor is the freeing of that basic majority of workers who are yellow, brown, and black." You have made the decision to do battle, and that is the only decision that you will make. WE shall decide the arena and the time. You will also be held completely responsible for all of the grave consequences arising from your racist actions.

Thank you again

General G. Baker, Jr.
0290-170

p.s. You have lit the unquenchable spark.

Chapter Two

Our Thing Is DRUM

1

There will always be people who are willing to work the 10-12 hour day, and we're going to look for them.

—James Roche, president, General Motors Corporation, quoted in William Serrin, *The Company and the Union*, 1973

Chrysler Corporation, Detroit's single-largest taxpayer and employer, is among the seven largest corporations in the United States. Since the end of World War II, like the entire auto industry, Chrysler has experienced wild fluctuations of sales, profits, and capital investments. Companies such as Hudson, Nash, Fraser, Briggs, Kaiser, and Packard did not survive the boom-and-bust cycle and were liquidated or bought out. Even GM, the patriarch of the auto industry and the world's largest private employer, made more capital investments in terms of real money in 1956 than it did 15 years later. More cars were produced by the industry in 1950, 1955, 1960, and 1965 than in 1970. Chrysler suffered more from the roller-coaster economic pattern than the other auto makers, for a number of reasons. Originally distinguished by superior engineering, Chrysler let its standards fall, settled for being a style-follower instead of a style-setter, and made poor domestic and foreign investments. This poor corporate record was capped by a management scandal in the late 1950s that nearly drove Chrysler into bankruptcy. In spite of these developments, Chrysler still had some outstanding profit years; and in Detroit, the prosperity of Chrysler was crucial to the prosperity of the city itself.

By the late 1950s, significant numbers of Americans had begun to buy well-built, small, inexpensive foreign cars, but the auto industry resisted the trend and continued its traditional policy of making big cars with high-priced (and highly profitable) accessories. Each new "compact" from Detroit tended to grow larger and less economical after its first year of sales. Instead of producing a single model that could be built for a number of years with increasing reliability, Detroit insisted on the annual model changeover, which put a premium on visual rather than engineering changes. Gas consumption per mile increased steadily. Cars were designed for quick obsolescence, and parts were designed to be replaced rather than repaired. The recall of cars for defects in production, a rare event in earlier periods, became routine in the 1960s and was a symbol of failing standards. The industry began to suffer from a saturated American market and from a host of problems related to advanced middle age, yet it still directly or indirectly employed one out of six Americans. Auto production remained a cornerstone of the U.S. economy.

The difficult post-war decades had brought one tremendous advantage to the Big Three (GM, Ford, and Chrysler): a chance to counter the effects of unionism. Frightened by the radical spirit and mass actions of the late 1930s, the Big Three made a deal with the UAW after the war. Their overriding managerial concern was maximizing profits, and the prime condition for doing that in the auto industry was control of the shop floor. All operations had to be evaluated in terms of worker-hour and worker-minute costs. Time-study experts investigated each job to eliminate wasted motion and to invent new procedures for increasing the work load. A worker at the GM plant at Lordstown explained the process in an interview printed in the September 9, 1973, issue of the *New York Times:* "They tell you, 'Put in 10 screws,' and you do it. Then a couple of weeks later they say, 'Put in 15 screws,' and next they say, 'Well, we don't need you no more; give it to the next man.'" This worker was giving a specific example of the way management tried to systematize speed-up on an unprecedented scale. Sometimes the entire assembly line was accelerated either on a permanent basis or for temporary periods. Sometimes the number of operations required of a single person was increased. And sometimes workers were forced to keep up with the precise rhythms of a new machine or tool. Management could not get back to the "good old days" of Henry Ford when workers were not allowed to talk during lunch; but washing-up times, rest periods, job-preparation periods, and other paid non-production times were reduced. The net result of all facets of speed-up was that more labor was extracted from each person during each working hour. This increased tempo of work was not confined to a 40-hour week. The companies discovered that the savings from not paying fringe benefits to additional workers made it cheaper for them to pay time-and-a-half rates for overtime than to increase the total workforce. Compulsory overtime was enforced throughout the industry during the 1950s. Auto workers were made to work one to four hours overtime after finishing their regular eight-hour shift, and many were made to work on Saturdays and occasionally on Sundays.

The union acquiesced to company demands and was rewarded by support in dealing with its own internal problems. One form of support was that the companies collected union dues directly from the workers' paychecks, freeing the union from the workers' tactic of withholding dues if dissatisfied with union performance. Company and union amiability went so far that, during the GM strike of 1970, the company allowed the union to delay payment of $46 million into the health-insurance program because of the enormous financial burden that would place on the union. GM was paid 5 percent interest by the union after the strike was over. In effect, the company had floated the union a loan in the middle of the strike and thus financed a work stoppage against itself. Such cooperation found further expression in three- and five-year contracts with which the mutual interests of company and union were insulated from annual crisis. The chief consequence of the long contracts was that there would be no work stoppages of any kind. Any unauthorized (wildcat) strike could be punished by the courts as a breach of contract, pitting the offending workers against the union as well as the company. William Serrin, the Pulitzer-Prize-winning reporter of the *Detroit Free Press*, summed up union-management relations in his 1973 book, *The Company and the Union*:

What the companies desire—and receive—from the union is predict-
ability in labor relations. Forced to deal with unions, they want to deal
with one union, one set of leaders, and thus they have great interest in
stability within the UAW and in a continuation of union leadership.
They also want to have the limits of the bargaining clearly understood
and subscribed to. "GM's position has always been, give the union the
money, the least possible, but give them what it takes," says a former
negotiator. "But don't let them take the business away from us." The
union has come to accept this philosophy as the basis of its relationship with the companies: it will get money, some changes in work procedures, usually nothing more. "We make collective bargaining
agreements," Reuther once declared, "not revolutions." Both the union and the companies, a mediator says, have one major goal: "They
want to make cars at a profit."

The only weapon left to the worker was the grievance procedure. If
a job was speeded up or an extra procedure added, if safety goggles or
gloves were inadequate, if a machine malfunctioned, the worker could
not fight it out on the factory floor in a direct confrontation with a superviser. The worker could only write out the complaint, file it with the
union "rep," and wait for the complaint to be processed. Meanwhile,
whatever the new procedures or safety violations might be, they remained in effect unless they were gross enough to trigger a walkout by
all the workers. The grievance procedure became yet another device by
which company and union eliminated worker participation in decision-
making. The companies and the union had developed a division of labor. The companies looked after the machines, and the union looked
after the workers. American auto workers were told by the mass media
that they had one of the world's highest standards of living. They were
not told that they also had one of the world's highest and most gruel-
ing standards of work.

The company-union agreements meant that American factories remained unnecessarily noisy, unhealthy, and dangerous. Rather than re-
tooling or rebuilding, the corporations, especially Chrysler, tended to
just patch up. White-collar workers in management considered air con-
ditioning in summer and heating in winter to be matters of course; but
in the shop temperatures in summer could soar to 120 degrees in some
departments, while in the winter they fell to near freezing in others.
Compulsory overtime meant that workers had to put in nine to 12

hours a day, six and seven days a week, at such factories. Safety infractions and contract violations mounted, but the grievance procedure was a joke. By 1970, there were 250,000 written grievances at GM alone, or one for every two workers. It didn't matter if a worker was employed at GM's new Lordstown plant, publicized as a model of progress and modernity, or at cranky old Dodge Main. Ultramodern Lordstown had a roof that leaked whenever there was a hard rain, and Dodge Main had been declared a fire hazard as early as 1948. Conditions in the auto factories of the 1960s were as bad as they had been in the days before the union. George B. Morris, Jr., a GM vice-president and director of labor relations, explained the situation in *The Unions*, a 1972 book by Haynes Johnson and Nick Kotz, Pulitzer-Prize-winning reporters working for the *Washington Post:* "I guess it was understandable when the unions were beginning to organize that they had to be militant and aggressive. And they adopted a vernacular vocabulary that was militaristic, aggressive, and inculcated into the minds of their constituents this idea of conflict, of war between the classes, between the worker and the employer. Hell, that day is gone. That's like nickel beer and button shoes. It's gone."

2

Few industries, if any, can match the auto industry in terms of the vast array of poisonous chemicals, gases, and other health and safety hazards which its workers are exposed to daily.

—Jannette Sherman, M.D., and Sidney Wolfe, M.D., *Health Research Group Study of Disease among Workers in the Auto Industry*, September 1973

A new explosive element in the factories of the late 1960s was the presence of a quarter of a million black workers. Except for Ford, which had a special policy of using large numbers of blacks as an anti-union ploy, none of the auto companies hired many black workers until the labor shortages of World War II. At that time, blacks, mainly fresh from the South, were hired by the tens of thousands. Chrysler's number of black women employees went from zero in 1941 to 5,000 by

1945. Detroit blacks often wisecracked that Tojo and Hitler had done more for the emancipation of black labor than Lincoln and Roosevelt. Many of these new jobs were taken away in the recessions of the 1950s. To cite Chrysler again, there were years when no blacks were hired at any plants. The company's blue-collar force fell from 100,000 to 35,000 and its white-collar force declined by 7,000. Other companies were in no better shape. In the General Motors Building in midtown Detroit there were two black workers out of a force of 3,500.

When the auto industry staged a comeback in the early 1960s, blacks began to be rehired. Since Ford and GM had moved most of their operations out of Detroit in various decentralization schemes, the bulk of the new black workers in Detroit were employed by Chrysler. They invariably got the worst and most dangerous jobs: the foundry and the body shop, jobs requiring the greatest physical exertion and jobs which were the noisiest, dirtiest, and most dangerous in the plant. Blacks were further abused by the 90-day rule, under which workers could be dismissed at will before coming under full contract protection. The companies made it a practice to fire hundreds of workers per week, creating a rotating and permanent pool of insecure job seekers. The UAW was kept at bay on the issue because it received a $20 initial fee and $21 in dues for each 89-day worker. The companies also received poverty program fees for the purpose of "training" parolees and welfare recipients. These individuals were often blacks and they were usually put on the least desirable jobs. Any protest could mean an end to government aid and possibly a return to prison.

The exploitation experienced by all workers was compounded for black workers by the institutional racism which pervaded every aspect of factory life. Dodge Main was typical: 99 percent of all general foremen were white, 95 percent of all foremen were white, 100 percent of all superintendents were white, 90 percent of all skilled tradesmen were white, and 90 percent of all skilled apprentices were white. All the better jobs were overwhelmingly dominated by whites, and when whites did have difficult jobs, there were often two workers assigned to a task that a black worker was expected to do alone. The company was not even subtle in its discrimination. Sick notes signed by black doctors were refused as inadequate. Organizations like DRUM emphasized how the company deliberately cultivated and institutionalized racism in order that white workers and black workers would face their workaday lives in racial conflict with one another rather than in class solidarity.

The large majority of white workers at Dodge Main were Polish Americans. They tended to dominate the union and to hold the better jobs. Many of them were immigrants or first-generation Americans who had acquired negrophobia as part of their Americanization. The plant itself was located in Hamtramck, an independent city totally within the city limits of Detroit and a city that had a Polish population larger than that of Poznan. Hamtramck was run by a Polish-dominated city government and a Polish-dominated police force. In addition, the Poles voted Democratic by margins of 70-90 percent, and their voter turnout was very high. This gave them enormous power in the Democratic Party, which needed to carry the Detroit metropolitan area heavily in order to win elections in what was otherwise a Republican state. The political power of the UAW was closely linked to its ability to get out the vote in areas like Hamtramck. The Polish Americans did not like working conditions at Dodge Main any better than the blacks did, but they had a power base in the union and in the local government that made them concerned with the prosperity of Chrysler as well. They had no apparent option but to view their own vested interests as interlocked with the vested interests of an already interlocked system of company, union, and government.

The Polish Americans had the reputation of being a conservative force. This conservatism, like the so-called conservatism of other white ethnic groups, was often a defensive response to deteriorating social conditions in urban life. Seeing hard-won gains threatened by increasing insecurity at work, inflation, and crime in the streets, many white ethnics began to act defensively in support of what they considered their own interests. In fact, however, the Polish-American politicians in the Democratic Party were often New Deal liberals who fought for progressive social legislation, especially legislation affecting the working class. Earlier in the century, the Polish Americans and Eastern Europeans had a tradition of being associated with the most progressive social movements. Even in the 1960s, Hamtramck still had a Polish-language communist newspaper and a restaurant which was a well-known meeting place for leftists; but these were only remnants of a former activism that had been effectively submerged in a climate of fear and insecurity.

The only other identifiable groups of workers of significant size were the white Appalachians and the Arabs. The Appalachians had come to the North from the states of Kentucky, Tennessee, and West Virginia at pretty much the same time as the blacks. They, too, tended to cluster in ghettos, to attend inferior schools, and to move back and forth to the South as employment waxed and waned. Factory conditions were not much better for them than for blacks, but racist feelings kept the two groups effectively divided most of the time. The independent, individualistic hill people were unpredictable, however. They liked the liberal Kennedy brothers, and they also liked George Wallace and the Ku Klux Klan. They fought blacks all the time; but during the Great Rebellion, they had joined blacks for looting purposes, and an amazed Detroit Police Department had discovered that the majority of captured snipers were not blacks, but white "hillbillies."

Possibly the only group exploited more than blacks at Dodge Main was the recently immigrated Arabs. In 1968, they already numbered 500, and in the next six years that number would multiply fourfold. These workers were often totally confused by American conditions, and they were fearful of losing their jobs or being deported. The bulk of them were men who lived alone and sent most of their pay to relatives in the Middle East. A 1972 bulletin put out by Spark, a radical organization at Dodge Main, described the situation:

> Chrysler figures that no one will try to help an Arab worker when Chrysler attacks him. So now Chrysler is attacking. Foremen tell Arab workers to do more work than their jobs call for. Eventually the "extra" work is "officially" added to the job. Other Arab workers are kept as floaters and continually put on the worst jobs, *despite* their seniority. Medical passes get put off. Reliefs are forgotten about. . . .
>
> It's the same kind of shit they have pulled for years with black people. At first, black people were given work *only* when Chrysler was trying to break a strike. Chrysler consciously set white workers against black workers—both fighting for the same job, during the desperate high unemployment of the Depression, when there was no union.
>
> Then when Chrysler finally did hire black workers regularly into the plant, it was *only* in the foundry (or the Body Shop a little later)—all the hot, heavy dirty work around. . . .
>
> Then in the fifties, the company finally figured it could get a greater advantage by letting black workers go on the line in other parts of the plant. And most white workers in the plant were suckered into

the company's plan—most of the whites sat down, to protest that black people were coming onto the line. . . .

Now today, Chrysler is trying the same thing again—bringing in still another group of workers. Chrysler hopes to make conditions worse for all of us by first attacking conditions for the Arab workers. And they count on turning us against each other so they can do this.

The composition of the workforce at Dodge Main was indicative of the workforce throughout the city. The older, established work group was made up of European immigrant stock, while the newer force contained blacks, white Appalachians, Arabs, and other, nonwhite minorities. Facile analysts often stated that the older force was conservative and the younger radical. While this was true as a vague rule of thumb, there were many serious exceptions and qualifications. The older workforce, for instance, tended to be far more union-minded and was less intimidated by corporate threats than some of the new force. Young white workers in the skilled trades could be just as socially conservative as their fathers and mothers. Yet Local 160 of the GM Technical Center, representing 4,000 mainly white skilled workers with the highest-paying jobs, was among the most militant locals in the UAW. Its members dropped nails, snarled traffic, and formed car barricades during the 1970 GM strike, and it was the only unit to defy a UAW directive to allow certain technical personnel through the union lines. Local 160 was also the base of Belfast-born Pete Kelly, one of the two chairmen of the United National Caucus, a multi-plant organization opposed to the UAW leadership and advocating worker control of the shop floor. Conversely, some young blacks who were quick to clench their fists and shout "Right on!" proved less reliable and militant in the long run than some older black workers schooled in patience and in the skills of protracted struggle. Black or white, young or old, male or female, the workers on the shop floor were angry, yet the UAW offered no solutions. An agitational leaflet put out by workers at Chrysler's Eldon Avenue plant in March 1971 quoted UAW President Leonard Woodcock as having told reporters: "If some company says to us tomorrow, 'Okay, you take it, humanize the plant,' we wouldn't know where to start. . . . We don't have the answers."

3

I never went on a strike in my life, I never ordered anyone else to run a
strike in my life, I never had anything to do with the picket line. . . . In the fi-
nal analysis, there is not a great deal of difference between the things I stand for
and the things that the National Association of Manufacturers stands for.

—George Meany, president of the AFL-CIO, in a speech to the
National Association of Manufacturers, 1956

By the late 1960s, the UAW had lost touch with its mass base, especially its minorities. At least 30 percent of the UAW membership
was black, yet the 26-person executive board had only two blacks, Nel-
son Jack Edwards and Marcellius Ivory. (Edwards was fatally shot on
November 2, 1974, when he tried to break up an argument at a west-
side Detroit bar.) In 1969, blacks filled only seven out of 100 key staff
positions. Fourteen percent of the UAW membership was female, yet
women had even fewer posts than blacks and only one representative
on the executive board, Olga Madar. Once considered the cutting edge
of militant industrial unionism, the UAW showed little interest in organizing the numerous non-union feeder shops in the industry, in moving for unionization in the South, or in fighting for substantial gains
such as 40 hours' pay for 30 hours' work. Walter Reuther, president of
the union until a fatal plane crash on May 9, 1970, Vice-President
Leonard Woodcock, and Secretary-Treasurer Emil Mazey had once belonged to the Socialist Party; but they had grown distant from dissident social movements, and they had come to power within the UAW
by leading a purge of Communist Party members and sympathizers.
Reuther, who had once run for Congress as a Socialist and who had
worked in a Soviet auto plant, did not like the militants of SNCC, the
white radicals of Students for a Democratic Society, or peace marchers
who insulted the nation's president. Rather than honest-to-goodness
slugfests with the corporations, Reuther staged elaborate rituals in
which neither side was badly hurt. He enjoyed having his photo taken
embracing nonviolent activists such as Martin Luther King and Cesar
Chavez; but under his leadership the UAW did little to combat racism,
anti-Semitism, or sexism, either within its own ranks or where it had

influence. *Detroit Free Press* reporter William Serrin made the trenchant comment that the UAW was a right-of-center union with a left-of-center reputation.

Reuther died in a plane crash en route to the $23 million Black Lake educational and recreational center which was the obsession of his later years. The center's price tag had swelled enormously from original estimates, and most of the financing was arranged without the approval of the union membership or the executive board. Angry DRUM leaflets attacked the project as symptomatic of what the union hierarchy thought was important. DRUM pointed out that at maximum the complex could accommodate 600 people at a time. At that rate, it would be seven and one-half years before all of the 1 million UAW members had a chance to spend one day at the resort, even if they went alone. Just one guest per member would double the time to 15 years. The center was obviously not intended for the workers' use at all, but as a hideaway for UAW executives and their inner circle.

Black Lake was only one gross example of how the UAW leaders acted like corporate executives. The executive board members drew salaries comparable to those of industry officials, and they affected the lifestyles of their business counterparts, even though they had begun their careers as production workers. Corporate headquarters was the sleek Solidarity House, built on the Detroit River at a cost of more than $6 million and having a healthy annual maintenance budget.

Like all business ventures, the UAW had labor troubles. In March 1971, custodial and secretarial workers went on strike, demanding pay increases of approximately $11 a week. The strike lasted three weeks; and just as important an issue as the wage increase, which was $3 more than the UAW wanted to pay, was the reputed paternalism of the UAW leadership. In *The Company and the Union*, William Serrin quotes Emil Mazey as calling the striking women "little bitches." Other officials called the 400 strikers "greedy," "blackmailers," "unrealistic," "selfish," and "pea-brained women." The heads of the UAW crossed the picket lines every day. Their only concession to collective bargaining was to inform all non-striking staff members and workers that they could honor the picket lines without fear of union retaliation, although, of course, they would receive no pay if they did so.

The UAW had a national reputation for having a progressive stance on racism, but the UAW looked good only when compared to the lily-white and stridently racist unions which composed so much of the organized labor movement. Racism had always been used as a weapon against unions in the auto industry, and Henry Ford had systematized the practice. Beginning in the late 1920s, Ford made it a rule to employ blacks in his factory at every job level in the same percentage as that of blacks in the general population. Ford helped finance the all-black suburb of Inkster and always provided low-paying jobs to any unemployed residents. This new-style "plant-ation" owner also cultivated a select group of black clergy and professionals. Ford was called a humanitarian for some of these actions, but his motives were strictly business ones. His personal views on blacks, Jews, communists, and other "un-American" elements were expressed in the *Dearborn Independent*, a paper he owned and personally financed for more than a decade, even though it lost more than $5 million. Ford considered the Jews to be the world's major problem, and in 1938 he went to Nazi Germany to accept an Iron Cross from Adolph Hitler. Dearborn, the city which Ford built, the home of the mammoth River Rouge complex, and the headquarters of the Ford empire, prohibited black residents. As late as 1970, Orville Hubbard, Dearborn's mayor since 1940, regularly used the word "nigger" in his public utterances.

Ford Motor Company was the last major auto firm to be unionized, and Ford's black policy was a factor in the delay. Most of the 10,000 black workers at Ford participated in the final organizing strike which began on April 1, 1941; but Ford's hand-picked coterie of black "leaders" agitated for black workers to break the strike. On April 3, one group of approximately 800 black workers made three serious physical assaults on the UAW lines in what was the only genuine worker resistance to the union. Racial antagonism and suspicion did not end with the strike. Two years later, Detroit erupted in the worst race riot in the history of the United States; and long after World War II had ended, white workers often staged walkouts when a factory or a department hired its first blacks. The corporations had virtually no black officials, and the situation in the UAW wasn't much better.

The strongest organized attack on racism within the auto industry came with the formation of TULC (Trade Union Leadership Conference) by angry black unionists in 1957. The major leaders were Horace Sheffield and Buddy Battle, activists from the giant Local 600 at Ford's River Rouge plant. Viewed with alarm by most of the union leadership at first, TULC eventually became part of the bureaucracy, although it often took independent political approaches, especially in the area of Detroit elections. TULC became instrumental in getting out a large vote for liberal Jerome Cavanagh in the 1961 contest in which Cavanagh unseated Louis Miriani, the latest in a series of conservative, police-oriented mayors. TULC had a membership of 9,000 at times, and it was consulted by the mayor, industrial executives, and leaders of various unions. TULC hoped to win jobs for black apprentices in the skilled trades and otherwise to advance the cause of black job upgrading and equal pay for equal work. In 1963, in a totally peaceful March for Freedom, Martin Luther King led some 200,000 mainly black Detroiters in a mammoth walk down Woodward Avenue, Detroit's main thoroughfare. Twenty years after the bloody 1943 race riot, Detroit gave the appearance of a commitment to racial harmony. King, Cavanagh, Reuther, and a host of dignitaries locked arms to achieve a local victory in the land of the New Frontier.

But the New Frontier kept receding into a forever-deferred tomorrow. The all-white unions and the all-white skilled trades remained all white. Blacks were sent to die in Vietnam in the name of democracy when they couldn't buy a home in Dearborn, Grosse Pointe, Warren, or many other Detroit suburbs. The most minor reforms met resistance from the companies, the union, and white workers. When DRUM's first leaflets addressed the question of unresolved black grievances, the UAW viewed the group as another bellicose rank-and-file caucus, a more radical version of TULC. B.J. Widick, a former union official associated with progressive leadership in the UAW, wrote off DRUM in his *Detroit: City of Race and Class Violence*, as simply "an important symptom of frustration among black workers over the lack of progress within plants." He thought DRUM "allowed social steam to blow off harmlessly." Emil Mazey didn't think DRUM was quite so harmless. He said the black revolutionaries represented the most dangerous radical thrust since the 1930s, and he was instrumental in having 350,000 letters sent to Detroit-area UAW members accusing DRUM of being a hate organization whose purpose was to divide the working class along racial lines.

Both Widick and Mazey were mistaken in their major premise that DRUM was a caucus. DRUM was not a caucus, at least not a caucus of the type the UAW had dealt with for 30 years. Caucuses fought within the union for control of the union. The United National Caucus, led by Pete Kelly of the GM Tech Center and Jordan Sims, a black worker at the Eldon Avenue Gear and Axle plant, hoped eventually to supplant the Reuther-Woodcock machine with their own. DRUM was something else. It bypassed the UAW to organize workers directly into a structure dedicated to principles which went far beyond simple trade unionism. DRUM's earliest leaflets stated its goals of gaining direct representation of black workers. More like the IWW of an earlier generation of radicals than like a trade union, DRUM had many aspects of a popular revolutionary movement that could go in many directions. Although not always clear about its tactical methods or all of its strategic goals, DRUM was an illustration of what James Boggs had written in 1963 in *The American Revolution:* "Historically workers move ahead by the new. *That is, they bypass existing organizations and form new ones uncorrupted by past habits and customs.*" DRUM had no intention of sharing the economic pie with Chrysler, and it had no interest in making cars for a profit. DRUM wanted workers to have all the pie and to produce goods only for social needs. DRUM concentrated its organizing efforts on black workers, but it was conscious of the long-term necessity of organizing all workers. Its immediate program was a combination of demands for the elimination of racial discrimination and demands for workers' control, which would be beneficial to all workers, regardless of race, sex, or age. DRUM publications regularly stated that the organization was working in the best long-term interests of all workers and that the overall struggle must be fought on class rather than racial lines.

For years, Detroiters had heard conservative Fulton Lewis, Jr., spar in back-to-back newscasts with the UAW's Guy Nunn. Lewis made the union sound like a dangerous and radical threat to "the American way of life," while Nunn made it sound like the fearless champion of every righteous cause in America. The programs were on the same radio station which brought Detroiters adventure stories like "Captain Midnight" and "Sergeant Preston of the Canadian Northwest Mounted Police." Like these serials, the hoopla about the illustrious UAW was mostly a matter of sound effects. The business of the company executives had always been the business of maximizing profits. They viewed the city and its people as a corporate resource. The business of the union executives had become labor control. They viewed the city and its people as a union resource. In the auto industry, as in so many industries, the company was the senior partner and the union the junior partner. A worker with a decade of seniority in the plants wrote an article for the October 1970 issue of *ICV* explaining the formation of DRUM in the context of this company and union partnership:

> More than an opportunist officialdom, the working class suffers from the conversion of the institution of the union itself into a part of the boss' apparatus. The sacred contract, once viewed as the register of the workers' gains, has become the written record of their subordination to the power of capital. The seniority system, once a defense against favoritism and arbitrary firing, has been adapted to give legal force to the white male monopoly of the better jobs. The automatic dues check-off system has removed the union entirely from any dependence on its membership. The huge treasuries, originally conceived to stockpile ammunition for class warfare, have put the unions in the banking, real estate, and insurance business. The closed shop has become the token of wholesale selfishness.
>
> In this wasteland of labor's twisted hopes, where else could redemption come than from among those whose interests were at every turn sacrificed so that another, more favored group could make its peace with the masters? Where else, indeed, but from among the black workers at the automobile manufacturing infernos of the city of Detroit?

4

Assuming control of the means of production essentially means that you are at the first stage of assuming state power.

—John Watson, interview in *Fifth Estate*, July 1969

The wildcat of May 1968 at Dodge Main was followed by a flurry of plant bulletins put out by DRUM. A series of meetings, demonstrations, and actions attracted hundreds of workers from Dodge Main and surrounding factories. The May strike had involved both black and white workers concerned about speed-up, but the administrative punishments were directed primarily at blacks, causing a swelling of black support for DRUM. In the sixth week of its official existence, DRUM demonstrated its strength by calling for a boycott of two bars outside the plant gates that were patronized by blacks but did not hire blacks and practiced other, subtle forms of racial discrimination. Near-unanimous cooperation quickly brought the desired concessions without the use of pickets, signs, or violence.

Three weeks later, DRUM attracted more than 300 workers to a rally held at a parking lot across from the factory. After speeches from DRUM leaders, the workers, accompanied by a number of neighborhood groups and a conga band, formed a line and marched to the headquarters of UAW Local 3, two blocks away. The panic-stricken executive board opened the union auditorium and listened to criticisms aimed at the company and the union. Unsatisfied with the clichés that President Ed Liska and Vice-President Charles Brooks, a black, responded with, DRUM stated it would close Dodge Main in defiance of the union contract.

The following morning, a Friday, workers were met at the gates by DRUM pickets who told them the situation. No attempt was made to interfere with whites, and the majority of white workers entered the factory. Many others honored the picket line out of years of working-class savvy. Sympathetic or not, they went home. Some 3,000 black workers did not go home or into the factory. They stood outside the gates as production all but halted. At noon, six DRUM members went to the local to meet with Liska and other officials. They presented their grievances a second time, emphasizing that having only 72 blacks out of a union-wide total of more than 1,000 paid union representatives was unacceptable to black workers. The UAW was expected to change its ways and to change them rapidly. The demands were then read to the striking workers as police began to arrive in sufficient numbers to make trouble. DRUM dispersed the strikers after organizing a hard-core group of 250 into car pools. The cars then drove five miles to Chrysler headquarters in Highland Park. There the demonstration was repeated, and the demands read to the company as they had already been read to the union. The Highland Park police soon arrived with gas masks and riot weapons. Satisfied with having shaken company and union and having caused the mobilization of two departments of police, DRUM transported its demonstrators back to their homes.

That Sunday, a dozen DRUM members were invited to the regular citywide meeting of black UAW representatives. Tempers flared. Even after guarantees were given that the black UAW officials would support specific DRUM demands, there was clearly a parting rather than a meeting of minds. The following Monday, picketing resumed at Dodge Main until John Doe injunctions were served by the Hamtramck police. DRUM felt it had done well with its limited forces in such a short period of time. Rather than continue the strike, the activists tore up their injunctions and either went into work or went home for the day.

In the weeks that followed, DRUM organized parties, demonstrations, and rallies which were attended by workers, students, and people from church and neighborhood groups. DRUM also threw up a picket line at Solidarity House to publicize its demands, just as, a year later, it was to demonstrate at a special UAW national convention to reach delegates from all over the country. DRUM stressed that one of the major historical lessons of the black struggle in the United States was that it had failed because of "traitors" from within. The "traitors" had often been white leaders who capitulated to racism among white workers or who habitually postponed meeting specific black demands until there was a more "favorable" political climate. Just as often, however, the "traitors" had been blacks. They had subordinated the mass struggle to their personal careers or had gone along with the cowardice of the white leadership. As a consequence, DRUM was unsparing in its condemnation of "Uncle Toms, honkie dog racists, and knee-grows." DRUM lashed out at the hypocrisy of the supposedly infirm Chrysler Corporation, which donated more than $1 million to black-owned banks and gave away vans to the Detroit police department while crying poverty to avoid meeting the demands of its workers. DRUM stated that it would be pleased if whites and moderate blacks would support its demands, but it would offer no concessions for that support and was prepared to fight alone. In *Finally Got the News*, a film made in 1969-1970 by black and white revolutionaries about the struggles in Detroit, Ron March described DRUM's policy toward alliances with white workers: "White workers came to support us. Some wanted to work with us. But we found out that management knew how to divide the whites. We decided that we could work best by organizing alone. We told whites to do the same thing. Once they did that, we could work with them on a coalition basis."

The weekly DRUM leaflets covered every aspect of working-class problems: the unaccountability of UAW officials, discriminatory hiring, unsafe machinery, capricious time studies, the exclusion of blacks from skilled trades, speed-up, holdups in pay, short paychecks, harassment over sick leave, the need for job upgrading, and increasing regimentation at the plants. DRUM attacked the salaries of UAW officials, the UAW grievance procedure, the policies of the UAW credit union. It advocated worker rather than company control of production, but the rhetoric was often that of a revolutionary black nationalism, a fact which tended to confuse people about the major issues. A union election in September provided DRUM an opportunity to test its strength at the ballot box. In the film *Finally Got the News*, Chuck Wooten recalled the experience:

> Our man was Ron March. Most of the old-line guys told us that we didn't have a chance. They said we didn't have experience—we didn't have a platform. All that kind of crap. We went out anyway. Ron pulled 563 votes. The next highest guy was a white worker who had 521. There were other candidates, so we had to have a runoff election. Immediately after that, the Hamtramck police department began to move in a much more open way. They gave us tickets on our cars and just generally harassed us. One day, about 50 of us were in the union hall, which is right across from the police station. The mayor of the city and the chief of police came in with guns in their hands. They told us to stop making trouble, and we said all we wanted was to win the election. We asked them why they weren't harassing the others. While we were talking, a squad of police came through the door swinging axe handles and throwing Mace around. That gave us an idea of the kind of repression black workers seeking to make a revolutionary organization would face. It tipped us off about what would happen when we tried to create a black labor struggle to be part of the black revolution.

March and other DRUM activists were candid in admitting that even if their entire slate of candidates won the election there would be no real improvements at Dodge Main. The major goal of DRUM was another demonstration of insurgent workers' power. All its resources were thrown into a similar campaign one year later. Leaflets were written in Arabic in hopes of picking up votes from the bloc of Arab workers, and an unsuccessful attempt was made to negotiate a compromise with a radical slate which was integrated; basically, however, DRUM relied on its ability to mobilize the black vote. John Watson recalled the results in *Finally Got the News:*

DRUM suspected the union would cheat. We arranged observers for every candidate and machine. Black workers were incensed when the levers for our candidates would not go down. We were in a toe-to-toe battle with the bureaucracy just to make it halfway fair. When the local saw that it could not steal the election, it called for help. George Merrelli, the regional UAW leader, stormed into the hall with his entire 50-man staff. They were armed and had the additional support of a contingent of police. They evicted the workers and occupied the hall. The voting machines had not even been sealed. The next day, the union said Ron March had come in third with only 943 votes. There wasn't even a runoff election. Of 35 candidates, only two DRUM people were elected. A week before, in another factory in the city, the ballot boxes had been confiscated by the police and held in the police station overnight. These acts demonstrated the UAW would risk outright scandal rather than let blacks assume any power. It didn't matter whether DRUM won or lost in this election. What counted was that the enemy lost by being forced to provoke the anger and raise the consciousness of thousands and thousands of workers.

The struggle led by *ICV* and DRUM could not be contained within one factory, much less within a single election. Although the leaders of DRUM had to cope with police harassment, union denunciations, and court injunctions, workers all over the city were forming RUM (Revolutionary Union Movement) units at their places of work. Students and other sympathizers continued to volunteer for picket lines and leafleting to minimize police, company, and union intimidation of plant militants. On the same day as the first Dodge election, a coalition of white and black supporters of DRUM took editorial control of Wayne State University's daily newspaper, the *South End*. The new editors immediately set about the task of transforming what had been a strictly student newspaper into a citywide daily voice for black and white revolutionaries, both on and off the university campus.

Chapter Three

We Will Take the Hard Line

1

You can't talk to them. They don't speak the same language. The previous editor hated my guts and I had an abiding contempt for him. I was glad to see him go, but when this new one, this Watson, walked in, he had the look of cool hatred in his eyes.

—Frank Gill, *South End* faculty adviser, quoted in the *Detroit Free Press*, November 1968

In the autumn of 1968, Wayne State University had almost 35,000 students. Most of them lived at home and most of them worked. Classes began at 8:00 a.m. and continued until near midnight. The school was open year round and there were some classes on Saturday. The first colleges of the Wayne complex were old land-grant institutions of the nineteenth century. They had undergone a number of name changes until they became a state university in the early 1960s. Wayne is located in the center of Detroit, midway between the downtown shopping area and the business district around the General Motors Building. It is surrounded by impoverished black and Appalachian ghettos dotted with some student housing. For years, blacks, immigrants, women, the working poor, and upwardly mobile first-generation white ethnics had found Wayne a convenient place to get an education. It was typical of Wayne that Walter Reuther and Leonard Woodcock had been students there and that the official UAW archives were housed in its Labor Relations Institute.

Wayne had a reputation for radicalism; but, in fact, the administration had driven all left-wing groups from the campus during the McCarthy period, as well as firing some professors. Even so, Wayne prided itself on its egalitarian and liberal traditions. There were between 2,500 and 3,500 black students at Wayne during the 1960s, giving it a higher black enrollment than all the schools of the Big Ten and Ivy League combined. However, the tough municipal university, like so many Northern institutions, did not understand how far it had fallen short of black expectations. Many of the black students only attended part-time and did not end up with a degree. The 10 percent black enrollment might compare favorably to the figures for conservative, "prestige" institutions; but Detroit's population was moving rapidly toward a black majority, and against that background a 10 percent enrollment in the city university was not impressive. A minor indication of Wayne's relative indifference to racism was the fact that the college newspaper had never been known to take up social issues. It functioned primarily as an extension of the journalism department and was run like a high-school paper. Few blacks wrote stories for the paper, and there had never been a black editor.

The police riot at the Democratic Convention in Chicago was fresh news in the frantic summer of 1968, and much of America wondered if the armed uprisings of the previous summer would be repeated. The Weatherman faction of SDS (Students for a Democratic Society), with its dream of using bombs to open a military front within the borders of the United States, was about to become a household word. The revolutionaries of *ICV* and DRUM were thinking in far more practical terms. Through adroit electioneering and persuasion, they managed to capture a majority on the student committee responsible for selecting the editor of the *South End*, Wayne's daily student newspaper. The choice of the committee for the academic year 1968-1969 was John Watson. DRUM had scored an important victory, for editor Watson had virtually full control of a newspaper with a daily run of 18,000, a printing budget of $100,000, an editor's salary of $2,400, and a staff payroll of $23,400.

Watson had a bold vision of how the *South End* could be used. His term as editor proved to be one of the most successful examples in the late 1960s of how a black could lead a principled coalition of black and white forces struggling within a major institution. Watson took the position that the *South End* did not belong to the university, the state, or even the students as students. Wayne State University was a public resource that belonged to the entire population, and its daily newspaper was also a public resource that must speak to the needs of the entire population. This meant the *South End* would deal with the needs of students as workers, as slum dwellers, as potential draftees, as taxpayers, as parents, and as performers of any other role the society expected of them. The various university departments sent trainees into the neighborhoods, schools, industries, and clinics of the city as a matter of routine. It was only logical that the newspaper should also burst the boundaries of the campus and reach into those same places.

Luke Tripp and Mike Hamlin, two key members of *ICV* (which was published irregularly during this period), immediately came over to work as paid staff members of the *South End*. Tripp had been involved in most of the organizations in which Watson had figured. He was a quick-tempered man who had gained university notoriety in the early 1960s when he and Charles "Mao" Johnson worked in the library mailroom, from which they enthusiastically spread news about China quoted directly from the *Peking Review*. Tripp spent several hours a day on a physical-fitness program, had been a participant in the 1964 Cuba trip, and was fond of explaining his attitude to the United States government by declaring, "I oppose everything you support and I support everything you oppose."

Tripp summed up the general view of the university held by the *South End* staff when he told the authors in August 1972: "The university serves as the ideological and technological servant of the American ruling class." The *South End* rebels proposed to make their part of the university do just the opposite. They would be advocates for all those insurgent groups that were challenging the power of the old white men who ruled American society. They rejected the definition of objectivity used by the mass media, saying that it was only a pretext for perpetuating the viewpoint of the system. Mike Hamlin taunted one critic by saying, "There are two views, of course. The right and the wrong. You wouldn't want us to print the wrong one, would you?" The first editorial of the Watson term appeared on September 26, 1968, and spelled out the *South End*'s goals:

> The *South End* returns to Wayne State with the intention of promoting the interests of impoverished, oppressed, exploited, and powerless victims of white, racist monopoly capitalism and imperialism. . . . We will take the hard line. . . . Our position in each case will be demonstrated to be logical, just, and concrete and we will always be prepared to defend any position we take. . . . Our only enemies will be those who would further impoverish the poor, exploit the exploited, and take advantage of the powerless.

Readers of that first issue might have written off the editorial as part of the typical rhetoric of the black and student movements of that era. Even the two black panthers on either side of the masthead and the inscription "The Year of the Heroic Guerrilla" could be seen as brave posturing. Watson and associates soon put an end to such illusions. The most important person on the staff, next to John Watson, was a lean, tough, white ex-paratrooper with a prison record named Nick Medvecky. Watson and Medvecky had met earlier that summer. Medvecky had belonged to the Young Socialist Alliance but had left after disputes over the group's rules on discipline, such as the one prohibiting the smoking of marijuana. The relationship between Watson and Medvecky was crucial to the action which swirled around the *South End*.

Most of the black radicals working on the paper were also involved in agitation at Dodge Main and other activities of the emerging League of Revolutionary Black Workers. Medvecky, heading a mostly white production staff of whom only a few were radical, was responsible for actually putting out the paper. Watson laid out its general strategy, looked over the stories that went in, made criticisms before and after the fact, and had the final word on everything; but Medvecky was the gruff managing editor who chewed out lazy reporters and saw to all the details of day-to-day production. When some radical new line emerged from the editorial office, Medvecky would often act as the buffer between uneasy white staff members and Watson. He would recall with amusement in 1972 how some of the whites would sometimes threaten "to go to John over this," as if he and Watson were not in complete accord to begin with.

The *South End* quickly became the voice of a de facto radical united front. Although articles on DRUM, the local Black Panthers, third-world guerrilla movements, women's liberation, and anti-war activities predominated, every progressive element on campus and in the city could get its views published. The situation was exactly the reverse of that in the daily press. Insurgent opinion set the tone of the paper and commanded the editorial columns, while conservative and status quo opinion was relegated to rebuttal articles and letters to the editor.

The cultural revolution at the *South End* was not without its minor compromises. Medvecky and Watson took a practical line on the questions of sports coverage, the reporting of social activities, and the use of questionable language. Very early in their regime, they informed the fraternities and sororities that they could write their own copy and would have unquestioned access to a full page of the paper whenever they wanted it. Wayne had de-emphasized sports for years, but the radicals allotted space and photos to whatever events the sports-minded students were interested in. Most importantly, they avoided obscene and blasphemous language. University President Keast, a liberal, saw this as a significant compromise in a day when the alternate-culture press was making nudity and profanity an important freedom-of-the-press issue. Medvecky and Watson had no personal or ideological objection to using obscene or blasphemous language, but they saw it as a side issue the university might exploit to shut them down. The important thing was the politics of the paper. About that, there could be no compromise.

Some days, less than a thousand copies of the *South End* were distributed on campus, while several thousand were transported to school, hospital, and factory gates. Sometimes members of the staff would pick up copies of the paper from the stands after they had been distributed by the "straight" elements; more often, they simply arranged for the papers to be transported directly to a target community. The big 12-page special issue about DRUM written by Luke Tripp was distributed in the thousands at factories throughout the city. New exposures of conditions at Detroit General Hospital continued the attack on that institution started in *ICV*; the issues were given away in and around the hospital and eventually brought action from the city government. Issues attacking the deteriorating conditions in the public schools were distributed at high schools; and, as the year went on, high-school students came to work in the *South End* offices to prepare centerfolds on education. These were often slipped out of the larger paper and distributed as broadsides.

Watson demonstrated his customary fairness and flexibility throughout the time of his editorship. Rather than holding the newspaper as a resource only for his own organization or solely for the black movement, he encouraged other forces to use it as much as possible. A striking example of this was the special issue put out by staff member Nick Boyias and other Greek Americans who wished to agitate against the colonels who had seized power in Greece on April 21, 1967. For one day, the second anniversary of the coup, two Z's replaced the usual black panthers and the masthead inscription read, "One Greek Freedom Fighter Is Worth 100 Idle Greeks." The issue reviewed the revolutionary traditions of the Greek nation and called for armed struggle against the colonels. Some 10,000 copies mysteriously found their way to anti-junta organizations throughout the United States, Canada, Europe, and Australia. Similar consideration was given to other movements and causes which met the criterion of opposing "those who would further impoverish the poor, exploit the exploited, and take advantage of the powerless."

The *South End* was an important resource for insurgents in another fashion. Some members of DRUM drew *South End* salaries yet rarely appeared on campus, since they were busy doing work elsewhere. The editors never flaunted this or similar practices that the university might have been able to use against them. The paper appeared each and every day, so there could be no question of incompetency. All university rules and regulations were scrupulously followed—at least on paper. The legally selected editor and his legally selected staff had insulated themselves from any technical avenue of university attack.

President Keast had been finessed, and he knew it; but he was under increasing pressure from the UAW, business forces, and the state legislature to do something to stop the paper. As early as November 1968, suburban newspapers such as the *Southfield Sun* were making vitriolic attacks on Watson. The Wayne State Fund, an alumni group which contributed $300,000 a year to the university, expressed its concern repeatedly. These people knew very well that special agitation issues running to tens of thousands of copies were being used to undermine the Detroit power structure. They understood that the state of Michigan had been put into the position of supporting an organ that called for revolution against that very state. President Keast had no easy options. The Great Rebellion was barely a year past and there was no telling what black reaction would be to the dismissal of the paper's first black editor by executive fiat. This was especially true given the power DRUM and its sister groups had recently demonstrated in the factories. There was also the fact that Wayne had never had a significant campus protest movement. As one faculty member explained to a *Free Press* reporter in November, "[Keast] is haunted by the examples of Berkeley and Columbia. That might happen here if he clamps down. But at the same time, he's got important people complaining and telling him he's got to do something." Unfortunately for the enemies of the *South End*, they had no recourse but to bide their time and hope that Watson would make a mistake.

2

The unions were born 100 years ago, and claim to be free associations of the workers to defend themselves against the bosses. But today, in every country in the world, they have become one of the main instruments that the bosses have to maintain their control over the working class.

—An Italian Fiat worker, writing in *Lotta Continua*, November 1970

Events in the Detroit factories were not unique, either in the United States or in advanced industrial society as a whole. During the late 1960s, strong student and worker groups emerged throughout Europe and became particularly powerful in Italy and France. Just as the American workers challenged the UAW, the European rebels challenged their traditional unions, despite the fact that the unions were usually under socialist or communist control. The new groups rejected the traditional political formations and liked to call themselves *extra-parliamentarians*. They searched the American political landscape for comparable phenomena. Most of them became attracted to the Black Panther Party, but others became interested in the revolt at Dodge Main.

The Italian Socialist Party of Proletarian Unity (PSIUP) was part of the movement against the established parties, even though it main-

tained a parliamentary role by electing deputies to the national and
provincial parliaments. PSIUP planned an international anti-imperialist
conference for December 1968 which would feature speakers from the
South Vietnamese National Liberation Front and a representative of
the American black liberation movement. Many of the organizers
wanted a Black Panther as the American speaker, while others wanted
someone from Detroit. As chance would have it, John Watson was then
a member of the Detroit Black Panther Party. His name satisfied both
groups, and he was issued an invitation.

Watson's membership in two separate revolutionary organizations,
DRUM and the Panthers, represented a short-lived compromise between black revolutionary forces in Detroit and California. *ICV* had
given publicity to the Panthers when they first came to prominence.
The Detroit group's original attitude had been positive, yet the Detroiters understood that the Panther label would be as attractive in
their city as elsewhere and that the organization could be a rival of consequence for DRUM if allowed to develop an independent power base
within the Detroit population. They tried to avoid a possible crisis by
having Luke Tripp and John Williams organize the local Panther chapter; most of the people associated with *ICV* and DRUM became the initial membership. The effort was not grounded in duplicity. The
Detroiters assumed that the Panthers would recognize that their long
experience in the city qualified them to head the local struggle. They
expected the national linkage to be flexible, so that their chapter could
enjoy semi-autonomy. This arrangement quickly broke down, but dual
membership was still possible during Christmas of 1968.

Watson's trip to Italy was no pleasure jaunt. He had less than $10
in his pocket when he arrived in Italy, and he had the flu. The major
benefit of the trip was that he came to have firsthand knowledge of the
dissident workers' movement in one of Europe's more industrialized
countries. Watson was amazed at what he considered the tactical and
ideological timidity of the Italian Marxists, especially given their enormous working-class base. After speaking at the conference in Naples,
Watson made brief stops in Sardinia, Rome, and Turin, Italy's major
automobile manufacturing center, a city often compared to Detroit.
During this trip, Watson made the acquaintance of individuals from
extra-parliamentary groups and the radical wings of established parties.
Many of these people followed up the contacts made that Christmas of

1968 with subsequent visits to the United States, where they made additional contacts and pursued mutual theoretical concerns with their fellow revolutionaries. Events in the Michigan plants were probably followed more avidly in Turin and other Italian industrial centers than anywhere in the United States.

Watson returned to Detroit with his flu worsened and his wallet flat. Within a short time, he was fired by the *Detroit News* for having taken a vacation while claiming sick leave. It was more than a little ironic that the editor of the *South End*, Detroit's third daily, was supporting his family by working in the delivery room of the paper which boasted of having the largest circulation of any evening newspaper in America. It was even more ironic that it was at the *News* that Watson had become good friends with Mike Hamlin and Ken Cockrel. Hamlin had been employed as a driver of a delivery truck, and Cockrel, then working his way through law school, had served as Hamlin's assistant. The *News* had a reputation among blacks of being "a racist rag," and in its delivery room were three of its angriest critics. One of their revolutionary aims was to put papers like the *News* out of business, and their activities soon carried them to the front page of the newspaper they had once stacked, tied, and delivered.

3

When John Watson and myself, as the Editor-in-Chief and Managing Editor of last year's South End, came out with a front page news/editorial statement on Al Fatah, little did we realize at the time what a Pandora's Box had been opened.

—Nick Medvecky, *Inner City Voice*, November 1969

The *South End* masthead for 1969 declared, "One Class-Conscious Worker Is Worth 100 Students," and the paper became increasingly aggressive in its attacks on the UAW and the Big Three. Although the *South End* was viewed by its editors as the daily organ of the DRUM forces, it continued its policy of publicizing all mass-based revolutionary movements. Special issues dealt with the thought and the lives of Malcolm X and Martin Luther King, as well as with local controversies involving Judge George Crockett and attorney Ken Cockrel. The special issue on Greece appeared in April, and articles on Marxism by various authors were featured in numerous issues, along with articles on women's liberation and the anti-war movement. President Keast made his first effort to remove Watson as editor by saying that he had failed to register for winter classes; but Watson had simply registered late and Keast was forced to make a frontal assault. This major thrust began in late January, following an article favorable to the Al Fatah guerrilla organization written by Nick Medvecky. Keast charged that the *South End* was anti-Semitic and "reminiscent of Hitler's Germany."

Keast's attack was soon seconded by city, state, and union officials, backed up by the *Detroit News*, the *Detroit Free Press*, and the television stations. Many otherwise liberal people who knew that criticism of Zionism often served as a cloak for anti-Semitism did not understand that such was not the case with the *South End*, whose criticism was political and not racist or religious. Letters to the editor and rebuttal articles supporting Israel were printed as regularly as material supporting the Palestinian viewpoint. Similar articles on African guerrilla organizations had never generated such a reaction, and the editors were genuinely surprised at the storm brought down on them by the Al Fatah piece. They reaffirmed their own views, but emphasized that they would continue to provide ample space for opposing opinions, as had always been their policy. In spite of this reasonableness, the attacks on the *South End* mounted from every quarter, and on February 3 there was an arson attempt on the paper's offices.

The 24-year-old Watson stood his ground. He noted that the forces now raging against him had never spoken out against the institutionalized racial and religious discrimination found in Detroit and its suburbs, especially in Dearborn, where the Ford Motor Company could get anything it wanted, or in the five Grosse Pointe communities with their unique point system which effectively excluded Jews, blacks, and other "undesirables." The prestigious Detroit Athletic Club, to which many of Watson's critics belonged, had only one Jewish member, while the *South End* had an impeccable record of militant opposition to all forms of bigotry. Numerous Jewish writers had contributed guest editorials, plays, news stories, and columns to the *South End* throughout the fall of 1968, and the Jewish members of the staff unanimously supported the political criticism of Israel. Watson charged that the American Civil Liberties Union had attacked him because of the influence of the UAW and Max Fisher, the chairman of New Detroit. The state leg-islature, which threatened to cut off $100,000 in aid if Watson was not removed, had never taken such tough action to enforce civil rights leg-islation. The Wayne State Fund, an alumni group which also opposed him, was in the same position. Watson questioned why those who were so outraged by the *South End* had never moved against Breakthrough's Donald Lobsinger, a city employee who went around organizing openly racist and anti-Semitic groups reminiscent of the Black Legion that had terrorized Detroiters in the 1930s. Watson further pointed out that the Detroit area and nearby Toledo had the largest Arabic-speaking com-munities in North and South America and that the *South End* was a voice for them as much as for anyone else. An article by Harry Clark which appeared in the February 7 *South End* summed up the feelings of most of the blacks on campus: "The furor is based on the fact that the black journalists refuse to religiously follow the inane routines and ceremonies necessary in the establishment media."

The tempest came to a dramatic head on February 10 in an inci-dent involving Joe Weaver, a newscaster for WJBK-TV2, the CBS affili-ate in Detroit. Weaver entered the offices of the *South End* to get a taped interview with the editor. John Watson responded with a curt "no comment" to all questions and closed the door to his office. Weaver promptly forced his way in, and even though Watson ordered him to leave, continued to ask his questions. When Watson and other members of the staff tried to block the cameras which were recording the entire scene, scuffling began. Weaver was considerably taller and heavier than Watson, but when he left the *South End* offices, he went to police headquarters, where he filed charges against Watson for assault and battery. "The mad editor" of the *South End* had irrationally at-tacked a simple newsman trying to get a story.

Watson's response to Weaver's charges was to take the offensive. Rather than defend his own actions, in a *South End* article published on March 5, Watson made Weaver defend his: "I was completely within my rights and was fulfilling my obligations and responsibilities as editor when I expelled Weaver from the office. He was trespassing, abusive, provocative, and disruptive to the operation of the office. . . . It is TV-2 and Recorder's Court which will really be on trial." Ken Cockrel repre-sented Watson and developed the defense strategy. The film made by WJBK proved more helpful to Watson's case than to Weaver's. The jury had little difficulty in reaching a decision of acquittal for John Watson.

Mike Hamlin wrote an article at the time of the trial in which he said that the attack on the *South End* had opened the closet and let loose all the Detroit power structure ghosts. He charged that the university and the UAW had entered into a conspiracy with Chrysler and the mass media to put the *South End* out of action. What the masters of Detroit were really upset about was not an article discussing a Palestinian guerrilla organization but the assault on their power in the factories. Just as Chrysler called out the Hamtramck police to try to stop DRUM, Chrysler and the UAW had called out President Keast, the *Detroit News*, and WJBK-TV to stop the *South End*.

4

If Crockett is right, we should change the law. If Crockett is wrong, we should change Crockett.

—Carl Parsell, president, Detroit Police Officers Association, quoted in *South End*, April 3, 1969

Watson's position at the *South End* was shored up on March 29 by an incident, apparently unrelated to the university, which showed the importance of the newspaper as a resource against oppression and the need for a united response to legal and military pressures. The incident occurred at Reverend C.L. Franklin's New Bethel Baptist Church on Detroit's west side, where the Republic of New Africa (RNA) was holding its first anniversary meeting. More than 200 people were at the meeting, which was protected by armed security guards, a practice fully within the Michigan law. The celebration had ended and people were starting home when a squad car pulled up to the security guards. Officers Michael Czapski, aged 22, and Richard Worobec, aged 28, came out of the car. The confrontation which followed resulted in Czapski being killed, Worobec being badly wounded, and four civilians being wounded. Police cars careened into the neighborhood from every direction and the church was surrounded by police, who began firing rifles and pistols. For a moment, it seemed the Great Rebellion would flare anew; but there was little return fire, and soon every black person in sight had been seized and taken to the nearest police station.

Republic of New Africa members would state in court that the police had drawn their weapons and begun to fire for no apparent reason. The RNA members stated that they remembered the Algiers Motel incident, in which defenseless blacks had been killed by police, and that three separate police attacks on unarmed civilians in the latter part of 1968 were fresh in their minds. They claimed to have returned the officers' fire in self-defense. Worobec contested this version of the incident. He testified that he and Czapski had come out of their car with their guns in their holsters and that the security guards had shot at them for no apparent reason.

Brother Gaidi (Milton Henry), who was then the leader of the Republic of New Africa, had left the area before the shooting began. When he heard what had happened, he contacted black State Representative James Del Rio, who in turn informed Reverend Franklin of the incident. These two men then called black Judge George Crockett, who proceeded to the police station, where he found total legal chaos. Almost 150 people were being held incommunicado. They were being questioned, fingerprinted, and given nitrate tests to determine if they had fired guns, all without benefit of legal counsel, in total disregard of fundamental constitutional procedures. Hours after the roundup, there wasn't so much as a list of persons being held, and no one had been formally arrested. An indignant Judge Crockett set up court right in the station house and demanded that the police either press charges or release their captives. He had handled about 50 cases when Wayne County Prosecutor William L. Cahalan, called in by the police, intervened. Cahalan promised that the use of all irregular methods would be halted. Crockett adjourned the impromptu court, and by noon of the following day, the police had released all but a few individuals who were held on specific charges.

Crockett's action touched off a bitter controversy that was to engage Detroit for weeks. The Detroit Police Officers Association (DPOA) charged that Crockett's behavior sprang from racial feelings rather than legal principles and that he had given black paramilitary organizations a license to kill cops. The *Detroit News* concurred, calling Crockett's actions "unwarranted leniency." The DPOA launched a petition campaign to have Crockett impeached or removed. It took out a full-page ad in the *Detroit News* to present its case, and it set up picket lines around the judge's court. Governor William Milliken and various state senators responded to the initial DPOA efforts by calling for a full legislative probe of Crockett's fitness to remain on the bench.

Crockett refused to repent his actions. He declared that the police had no right to declare martial law whenever it pleased them. The mass arrests and unconstitutional procedures were typical of the police lawlessness which had victimized Detroit blacks for years. The police actions, he said, might have set off massive counter-violence in the streets if he had not intervened on behalf of due process. The *South End* of April 10 quoted him as saying: "Can any of you imagine the Detroit police invading an all-white church and rounding up everyone in sight to be bussed to a wholesale lockup in a police garage?"

The black population in the city rallied behind Crockett by forming the Black United Front, a group which included 60 organizations ranging from Christian churches to a black policemen's organization to DRUM. The Black United Front was an extra-governmental response similar to the People's Tribune set up to investigate the Algiers Motel killings. Dan Aldridge, a radical intellectual who had been active in the People's Tribune, became the chairman of the Black United Front. He articulated the four major premises of the organization, saying that the police failed to respect religious institutions, that the police failed to respect black women and children, that the police failed to respect the rights of those opposing institutionalized racism, and that public opinion was being misled by Governor Milliken, Police Commissioner Johannes F. Spreen, Mayor Cavanagh, Prosecutor Cahalan, the DPOA, and the *Detroit News*, all of whom were guilty of racism.

The *South End* devoted an entire issue to the New Bethel case. It reprinted statements from all sides, including those of Crockett, Del Rio, Franklin, the DPOA, and anti-Crockett reporters. Lengthy attempts were made to reconstruct the events accurately, and editorials probed the nature of the forces seeking to remove Crockett from office. If there were any doubts about where the *South End* stood editorially, a centerfold portrait of Judge Crockett put them to rest. Once more, thousands of copies of the paper left the university campus, reaching the streets, neighborhoods, and schools of the city.

The jurist at the center of the storm was no newcomer to political turmoil. George Crockett belonged to an earlier generation of Detroit black radicals. He had been one of the defense attorneys for the Communist Party in 1948 and 1949, when its leaders were prosecuted under the Smith Act. During the heated trials, Crockett had been cited for contempt of court by Judge Harold Medina, and he had served four months in a federal prison. In the 1950s, Crockett had defended Coleman Young and other blacks involved in trade union work when they were attacked by the House UnAmerican Activities Committee. Through the years Crockett had remained an active participant in a wide range of social movements; but because of his radical past he had been unable to gain elective office until 1966, when the surge of the black liberation movement had brought him to Recorder's Court. His friend Coleman Young had been elected to the state legislature in 1964 and had begun to build the power base that would carry him to the Detroit mayor's office in 1973. In the April 10 *South End*, Crockett spoke of the New Bethel problems as only the latest of a long sequence. "The causes are steeped in racism—racism in our courts, in our jobs, in our streets, and in our hearts."

On April 3, 1969, the Black United Front called for demonstrations in support of Crockett, and some 3,000 people responded. Among the cooperating groups were two white organizations, the Ad Hoc coalition, led by Sheila Murphy, and People Against Racism, led by Frank Joyce. Two weeks later, the Detroit Commission on Community Relations issued a report which was generally favorable to Crockett. On the same day the report appeared, the *Detroit Free Press* published an unusual editorial apologizing for inaccurate information in earlier stories which had been damaging to Crockett. A short time later, the Michigan Bar Association and spokesmen for the UAW and New Detroit defended Crockett's legal positions. Governor Milliken and other officials reversed some of their original views and attacked the political opinions being expressed by the DPOA. The storm was passing for the 59-year-old judge, who was completely vindicated. The sensational New Bethel trials lay in the future; but the black community had fought for its judge, and some of the spillover aided the embattled John Watson at the *South End*. It did not take a political pundit to note that many of those who had opposed Crockett most vociferously also opposed Watson.

5

*ONE QUESTION—The facts in this paper are in the hands of the
news media—why do you not see them? THINK.*
    —*South End* masthead, June 1969

Watson had committed the *South End* to the Crockett fight without any reservations. Crockett's subsequent victory, coupled with the
court victory over Joe Weaver, strengthened Watson immeasurably.
The paper's policy of printing pro-Israel articles, the support of students and faculty, and the general cooling of temperatures brought
more people to the realization that a newspaper could criticize the state
of Israel without being anti-Semitic, just as an individual could be personally anti-Semitic yet support the domestic or foreign policy of the
state of Israel for business or political reasons. Watson agreed to hold a
weekly public coffee-hour meeting with President Keast in the Student
Center cafeteria to keep communications open and promote student
body participation in the decision-making. Even so, articles favorable to
the guerrilla organizations continued; and on May 15, a special eight-
page issue dealt with the Palestinian question in much the same terms
as had the issue of January 29 which set off the confrontation. The
radicals had won.

The importance of Watson's editorship of the *South End* would be
hard to overemphasize. A group of white and black radicals had consciously wrested an important resource from the state, and they had successfully warded off a serious attempt to dislodge them. The radicals had
transformed a lifeless student publication into a daily mass-circulation
paper. The principled use of the *South End* had strengthened the alliance of radical forces under black leadership, an alliance that did not
indulge itself in sycophantism or appeals to white guilt feelings. The
South End had worked because its readers had seen the journal as being
written for them rather than against them. In a very real way, Watson,
Medvecky, and the others had realized Wayne's often-expressed goal of
being relevant to the larger Detroit community. Their sense of what
was relevant, however, differed drastically from that of Keast, the university, and liberals. Watson had explained his views in an interview
printed in the July-August 1968 issue of *Radical America:*

We are no more for integrated capitalism than for segregated capitalism. Neither are we in favor of a separate state, based on the same class lines as in this society. We are against a separate state in which a black capitalist class exploits a black proletariat. We are opposed also to all sorts of haphazard talk which doesn't tell us what to do with the United States, capitalism, and imperialism. . . . We had studied the history of the Russian Bolsheviks and found a specific pamphlet by Lenin called *Where To Begin*, written in 1903, before he wrote *What Is To Be Done?*, where he described the rôle a newspaper could play. A newspaper was the focus of a permanent organization. It could provide a bridge between the peaks of activity. It creates an organization and organizes the division of labor among revolutionaries. Revolutionaries do something, not just a meeting on Sunday, making speeches, and passing resolutions. It creates the kind of division of labor needed not just for the newspaper but for a revolutionary organization.

Two years after his work on the *South End* finished, Nick Medvecky evaluated the Watson editorship for the authors of this book. He stated that the Trotskyist group to which he had belonged had responded to the political stance of the pre-Watson *South End* by proposing a critical newsletter to be distributed on campus. Watson's response to the same situation had been the more dynamic one of taking over the paper entirely. One view reflected the oppositionist mentality which dominated most of the radical and student movements, while the other assumed that a serious bid for power might become a short-term objective. Medvecky noted that although the *Fifth Estate*, Detroit's alternate-culture paper, had done good work since being founded in 1966 and deserved its reputation as one of the best underground papers, it was still cemented in an essentially oppositionist framework. It had not gotten its own production equipment and thus remained dependent for survival on costly printers and other outside technicians. Its goal was to be a perpetual weekly alternate-culture news and "freak" sheet rather than a widely read popular paper capable of fomenting deep social change. Harvey Ovshinsky, the founder of the paper, had said as much when asked to comment on the role of the *Fifth Estate* for Robert J. Glessing's *The Underground Press in America*, a book published in 1970: "There are four estates, the fourth of which is journalism. We are the fifth because we are something different than . . . other newspapers. We hope to fill a void in that fourth estate. . . . A void created by party newspapers and the cutting of those articles which express the more liberal viewpoint. That's what we really are— the voice of the liberal element." (Ovshinsky's views dominated throughout most of the paper's history, even though staff members such as Peter Werbe tried to take a more radical political line. The paper's policy changed slowly. Unlike most underground papers begun in the 1960s, the *Fifth Estate*, under changing editors, survived into the 1970s and in July 1974 became a weekly. An editorial of June 8 expressed the politics of the paper at that time: "The *Fifth Estate* is simply a newspaper which is owned and operated by the people who work there. Our politics are simple: everybody's lives and tools for survival should be owned and operated by those who expend labor—not those who manage and take a cut (profit) of the labors of others.")

The differing perspectives of Ovshinsky and Watson reflected a real division between advocates of an alternate lifestyle and hardcore political revolutionaries. Nationally, individuals such as Abbie Hoffman and Allen Ginsberg practiced a cultural revolution from above, based on the glorification of a few thumb-nosing superstars in a Hall of Fame conception of history. They mythologized the mammoth musical concert held at Woodstock, New York, in August 1969 as a political convocation of a youth nation. They believed the mass media could be infiltrated and manipulated into popularizing their views. William Burroughs, author of *The Naked Lunch*, summarized the possibilities of media manipulation as a cultural weapon in an interview given to one of the authors in 1970 and subsequently published in *Something Else Yearbook 1974*: "There's an extremely chaotic situation which revolutionaries can take full advantage of. For instance, there's a gap between the mass media and the administration. We're beginning to get an overlap between some liberal elements in the mass media and the underground press. I think this is an important development. It should be encouraged."

The forces around DRUM were never sympathetic to the notion of manipulating the established media because they believed that the media could publicize any number of revolutionary acts without threatening the established power structure. By giving some exposure to radical ideas, especially those which were moral and cultural rather than economic, the media solidified the liberal mystique of open debate and discussion of challenging ideas. Burning cities, guerrilla spokesmen, and gurus of every creed could be and were reduced to a ten-minute specta-cle on the evening news or a talk show.

Their struggles with the *Detroit News*, WJBK-TV, and other news vehicles had led the Detroiters to the conclusion that they needed total control of their own cultural apparatus if they were serious about con-tending for power. The problems in printing *ICV* and the attempted suppression of the *South End* had indicated the necessity of owning printing equipment and having trained personnel to operate it. DRUM was about the business of gaining power for its constituency, rather than merely acting as a moral witness for it. The sharpening conflict with the Black Panthers involved some of the same issues regarding the media. The black leather jackets and berets of the Panthers were good media fare, perhaps too good. The DRUM forces believed in keeping their membership under cover as much as possible, especially those in-volved in military operations. They felt that the masses should be pre-sented with images that were realistic rather than those of superheroes whom they might admire but would be afraid to imitate. DRUM activ-ists and their allies did not refer to themselves as "freaks" or "move-ment heavies." Rather than making a spectacle in the courtroom, they wanted to be in a position to control that courtroom, to control the judge, and to control the jury selection. Rather than shouting "Off the Pig!" as some others did, DRUM worked for the power to control the police department. Gestures made for a capitalist headline, even a "hip" capitalist headline, were perhaps counterproductive and in any case were secondary to amassing the resources, trust, and talent to pro-mote a cultural revolution from below.

The major error made by the *South End* leaders concerned the con-tinuity of control. Fighting off the charges of anti-Semitism and in-volved in one political struggle after another, Watson and his associates did not pay attention to the 1969-1970 appointments. Since the paper was never used to organize the student body and the rules for selecting the editor had been changed in midyear, no candidate who could slip through the process was put forward until too late. There was, in fact, a revolt of part of the staff late in the year. Calling themselves the *South End* Revolutionary Union Movement, some whites on the staff, includ-ing the woman who would become summer editor and the man who would become editor for 1969-1970, asked for more collectivity in de-cision-making. The rebels supported the general editorial direction of the paper but complained that Watson and Medvecky operated in a dictatorial manner. When all efforts at compromise failed, Medvecky fired all the dissidents and Luke Tripp threatened to throw them out the window if they didn't vacate their offices. Most were quickly re-hired, but the possibility of the Watson group retaining control for an-other year had been lost. The summer editor got the paper closed down for obscenity after only a few days of publishing, and the 1969-1970 editor began a transition to safer ways. Even so, the *South End* would never quite return to its former political irrelevance. Periodically, the paper would fight as it had fought under Watson, and during the stu-dent agitation over the invasion of Cambodia, Medvecky and the Wat-son stalwarts returned to the paper for a brief period of control. In retrospect, Watson saw that losing control of the *South End* was a costly mistake, but by the spring of 1969 the DRUM and *ICV* forces were in-volved in various funding projects that gave every indication of being able to finance a totally independent print shop which could produce *ICV* at will.

6

Father, I know you came
Out of a long mountain
Wide thumbed, brimming with mustache
Your shoulders stuck in a tight coat
Pieces of bread in your pocket. . . .

—Abdeen Jabara, "Father"

The furor over the alleged anti-Semitism of the *South End* tended to obscure a far more substantial link developing between the black revolutionaries and Detroit's Arabs. The Detroit Arabs, like most of the Arabs in the United States, were a more or less invisible minority. The earlier, established immigrants tended to be white skinned, 90 percent Christian, and involved in small business. Due to their relatively small numbers, they had been absorbed into the American melting pot more easily than most immigrant groups. A popular television comedy series starring Lebanese American Danny Thomas was about as much play as their Arabness ever got. One of the mainstays of the program was a quaint old uncle still imbued with the customs and habits of the Middle East.

The Arab immigration pattern changed abruptly in 1966 when the federal laws were revamped to allow easier immigration of people who were relatives of American citizens. The new wave of Arab immigrants who took advantage of the change were primarily dark-skinned Muslims with little formal education. The newcomers invariably worked in heavy industry, where they got the same dangerous and arduous jobs as blacks. The Arab community in Detroit swelled to 85,000 and began to take on a dual quality. On the one hand, it was like the established European immigrant communities of an earlier epoch; and on the other hand, it was like the racially defined ethnic minorities such as Native Americans, Asian Americans, and Hispanic Americans.

The most coherent Arab community was in a section of Dearborn which had the same name as Wayne's newspaper, the South End. This area, immediately to the east of the Ford River Rouge complex, housed more than 6,000 people who were almost entirely immigrants or first-generation Americans of various nationalities. Approximately half of this population was Arabic, with a heavy proportion of Yemenites. In many cases, 400-600 people from the same village in Yemen had come to the South End. Mayor Hubbard had never made it a secret that Dearborn was a "white man's town," and the Arabs were considered to be so many "white niggers." Beginning in the early 1960s, Hubbard had harassed home-owners by restricting building and repair permits, strictly enforcing an onerous housing code, and scaring off federally guaranteed financing. These moves effectively eliminated the private real estate market and all but forced people to sell their property to the city, which promptly tore down all buildings in an effort to push out the immigrants and convert the South End to industrial use. The mayor's actions had been challenged in a class-action lawsuit begun by a Community Council headed by Arab American Alan Amen.

The personal history of Alan Amen's family illustrates the kind of lives Dearborn Arabs led. Amen's grandfather had been born in Lebanon and had worked 42 years for the Ford Motor Company. His father was working in his 34th year as a janitor at Ford in 1973 and had never had the opportunity to learn to read or write English. Alan Amen's older brother, Ron, a Vietnam veteran, had lost the use of his left hand when it was crushed by machinery at the Premier Steel Company. Like many of the working poor before him, Alan Amen tried to break his family cycle of factory work by taking courses at Wayne State University. His mother, Katherine, who had been a secretary and was active in community affairs, drew him into the struggle against the city. The Amen family, like many Arab Americans, saw Dearborn's efforts as one more contemptuous act by a society that viewed Arabs as dirty il-literates without culture or common sense. Alan Amen's personal dream was to see the South End become a center of Arabic life that would promote Arab culture in the way Chinese centers did in San Francisco and New York. His mother became the plaintiff in the class-action suit brought against the city of Dearborn, and the pressures on Alan Amen became so strong that his wife, Karen, a nurse, had to sup-port the family.

Amen became treasurer of the Community Council in 1968 and president in 1970. Other officers were Nick Koicheff, a Greek in his sixties, Jerri Rallis, a Cherokee Indian in her thirties, and Helen Okdi Atwell, a mother of eight who, although a Muslim of Lebanese descent, hoped to become an anti-Hubbard member of the Dearborn City Council. Under their leadership, the community achieved a landmark victory on August 14, 1973, when federal Judge Ralph Freeman ruled that Mayor Hubbard had improperly conducted a ten-year campaign of harassment. The judge gave 350 former home-owners affected by the class-action suit the right to sue the city for the difference between the price paid to them for relocation and the true market value of their property. Judge Freeman agreed with 28 of the plaintiff's 33 grievances in a decision that saved the South End community from further de-struction. The Community Council was legally represented by Abdeen Jabara and by the Center of Urban Law and Housing at the University of Detroit Law School, a Jesuit institution. Zakhour Yousseff of the Psychology Department of Eastern Michigan University and Barbara Aswad of Wayne's Anthropology Department offered key testimony on the disruption of cultural vitality by the city's actions.

Attorney Jabara was representative of yet another new force in Arab-American life. Born in a small town in Michigan, he had served in a number of Arab cultural organizations and had been the Arabic-speaking lawyer on the defense team of Sirhan Sirhan, the Palestinian immigrant convicted of assassinating Robert Kennedy. Rather than seeking to further Westernize their lifestyles, Arab Americans like

Jabara took pride in their distinct political, culinary, literary, and musical heritage. They felt that Arabic culture, far from being a slave culture, was at least equal if not superior to Western culture. At Wayne, they sought to create an Arabic Cultural Room to be a showcase of Arab accomplishments, and they were active in a series of ethnic festivals held annually in the city of Detroit. One goal of the Arabs in Detroit was to establish an Arabic Community Center for Economic and Social Services with a bilingual staff to deal with the roster of labor, health, legal, and housing difficulties facing the Arabic community. Jabara was not as pleased with the court victory as might be expected. He told the authors in February 1974 that the lawsuit "wasn't won on community rights, but on the constitutional principle of due process of law to protect the taking of private property."

The problems of the Dearborn Arabs were reflected in the rest of the metropolitan area as well. In an article in the *Arab-American University Graduate Newsletter* of October 1973, Amen stated that 2,000 of the 35,000 workers at Ford Rouge were Arabs. He was incensed that Ford Local 600, the largest local in the UAW, had bought $300,000 worth of Israeli bonds without rank-and-file approval. The UAW as a whole had bought more than $750,000 of the 5.5 percent bonds, and by mid-1973 Arab members of the UAW were trying to organize a serious opposition to the union leadership, which they felt did not represent or respect them. They had many of the same on-the-job problems as blacks, and they asked blacks how they would feel if the UAW had bought the national bonds of the Union of South Africa or Rhodesia. The potential power of the dissident Arab workers was something to be reckoned with. An informal UAW count in three plants disclosed that Chrysler's Jefferson Assembly plant had 1,400 Arab workers, its Mound Road plant had 800, and the Hamtramck complex that included Dodge Main had almost 2,000. The UAW's national membership included at least 15,000 Arab workers, most of whom were in the Detroit area.

During the peak of activity of DRUM, many of the Arabs at Dodge Main had crossed DRUM picket lines for fear of losing their jobs. By 1973, they had gained in numbers and militancy, both in their neighborhoods and in their workplaces. On October 14, marching 70 abreast, 3,000 Arabs staged a militant parade from the streets of the South End in Dearborn to the offices of Local 600, where they protested the UAW bond purchases. On November 28, when Leonard Woodcock was being presented the Humanitarian Award of B'nai B'rith at a $100-a-plate dinner attended by a thousand guests, 2,000 Arabs and their supporters demonstrated outside. Most of the demonstrators were workers who had walked off their jobs and had agitated to get other workers to do the same. The result was that both lines of Dodge Main's afternoon shift were shut down that day for the first time since the DRUM wildcats. In the next issue of *Solidarity*, the union paper, Emil Mazey denounced the demonstration as communist inspired. He said that the disputed bonds had been purchased in the 1956-1966 period and had been converted in 1967 to bonds payable in 1986. He said that they did not indicate support for Israel against the Arabs but were simply a good investment, backed by "the only country in the Middle East with a free and democratic labor movement and a freely elected Labor Party government."

The new Arab immigrant workers of the late 1960s felt that the UAW, like most American institutions, was hostile to them. The Arabs believed that they were regarded as so many transplanted "camel jockeys" who had the additional handicap of being not quite white and not quite black. They were like the Puerto Ricans, Chicanos, Filipinos, and West Indians employed in other American industries and localities. They were also part of a larger world pattern. Beginning in the 1950s, European capital had made massive use of cheap immigrant labor. Black Africans, Turks, Greeks, Arabs, Yugoslavs, Italians, and Spaniards had found work in northern Europe, France, Switzerland, and northern Italy. They frequently were forced to live in separate compounds and were paid wages inferior to those of domestic labor. In a French auto plant it was not uncommon to find five or six nationalities who literally did not speak the same language interspersed on an assembly line. Similarly, in the early 1970s, American capital began to import cheap labor for specific industries. In the East, along with Puerto Ricans, who had been immigrating for years, there were large influxes of South Americans and various Caribbean peoples, particularly Haitians, Jamaicans, and Dominicans, each with their own culture and language. On the West Coast, the cheap labor was primarily of Mexican and Asian ancestry.

The migrant-labor pattern was so invisible to most Americans that it came as a shock even to knowledgeable people that the first farm worker killed by police in the decade-long struggle to unionize the farm workers was not a Chicano but a young Yemeni immigrant named Nagi Daifullah. On August 17, 1973, 10,000 people marched in Delano, California, in a memorial service for the slain Daifullah and for Juan de la Cruz, a 60-year-old Chicano killed one day later. United Farm Workers National Director Cesar Chavez called for a national three-day fast for the two men. At the memorial service for Daifullah, Chavez said, "He came to this country seeking opportunity and fell into a trap of poverty and powerlessness that has enslaved so many migrant farm workers in our country. Nagi was not content to be a slave in a free country. He joined the United Farm Workers union and gave of himself fully to the grape strike and the assertion of farm workers' justice. Nagi Daifullah is now dead at the age of 24, a victim of violence by a sheriff's deputy of Kern County."

In Dearborn, the Arab community held two marches in honor of Daifullah. They learned from speakers that the thousands of Arabs working in the California fields were mostly men without skills or knowledge of English who lived in company "camps" often lacking the most basic sanitation. The workers were completely alienated men—alienated from their families, from their community, and from American society. Few of the Arab workers could even communicate directly with the Chicanos, Filipinos, and Portuguese who shared their lives in the fields and on the picket lines.

The killing of Daifullah in a California grape strike also reinforced the fear many Arabs had of the American government. They knew that "Operation Boulder," set up by the U.S. State Department in 1972, had brought federal pressure on all Arab travelers and visiting students. Everyone knew of people visited in their homes and places of work by the FBI and of students deported for their political views. In the harbor of Detroit, sailors from the ships *Kuwait Horizon* and the *Star of Kuwait* had not been allowed shore leave in the United States. In the latter case, the captain of the ship was emotionally unstable, and the vessel had to dock on the Canadian side of the river so that he could be dismissed and the seamen's needs met. Many Arab Americans began to fear that if the Middle East wars should ever involve U.S. troops on a serious level, they might be treated as the Japanese Americans had been during World War II. These fears, justified or not, combined with the problems facing Arab workers, paved the way for a working alliance with revolutionary black workers. From the standpoint of organizations like DRUM, the Arabs were only one example of several racial minorities that might be persuaded to work on a fraternal basis with blacks.

Chapter Four

The League of Revolutionary Black Workers

1

A union of workers is power. They can, if they so decide, control the economy of a country as large and powerful as the USA simply by calling a general strike.

—League of Revolutionary Black Workers, in a special UAW convention issue of *Inner City Voice*, November 1969

The success of DRUM bred a score of RUMs in other factories, as well as an UPRUM (among United Parcel Service workers), an HRUM (among health workers), and a NEWRUM (among *Detroit News* workers). The elections at Dodge Main had demonstrated that a whole range of media, legal, and neighborhood support mechanisms would be necessary if DRUM and its offspring were to survive even the first counter-attacks of company and union. Almost from the first wildcat, there were discussions on how to weave an umbrella organization to unite the local RUMs and their support groups and allies. The final result was an organization named the League of Revolutionary Black Workers, which was legally incorporated in June 1969 and opened its headquarters at 179 Cortland Street four months later.

The League published numerous documents and position papers and had a finely drawn organizational chart, but it never functioned with the precision of a capitalist corporation or a Marxist-Leninist party. Rather than having a strict hierarchy, the League was organized into several components which had specific areas of work. Each component had a semi-autonomous character which often reelected the particular personalities of the individuals in charge. There was a central staff which grew to 80 members, but the organization was tightly controlled by a seven-man Executive Committee made up of General Baker, Kenneth Cockrel, Mike Hamlin, Luke Tripp, John Watson, John Williams, and Chuck Wooten.

The relatively loose structure of the League did not prevent the organization from developing a clear sense of strategy. The League viewed company, union, and government as an interconnected system of power that gave an appearance of intransigence but actually did not regard any one battle as critical. The stakes were much higher than those involved in any single confrontation, and the system was flexible enough to allow ample room for error, limited failures, some accommodation of worker demands, and grudging change. The League also appeared intransigent; but it, too, viewed no single election, strike, or activity as more than one operation in a broader campaign. One reason the League was able to flourish was that its opponents, who were so precise in describing their own actions and motivations, habitually abstracted the League's actions from their historical and organizational context. They saw local League actions centering on limited demands as the sole concern of the organization. They never imagined that a leaflet at Jefferson Assembly and a poster at Northern High School and a door-to-door petition on Dexter Avenue were all part of a system of interlocked centers of power and influence. They did not understand that the League sought to create a multilevel power apparatus parallel to the power apparatus of the system it sought to destroy.

The most publicized League activity was the in-plant organizing led by General Baker and Chuck Wooten. The approach, following the pattern of DRUM, was to move plant by plant, building small core groups and perfecting models of organization, discipline, and ideology. DRUM led to the birth of ELRUM (Eldon Avenue Revolutionary Union Movement) in November 1968, and soon ELRUM had an even larger membership than DRUM. There was also a FRUM at Ford's

River Rouge complex, a JARUM at Chrysler's Jefferson Avenue Assembly plant, a MARUM at the Mack Avenue plant, a CADRUM at Cadillac's Fleetwood factory, a DRUM II at Dodge Truck, and a MERUM at the Mound Road Engine plant—as well as units at Chevrolet's Livonia factory, at Ford's Wixom plant, at the Huber foundry, at the Winfield foundry, at Chrysler's Forge plant, and at the Plymouth Assembly plant. Had each of these new RUMs been as broadly based and popular as DRUM and ELRUM, the League would have had the strength of a fledgling political party or an alternate union. The reality, however, was that many of the RUMs reflected potential rather than solid organizations. Sometimes only a handful of workers were involved. A few bulletins or a single action might be the extent of their activities. The situation at each factory was unique. At Paragon Steel in Detroit, there was no RUM organization as such, but people in contact with the League carried out a small strike. In CADRUM, at the Fleetwood Cadillac plant, there were many older workers who had a long and militant history of shop-floor activism, including struggles with Ku Klux Klan elements in the local union. Often the new RUM units contained company, union, and police spies. The ranks also contained many confused sympathizers, vacillators, and strident black nationalists. Careful work was required on the part of the top leadership to filter out these elements and to make a reliable unit. One of the ever-present dilemmas during the first year of League operations was whether to answer a new inquiry or to devote extra time to an existing RUM. The League leadership's time and energy were spread thin and the organization's structure was as fragile as a pyramid of playing cards. Funds were limited and the task enormous, but requests for aid and information kept coming in, not only from the Detroit area but from all parts of the United States. There seemed to be no limit to how far the RUM idea might reach. The League constitution itself declared, "We must act swiftly to help organize DRUM type organizations wherever there are black workers, be it in Lynn Townsend's kitchen, the White House, White Castle, Ford Rouge, the Mississippi Delta, the plains of Wyoming, the mines of Bolivia, the rubber plantations of Indonesia, the oil fields of Biafra, or the Chrysler plant in South Africa."

The Baker group heavily emphasized the need to galvanize the new RUMs into tough and dependable units. They wanted all out-of-plant activities subordinated to this primary task. A number of other

League leaders believed that it was just as essential to organize people outside the factories—in the neighborhoods, schools, and places of recreation. These leaders stressed the interrelationship and interdependence of all League activities. Mike Hamlin, in particular, was concerned about the possibility of the individual RUMs becoming isolated. Perhaps the most patient and low-keyed personality in the leadership, Hamlin spun a web of alliances and relations for the purposes of creating a good public image for the League and strengthening the links between the various League components. Hamlin emphasized the need for student and community groups which could carry on public demonstrations when court injunctions and other considerations barred workers from public activity. Hamlin also was anxious to see the white radicals in the city form some organization which could act in concert with the League, and he wanted to find a device to link up Detroit activities with those of the similar groups emerging in other locations. Hamlin recalled some of the early League days in an interview given to the authors in 1972:

> We came to believe that the working class had to make the revolution, had to lead the revolution, and that we had to concentrate our energies on workers. We didn't really understand what making a revolution entailed, what a proletarian revolution was, how it took shape, and how it developed. . . . I began to feel we must broaden our contacts within the community. We needed support to continue the struggle. I also felt we should build several kinds of resources to serve the struggle. We needed a printing operation, a legal apparatus, and stepped-up political education. . . . The League began to recruit large numbers of students and professionals. I think that our understanding of proletarian consciousness at that time was very low, and we did not do a good job of transforming the understanding of our new members. We were held together by personal loyalties rather than ideology. People were coming to us for the same reason we had started. They wanted to find ways to struggle. They would come in and we would do work, but our ideology remained unclear. Word of what was happening in Detroit got to workers in other cities. They began to wage similar struggles and they began to communicate with us. We started to discuss ideas about coalitions, affiliations, national caucuses, black worker organizations, and so forth. . . . Community organizing and industrial organizing are linked up. They go together. The working class should lead the community effort.

Watson shared Hamlin's views and added his own ideas on the use of media to build a secondary leadership and to combat the ideological underdevelopment of many rank-and-file League members. Watson considered it impractical and wasteful to have a few individuals scurrying from one plant to another in what amounted to a permanent state of frenzy. He had already demonstrated, with *ICV* and the *South End*, that a revolutionary newspaper could be an organ of mass political education. He wanted to extend that education by moving into films, radio, printing, and television. Watson felt that if the League could acquire its own media facilities, it could conduct mass political education on a scale unprecedented in Detroit or elsewhere. In a speech delivered on June 8, 1971, at a public meeting held in Detroit's Central Methodist Church, Watson gave his views of the need for political education:

> I want to emphasize that education and knowledge are the most powerful tools that we have available in engaging in the struggle to make a better world. It is through the control of knowledge that the ruling class maintains its power. The struggle over the control of knowledge itself is a political struggle. The ruling classes have for many centuries understood this very clearly. Back to the days when the typical statement that you might hear from a slaveowner was, "Hell no, I don't want my slaves to learn how to read and write because educated niggers become uppity." That's exactly correct, and the man understands it very clearly today.

Ken Cockrel, who was admitted to the Michigan Bar in 1968, was closely associated with Watson and Hamlin. Outsiders tended to view Cockrel as the League's "intellectual in residence," but his biography was similar to that of the other League leaders. His parents had come from the Deep South during World War II, and his first home was in one of the army barracks thrown up around 8 Mile Road, the northern city limit, to house blacks brought to work in the factories. Cockrel's father had a job at Ford, and his mother was the first black woman to graduate from Lincoln High School in Ferndale. Both parents died when Cockrel was 12, and he was brought up by an aunt who worked as a supermarket cashier and an uncle who worked in various industrial plants around the city. Cockrel quit high school in the 11th grade and hung around the streets for a while. His state of mind at that time was like that of many Detroit blacks; he was quoted in an October 14, 1973, article in the *Detroit News* as saying: "I just knew I wasn't going to bang metal in some factory all my life. But I was in a general course in school and wasn't aimed at anything particular. So I joined the Air Force, like my brother Sye had done."

In the Air Force, Cockrel got top security clearance and trained as a nuclear weapons technician. When he got out, he thought he might try college. Turned down by Highland Park Junior College because he was a high school dropout, he was admitted to Wayne in 1959 as a conditional adult student in a special program for those who had not completed high school. Cockrel got a B.A. in 1964 and a law degree in 1967, just one month before the Great Rebellion. He soon joined a racially integrated law firm headed by Harry Philo. Cockrel and some of his law partners acted as the League's de facto legal component. In spite of the numerous criminal and civil actions involving League members, it was Cockrel's boast that no one, including himself, was ever convicted. Much of this remarkable record was a result of the brilliant courtroom performance of Cockrel himself, but various League policies were also helpful. The League discouraged inflammatory statements that could not be backed up, and it made a practice of investigating the past personal history of anyone wanting to join the League, especially anyone expressing extreme political views. Cockrel understood better than anyone else in the League the gamut of legal ploys that could be used against the organization. He was convinced that to survive and prosper it was essential to have a powerful presence within the media and within the community. In a retrospective interview given to the authors of this book in 1972, Cockrel said:

> If you are only dealing inside [the] trade union context, then you are not able to have the kind of pressure from the people who are affected by working-class struggle who are not workers. You don't have any criteria that are developed. . . .
>
> The situation at the point of production itself is such that the kind of controls, the kind of political discipline that is necessary for struggle to advance doesn't seem to me to be susceptible of being developed at the point of production independently of some interaction with other struggles inside the community and broader, more class-conscious, more programmatic input. . . .
>
> We had to develop a concept of what to do when workers are fired for doing organizational activity, and you are not in a position to feed

them, and you are not in a position to force the management to take them back, and you are not in a position to relate concretely to any of their needs. We had to confront incredible tactical questions. You are confronted with the questions of whether to try to force the union to get their jobs back; and if the union succeeds, then the union is assisted and your influence diminished. On the other hand, if you make no response, you are in a position of having led workers out of the plant on the basis of an anti-racist, anti-imperialist, and anti-capitalist line, and having the man respond, and you can't do anything. . . .

When Chrysler is attacked in America, it pushes a buzzer and gets the Hamtramck Police Department. The whole city structure goes into action. At Ford, you are dealing with Dearborn. The fact that we closed down Dodge Main, the basic assembly plant for Chrysler operations in this entire country, means we got a response. We got police. We got injunctions from the courts. They tried to destroy our organization. They tried to kill leaders like General Baker and Chuck Wooten. Most all of the members of our central staff had to go to trial sometime in the year of 1969.

Luke Tripp and John Williams held a middle position between those emphasizing in-plant organizing and those who saw the different League activities as equally important. Tripp and Williams were concerned about the political level of the average League supporter, but they were hesitant about moving too rapidly in too many different directions. They thought that political education might be best served by a more intense contact with individual workers in small social and study groups, rather than by the ambitious plans Watson, Hamlin, and Cockrel began to advance. Tripp and Williams were the initial leaders of the Detroit Black Panther Party and did not want to see the mistakes of the BPP repeated. They were not pleased by talk of spreading the League to other cities, and they did not always approve of the interviews given by Watson, Cockrel, and Hamlin in which DRUM and the League were projected in glowing terms. As members of the Detroit BPP, one of their quarrels with the California headquarters was over the issue of working with John Sinclair, a white local counter-culture poet with a flair for publicity on the issues of marijuana, psychedelic drugs, and the new music. They feared that the growing involvement of the League with white radicals might give rise to similar mismatches of interest and commitment. Tripp kept saying that the local organizational model must be perfected before it was ballyhooed around the nation. He summed up his view in the January 23, 1969, issue of the

South End by saying that political education should "cultivate a firm and correct political orientation, an industrious and pure style of work, and flexible strategy and tactics."

A concrete example of what the out-of-plant organizers had in mind occurred during the period of 1969-1970 when the Detroit Board of Education announced a plan to decentralize control. The West Central Organization (WCO), a coalition of neighborhood groups based at first on the ideas of Saul Alinsky, had appointed John Watson as its director. WCO was concerned about whether the decentralization plan would be an improvement or a backward step for blacks. Watson organized a conference attended by 300 representatives from 70 organizations. Some of these were black groups and some were white or integrated groups willing to work under black leadership. They formed another coalition called Parents and Students for Community Control (PASCC). The immediate issue was community control of schools, a matter which involved community groups in almost every major American city; but, under League urging, PASCC began to be more than a community-control group. PASCC came to see itself as the beginning of a permanent citywide network of communications and action. Hundreds of rallies and meetings took place, and PASCC representatives made regular appearances on radio, on television, and in schools. PASCC soon found itself in strong opposition to the Detroit Police Officers Association, Donald Lobsinger's Breakthrough, the homeowners' associations, and citizens' councils.

A Black Student United Front came into being, with Mike Hamlin as its adviser. The organization soon developed branches in 22 high schools and published a citywide newspaper. The same ideological mixture of socialism and black nationalism which was found in RUM publications characterized the work of the students. One example of the organization's activity was a campaign launched to revoke the suspension of students who had taken part in a revolt at Northern High School in September 1969. Some of the demands were purely nationalist, such as the one that a black, red, and green liberation flag be substituted for the stars and stripes at the daily flag raising. Other demands dealing with curriculum, police in the schools, and selection of faculty amounted to calling for full student and community control of the schools, which was an educational counterpart of workers controlling the factory. More important than any specific struggle, Black Student

United Front was a municipal student organization which served as a youth section for the League of Revolutionary Black Workers. It extended downward to junior high schools and had connections with college groups. Students sometimes did leafleting and picketing chores at plants, and some were in training at the print shop and other League facilities. The publications of Black Student United Front stressed self-reliance. One original comic book which was given wide circulation contained a strong attack on substituting the heroism of a few individuals for action by masses of people. The student organization had a role independent of PASCC, but, at the same time, it was an integral part of the plan to gain control of the public school system.

PASCC struggled continuously with the Detroit Board of Education, which was controlled by white liberals and was presided over by Abe Zwerdling, who had close ties to the UAW. Unable to reach a satisfactory compromise with the board, PASCC was forced to organize for the local school board elections. Summer programs were set up in black history, photography, printing, and journalism to build skills. Three PASCC offices operated in Detroit and one in Highland Park, a suburb adjacent to Hamtramck. The PASCC plan was to have production line workers as candidates for the community boards and to have students do most of the actual campaigning. Although 70,000 votes were recorded for PASCC slates, the effort ended in failure. In addition to the chronic problems of insufficient cadre, insufficient funds, and insufficient experience, PASCC faced the opposition of UAW and Democratic Party officials who understood that if PASCC succeeded it would create a political machine comparable to their own. Some members of the League's central staff argued that the PASCC bid for control of the schools was premature and only drained off resources. Others, like Watson and Hamlin, were disturbed that not all of the executive board responded with sufficient enthusiasm to a plan that would have given them a foothold on local political power. Even in failure, PASCC illustrated the depth and vision of the League's approach.

PASCC activity had counterparts in other areas with greater and lesser success. John Williams headed a Catholic school complex in the North End for a time; Ken Cockrel was research director for a religious foundation; and Larry Nevels, a League stalwart, headed UNICOM, a neighborhood group which dealt with youth and various areas of social service. Edna Watson, John Watson's wife, initiated a hospital organizing drive which involved her with the predominantly white Medical Committee for Human Rights. Solid relations were built with the Guardians, a black policemen's association. Bridges were built to white radical organizations such as the local branch of the National Lawyers Guild and indigenous Detroit groups such as Ad Hoc, People Against Racism, and the Detroit Organizing Committee. Meetings were held continuously with other black militant organizations and with sympathetic black trade union leaders who were willing to cooperate with the League on one level or another. The rudiments of an overall revolutionary strategy were present in the League's policies from the outset, but it was not always clear how the embryo was to develop to the point of contending for power.

2

We demand $500,000,000 in reparations.

—*Black Manifesto*, issued in Detroit, Michigan, May 1, 1969

A specific instance of how the League dealt with strategic and tactical problems was its role in the Black Economic Development Conference (BEDC) held in Detroit, April 26-29, 1969. Financing for the conference was obtained through a grant from the Interreligious Foundation for Community Organizations (IFCO), a nonprofit foundation begun in 1966 by one civic foundation and nine Protestant, Catholic, and Jewish agencies. BEDC (pronounced "bed-c") was to explore various economic strategies for black people in America. League personnel had major roles in inviting guests, arranging panels, and influencing the ideological direction of informal discussions. The Interreligious Foundation for Community Organizations may have hoped for a kind of black capitalism or black welfare state approach from the conference; and Michigan Congressman John Conyers and Georgia State Representative Julian Bond got most of the official media limelight. But the real tenor of the meetings was articulated by speakers such as James Boggs, who talked on "The Myth and Irrationality of Black Capitalism." What finally emerged from the conference was a call for black socialism. BEDC was to become a permanent independent national organization guided by a 24-member steering committee. Ken Cockrel,

Mike Hamlin, Luke Tripp, John Watson, John Williams, and Chuck Wooten were named to that committee. Most of the others on the committee were people associated with James Forman, who had been a major leader in SNCC for six years and had recently resigned from a brief membership in the Black Panther Party. Forman had been instrumental in bringing the BEDC proposal to the attention of the League, and he was given the task of reading the *Black Manifesto* on May 1, 1969.

The *Black Manifesto* called for $500 million in reparations to be paid by white religious institutions to BEDC to provide blacks with economic self-sufficiency. The sum was considered an atonement by the moral guardians of white America for the way "white America has exploited our resources, our minds, our bodies, our labor." The *Manifesto* asserted that the mammoth sum came to only $15 per black person based on the official government figure of a black population of 30 million, a count which most blacks considered a low estimate. The churches and synagogues were expected to pay up at once or black militants would enter places of worship all over the country to disrupt services by reading the *Manifesto* directly to the congregation.

The economic proposals of the *Manifesto* itself were divided into ten specific projects whose radical political purposes were left unstated. Of the $500 million in reparations, $200 million was to be used to set up a Southern Land Bank which would establish cooperative farms throughout the South. $80 million was to be divided between four new publishing ventures to be located in Detroit, Los Angeles, Atlanta, and New York and four audiovisual centers to be located in Detroit, Chicago, Cleveland, and Washington, D.C. $30 million would be spent to create a research skills center and $10 million for a training center in communication industry skills. $130 million would be spent to establish a black university in the South. $10 million would be granted outright to the National Welfare Rights Organization to further its work with welfare recipients. $20 million would be used to establish a National Black Labor Strike Fund, and $20 million more would go to the United Black Appeal (soon to be called International Black Appeal), which would be charged with developing additional funds for BEDC. A final demand of the *Manifesto* was that whatever sums were left over from the conference budget should be used to get the permanent BEDC organization started.

Shortly after the first reading of the *Manifesto*, James Forman entered New York's Riverside Church to make the first disruption of a religious service. Although there was all but universal disapproval of the tone of the *Manifesto* and the tactic of disruption, many of the churches affiliated with the Interreligious Foundation for Community Organizations promised to make some payments to BEDC to avoid such pressure and to satisfy insurgents within their own ranks. The American Jewish Committee was the sole exception. That organization refused to be intimidated into contributing toward an enterprise it did not approve of and it withdrew from IFCO altogether, citing the *Manifesto* and BEDC as the causes of its departure. The monies that eventually went to BEDC did not begin to approach the multimillions demanded, but they were considerably more than most radical groups had to work with. BEDC itself was awarded $80,000 by IFCO, and its allied research group got an additional $79,000. Local organizations in every part of the United States received IFCO grants following BEDC approval. Many of these organizations were worker caucuses or groups with former SNCC activists personally associated with Forman. DRUM got an $8,000 grant for its work at Dodge Main, and several other Detroit groups got similar aid. The West Central Organization received close to $30,000 to organize block clubs and neighborhood councils and to provide a citywide police-community relations program, food co-ops, employment services, and related programs. Eventually, IFCO earmarked an additional $200,000 for BEDC use in 1969.

In spite of the funds generated by the *Manifesto*, many of the in-plant League organizers considered BEDC a lot of pie in the sky. General Baker was suspicious of the political line of those who tried to con the system through a spectacular media campaign rather than sticking to the arduous task of organizing workers, and he refused to be on the BEDC steering committee. Baker was also wary of famous "outside" individuals who did not love DRUM the way Detroiters did and who had no permanent stake in the city. Cockrel, Hamlin, and Watson dismissed the objections of Baker as short-sighted and provincial. For them, BEDC was a way of acquiring the funds needed to orchestrate the full range of League possibilities. Others in the leadership shared some of Baker's misgivings but were willing to go along with BEDC for the same reasons as Cockrel, Hamlin, and Watson.

All the League leaders did agree that the proposal for an International Black Appeal (IBA) was one of BEDC's most important contributions. IBA was to become a national tax-exempt charity on the scale of Detroit's annual Torch Drive or the United Jewish Appeal. Factory workers and other hourly employees could allocate tax-deductible donations for IBA directly from their paychecks. Cockrel began a successful effort to get IRS approval for IBA's tax-exempt status at once, and John Williams was named its director. The UAW was approached about the possibility of taking contributions directly from paychecks and proved less hostile than expected. The UAW may not have realized that IBA would put potentially enormous financial resources into the hands of black revolutionaries, or the UAW may have been gambling that IBA was the first step toward the incorporation of League militants into the established system. IBA meant something quite different to the League. If each of the 250,000 black members of the UAW gave only $1 a month, the League would have a monthly budget of a quarter of a million dollars. This money could be used as a strike fund if it was funneled to friendly charitable agencies that could hire fired workers and support strikers. The possibilities were as broad as imagination could make them, and imagination was one ingredient the League had never lacked.

The *Black Manifesto* and IBA actually represented two contradictory approaches to financing. The *Manifesto* was an attempt at an outright "rip-off," depending upon white guilt for its success, and essentially it meant going back to the master's table for a handout. IBA was a self-financing approach dependent only upon the goodwill of black working people. The League considered BEDC and the *Manifesto* useful primarily because they started other projects capable of self-sufficiency. The ultimate peril of BEDC was that it had no organized mass base either to keep pressure on the churches or to control its leadership. The possibility that black clergy, "professional organizers," and others might usurp control of local or national BEDC operations was a clear and present danger. IBA, on the other hand, would be dependent on and responsible to a mass base.

One of the immediate concrete benefits of BEDC was the establishment in Detroit of Black Star Publishing under the leadership of Mike Hamlin. Black Star bought a building, purchased some equipment of its own, and shared in purchasing other equipment which was

housed at a white printers' cooperative run by Fredy Perlman. Helen
Jones, a League member, was in charge of the day-to-day operations at
Black Star and had considerable decision-making authority, although
she was ultimately responsible to Mike Hamlin. Black Star's major duties were to publish the newsletters and periodicals of the League's various components. Helen Jones also initiated a program to train League
members in printing skills. She and Hamlin hoped to develop Black
Star to the point where it could do commercial work well enough to become financially self-supporting. Black Star would then not only be
able to carry on the League printing chores, but also to provide paid
employment for League activists.

The printing and folding equipment shared with Perlman was another indication of the good and honest relations the League was able
to maintain with many Detroit whites. Perlman had been greatly affected by his experiences in the French uprising of May 1968 and had
set up the Detroit cooperative printing center to advocate libertarian
principles. One of his goals was to make the print shop more than a
service and convenience for radicals. Like Helen Jones, he wanted to
train people in the various skills associated with printing in order to
make them independent of commercial printers. Upstairs from the
print shop were the offices of the Radical Education Project, a spin-off
from SDS which distributed low-cost radical literature locally and nationally. Perlman also printed *Radical America*, a journal edited first in
Madison, Wisconsin, then in Boston, which began as an SDS publication and came to advocate a nonauthoritarian, worker-controlled com-
munism. Other individuals in the cooperative were associated with the
Detroit Organizing Committee, another SDS spin-off, which was trying
to organize white workers into RUM-type groups. The haphazard connections between the various radical forces in the city puzzled government and police agencies. In August 1970, a Senate subcommittee
headed by Senator James Eastland and Senator Thomas Dodd investigated the Detroit radicals and tried to tie in BEDC, the League of
Revolutionary Black Workers, the Radical Education Project, and the
Interreligious Foundation for Community Organizations with the activities of the American Communist Party and an alleged Cuban plot to
subvert the stability of the United States through terrorist bombings.

The fantasies and paranoia of the U.S. government aside, participation in BEDC was a significant step for the League. It was the first

time the League had helped convene an important national gathering, and it was the first time it had reached out for substantial funding. IBA promised to become an instrument that could solve any number of financial problems on a permanent basis within a structure that would further develop the League base. BEDC had also given the League its first nationally famous "convert" in the person of James Forman. Following the April conference, Forman promised to move his personal residence to the Motor City, and he was named to the central staff of the League of Revolutionary Black Workers.

Chapter Five

Niggermation at Eldon

1

I work at a small shop in Troy. . . . Three weeks ago, a woman on the day shift got her arm chopped off in a press. The week before this happened, the press repeated and they said they'd fixed it and kept people working on it, and then this lady got her arm chopped off. People were really freaked out; some of the people on days ended up quitting.

—Denise Stevenson, in a statement to a People's Court convened by the Motor City Labor League, April 3, 1973

One of the major concerns of the League of Revolutionary Black Workers was the deteriorating working conditions at the point of production. In 1946, some 550,000 auto workers had produced a little more than 3 million vehicles, but in 1970 some 750,000 auto workers had produced a little more than 8 million vehicles. Management credited this much higher productivity per worker to its improved managerial techniques and new machinery. Workers, on the other hand, claimed the higher productivity was primarily a result of their being forced to work harder and faster under increasingly unsafe and unhealthy conditions. The companies called their methods automation; black workers in Detroit called them niggermation.

Niggermation, not automation, was clearly the watchword at Chrysler Corporation's Eldon Avenue Gear and Axle plant. Clustered alongside four other Chrysler plants—Huber Foundry, Winfield Foundry, Chrysler Forge, and Plymouth—Eldon employed a workforce of more than 4,000, of which 70 percent was black. Eldon covered more than 1 million square feet, was surrounded by another 500,000 square feet of storage and siding areas, and housed 2,600 machine tools of 170 types. In a report to the National Labor Relations Board on November 30, 1971, Chrysler Corporation described Eldon as "engaged primarily in machining metal parts for rear axles of most Chrysler-built automobiles, for which it is the *sole* source, and assembling the parts into completed axles." Workers considered this key plant the most nig-germated factory in Detroit.

Even though Chrysler acknowledged how vital Eldon was to its operations, working conditions at the plant continually deteriorated. These poor conditions reached such proportions that by 1970 harassment, industrial illnesses, injuries, and deaths on the job pushed Eldon workers to the breaking point. After James Johnson shot and killed two foremen and a job setter, his attorney, Ken Cockrel, said, "We'll have to put Chrysler on trial for damages to this man caused by his working conditions." The Johnson jury was taken to Eldon, the "scene of the crime," to observe for itself the conditions which Judge Philip Colista had called "abominable" and which UAW Safety Director Lloyd Utter termed "inexcusably dangerous" and evidence of "a complete neglect of stated maintenance procedures." The jury agreed and concluded that James Johnson was not responsible for his actions. That August, during the local contract negotiations, Chrysler admitted to 167 separate safety violations at Eldon; yet a year and a half later, in January 1971, the Michigan Department of Labor found hundreds of violations of the Michigan safety code still uncorrected. In a separate case brought against Chrysler by Johnson, he was awarded workman's compensation of $75 a week, beginning from the day of his "breakdown."

Eldon workers knew that James Johnson was not an isolated case. Serious provocations, injuries, illnesses, and deaths were the realities of their everyday work. On May 26, 1970, less than two months before Johnson fired his M-1 carbine, another death had occurred at Eldon. Gary Thompson, a black 22-year-old Vietnam veteran, had been killed when his defective jitney overturned and buried him under five tons of steel. UAW Safety Director Utter investigated the cause of the accident. On November 12, 1970, his written conclusions were sent as an official union inter-office communication to Art Hughes, the assistant director of the National Chrysler Department:

I examined the equipment and found the emergency brake to be broken; as a matter of fact, it was never connected. The shifter lever to the transmission was loose and sloppy. The equipment generally was sadly in need of maintenance, having a lost steering wheel in addition to other general needs. I also visited the repair area and observed other industrial trucks in this area that were sadly in need of repair, noting: no lights, lack of brakes, horns, broken LP gas tank fasteners, loose steering wheels, leaky hydraulic equipment, etc. I was informed that there is supposed to be a regularly scheduled maintenance procedure for this equipment in this plant. I was also informed that operators are instructed to take trucks to the garage and tag them when they are in need of repairs. However, it seems to be the practice of foremen, when equipment is needed, to pull the tags off the equipment in the repair area that badly need corrective maintenance and put them back into service on the floor. . . . Finally, a general observation as we passed to and from the location of the fatal accident: there seemed to be little attempt to maintain proper housekeeping except on the main front aisle. Water and grease were observed all along the way, as we proceeded. Every good safety program has its basic good-housekeeping procedures. Proper steps should be taken immediately to improve conditions within this plant.

Thirteen days before Gary Thompson's death, Eldon had claimed the life of Mamie Williams, a 51-year-old black woman who had worked for Chrysler for more than 26 years. Mamie Williams had been ordered by her doctors to stay home because of a dangerous blood-pressure condition. Chrysler, however, had sent her a telegram telling her to return to work or be fired and lose all the benefits she had accumulated in almost three decades of employment. An intimidated Mamie Williams had returned to her job on the first shift in Department 80. One week later, she passed out on the line and died shortly after being taken home.

A year before the deaths of Gary Thompson and Mamie Williams, Eldon had taken the life of Rose Logan, a black janitor. Rose Logan had been struck in the plant by an improperly loaded jitney whose driver's vision was blocked. Her doctor told her to stay off her feet, but Chrysler's doctors ordered her back to work. She returned to Eldon from fear of losing her job, developed thrombophlebitis in her leg, and, like Mamie Williams, ended her service at Eldon in a coffin.

Higher production at Eldon had not been achieved with advanced technology and automated assembly line procedures, but through the old-fashioned method of speed-up. The single goal of the company was to increase profit by getting more work out of each individual worker. Eldon conditions were typical of conditions in the industry. Even when there were technological changes, usually only one segment of the assembly line was automated, so that the workers on other segments had to labor more strenuously to keep up. Often, the automation eliminated interesting jobs, leaving the more menial and monotonous tasks for people. Many of the "new" machines were not technological advances at all, but simply updated models of tools introduced as early as the 1920s and 1930s. Health and accident data on the auto industry were difficult to obtain. Only in the early 1970s did the UAW and the Department of Health, Education, and Welfare begin to make studies in this area. One important report did appear in 1973. Called the *Health Research Group Study of Disease among Workers in the Auto Industry*, it was based on figures compiled by the National Institute of Occupational Safety and Health and was written by two medical doctors, Jannette Sherman and Sidney Wolfe. The report estimated 65 on-the-job deaths per day among auto workers, for a total of some 16,000 annually. Approximately half of these deaths were from heart attacks. There were also some 63,000 cases of disabling diseases and about 1,700,000 cases of lost or impaired hearing. These statistics did not include many long-term illnesses endemic to foundry workers and others exposed to poisonous chemicals and gases, nor did they include deaths and injuries by accident. Even these limited figures made it clear that more auto workers were killed and injured each year on the job than soldiers were killed and injured during any year of the war in Vietnam.

The hazardous conditions were supposedly compensated for by high wages. Auto workers were among the highest-paid workers in the United States, yet wage rates were deceptive. In the 1920s, Henry Ford made headlines by promising $5 a day to every worker in his enterprises. Ford workers soon discovered that it was not quite $5 a day for not quite everyone. Fully a third of all Ford workers never got the $5 a day. Likewise, at Eldon, the 1969 $4-an-hour average Chrysler wage proved a fiction. Before any deductions and without the cost-of-living allowance, which did not cover all workers and was never more than 21 cents an hour, most job categories at Eldon paid around $3.60 an hour

and none paid more than $3.94. Workers found it difficult to get fig-
ures on hourly pay for their particular job, and they were often cheated
out of increases by complex union and company clerical procedures.
What the workers did know was that overtime had become compulsory
and that most of them needed the time-and-a-half paid for overtime to
keep pace with inflation. Census Bureau figures revealed that the value
of the products shipped out of the plant, minus the cost of materials,
supplies, fuel, and electricity, came to $22,500 a year per worker, as
compared to an average wage of $8,000 for a worker putting in a 40-
hour week. During the period 1946-1969, wages had increased by 25
percent, while profits went up 77 percent, dividends 60 percent, personal corporate incomes 80 percent, and undistributed corporate profits 93 percent. The industry moaned about its cycle of booms and
busts, but in 1970 General Motors remained the nation's (and the
world's) largest manufacturing enterprise. Ford was the third largest.
And Chrysler, "the weak sister," was fifth.

Niggermation at Eldon gave rise to three separate rank-and-file opposition groups. The one with the longest record in the factory was a
militant trade union group led by Jordan Sims, the black chairman of
the shop stewards' committee. A radical group called Wildcat began
publishing a newsletter in February 1970, and ELRUM, the local unit
of the League of Revolutionary Black Workers, made its official appearance in November 1968. The three groups, separately and in various
combinations, produced a steady barrage of information for the workers and succeeded in closing down the plant in several successful wildcat strikes. Chrysler was more than a little concerned about this
activity. If Eldon were closed for any lengthy period, all gear and axle
production would stop; and with that stoppage, all of Chrysler would
stop. Chrysler remembered how General Motors had been forced to
recognize the UAW in 1937 when it occupied the Chevy motor plant
in Flint, the only place in the country making Chevy motors. Eldon
had the same sort of pivotal role in Chrysler production. At this point
of maximum vulnerability, Chrysler faced one of the largest concentra-
tions of black workers in the industry. Eldon was Chrysler's Achilles'
heel. Chrysler knew this, and so did the League of Revolutionary Black
Workers.

ELRUM's history was similar to that of DRUM. Meetings, rallies,
and newsletters built up a hard core of supporters and a much larger

number of sympathizers. Leaders of ELRUM such as Fred Holsey and
James Edwards found themselves under continual pressure from company, police, and union. Physical assaults were frequent, but the EL-
RUM leadership did not crack under the pressure. On January 22,
1969, ELRUM led more than 300 workers to confront the local union
leadership with a grievance list in much the way DRUM had confronted the leaders of Local 3. Five days later, ELRUM called a strike
to back up its demands. ELRUM kept out 66 percent of the workers
the first day of the strike and 50 percent the second. The company's retaliation was to fire some two dozen workers and to discipline 86 others.

In retrospect, the League evaluated the January 1969 strike as premature. Too many ELRUM members were knocked out of the plant,
and the remaining base of support was insufficient to maintain the
struggle at the same level as in the previous six months. Despite these
facts, ELRUM continued to fight, and it continued to have a cadre and
sympathizers in the plant. During the early part of 1970, ELRUM once
more took a leading role in plant struggles, and it arrived at a working
coalition with other militants.

2

*You don't read about them in Newsweek or see them on television. They're
too dangerous. They're too dangerous to the system to have information about
the kind of work being done at Eldon to be disseminated widely. This is a war
we're talking about. There is literally a war going on inside the American factories. This is a violent struggle. Sometimes it is organized and guided. Most
times it is unorganized and spontaneous. But in the course of this struggle more
American workers have died than in all the four major wars.*

—John Watson, interview in *Quaderni Piacentini* (Italy), Winter
1970

One of the key figures in the new series of events at Eldon was a
white worker named John Taylor. In August 1972, he gave the authors
of this book a retrospective account of the events at Eldon as he had
experienced them. At the time of the interview, John Taylor was a
member of the Motor City Labor League. His personal testimony regarding the period from 1968 to 1970 is a textbook of what was wrong

with the company and the union. It also presents a candid view of the problems within the ranks of the insurgents themselves:

My name is John Taylor. I wasn't born in Detroit. I was born in West Virginia. My father was a coal miner who worked in the mines for 17 years. My grandfathers on both sides were coal miners. My grandfather on my mother's side was the recording secretary for the first miner's local in that part of the country back in 1916. We moved to Detroit in 1949 as part of the migration of white Appalachians northward. My father started to work at Chevrolet gear and axle plant as a production line worker in October 1949 and he retires in 1975. My mother works at the Federals Department Store putting price tags on clothes. She's worked there since 1952 and expects to retire soon. I went to the Detroit public schools and Wayne State University. I came out with a bachelor's degree in English and a law degree. Along the way, I worked eight years for the Better Business Bureau in Detroit, a capitalist front organization, and I worked for Chrysler Corporation on the management side as a workman's compensation representative. That job took me into almost every Chrysler plant in the Detroit area. It put me into contact with literally hundreds of injured workers per week. I worked there from June 1966 to September 1968. In November of 1968, I got a job as a production line worker at Chrysler's Eldon Avenue Gear and Axle factory, the same factory where I had worked for management.

I was asked to resign my management job because of what they called a "bad attitude." The truth is that the company was fucking the workers on compensation. One of their devices was to refuse to discuss the cases with the union. They claimed workman's comp was covered by statute and therefore not part of the contract and therefore not negotiable. My feeling was that, while the substance of the decisions was not negotiable, the administration was and was therefore grievable. I thought I should discuss these cases with the various shop stewards. I did what the union should have done. I gave the stewards an outline of the rights of workers—their constituents. I noticed that, during a period of nine days, about every steward in the place was in my office. I didn't find out until several years later that Jordan Sims had noticed what I was doing and had made it part of his program as chairman of the Shop Stewards' Committee to send all of the stewards to see me. Finally, he came in himself and we had a long rap. I gave him a copy of the statutes. I used to have almost daily relations with the Labor Relations Committee. I remember on more than one day how they would say, "Oh, we're going to have a rough afternoon coming up because Sims is coming to bargain." That's the kind of reputation Sims had.

After I got kicked out of Chrysler management, I went back to Wayne State; but I didn't want to be a lawyer or a teacher. I wanted to organize, and the logical place seemed to be the plant. I had the reputation in the Eldon Personnel Department of being the best comp man they had ever had. I talked them into letting me work hourly, and they put me into Department 75, first as a conveyer loader and then I worked up to being a precision grinder. That's the best job I ever had in my life. I didn't have any organizing agenda at that time. The only politics I had came out of the *Fifth Estate*, Detroit's underground paper. I had never read Marx or Lenin. The first time I read the *Communist Manifesto* was late 1969. I thought, "This is far out. They are talking about this plant." That was an important event for me.

One funny coincidence from that time is that I entered the plant on November 8, 1968, and on November 10th some black workers in other departments founded ELRUM, the Eldon Avenue Revolutionary Union Movement. They had been turned on by the agitation at Dodge Main and became an affiliate of the League of Revolutionary Black Workers. I would like to relate these events in the sequence I lived them, rather than strict chronological order. I will come back later on and fill in the most important dates and events.

Our steward in Department 75 on the third shift was a man named Frank McKinnon. I got to know him when I was in workman's comp because McKinnon was a witness in a case involving a fight. Chrysler had a policy of firing the aggressor, so the question of who started the fight was important. McKinnon gave me a statement that the worker had started the fight. I found out later he lied to me. That was the kind of steward he was. When I got to be a worker, he refused to write up my safety grievances. A number of us also had grievances relating to pay raises due us because of promotions. We were supposed to get a 5-cent-an-hour raise within a week, and it took me six weeks to get mine because the foreman wouldn't do the paperwork. He was trying to save on his own budget, and McKinnon wouldn't write up the grievance about it. That's how things worked at Eldon.

My safety grievance typifies the problems in that factory. I worked on what they call a modern grinder. We used to laugh about it because there was nothing modern about it at all. It was ancient. We had to burn off the rough edges of rangers, which looked like donuts with metal teeth. This part went into the differential. There was a lot of fine dust generated by this grinding. The company put vents on the machines to hold this down, but every shift the filters would get clogged. The supervision would never give us the little time needed for someone to come and do some maintenance on them. I requested a mask. I got this thing that didn't look right and asked for the box it came in. It turned out to be for paint and gas fumes and was no help against dust. I ran all this down to McKinnon, but he refused to deal with it. So, I called for a department meeting. I organized around him. The union president wouldn't schedule the meeting for more than two weeks because he said we had one word wrong in our petition. Richardson [the president] was just pissed because he had just taken office, and now, less than two months later, there was dissatisfaction with one of his stewards. Richardson told me straight off he wanted people to cool off because he didn't want angry people in the union hall. That's another indication of the union's attitude. They do not want to deal with angry workers.

I started seeing Sims in the cafeteria every morning. This was in early 1969, and he suggested I get on the union bylaws committee. I worked on that for a year with Sims and a guy named J.C. Thomas. We drew up some bylaws that would have made that union as honest and democratic as unions can be in this period. Needless to say, those bylaws were never presented to the membership.

By 1970, we had gotten to a situation where Chrysler was making most of its money off small cars, the Valiant and the Dart. One reason things got so bad at Dodge Main was that is where they made those cars. Behind the need for increased production and because they wanted to harass the union, Chrysler did a lot of firing, disciplinary actions, and all sorts of bullshit. There was attempted speed-up in my department at Eldon. One foreman arbitrarily raised the quota on the grinder machine, which was totally against the contract. What we did was lower to 400 instead of the usual 700 gears and that cooled his ass about a speed-up.

On April 16, 1970, things built up to what we call the Scott-Ashlock Incident. There was a black worker named John Scott who was a physically small man. His foreman was a fairly large guy from Mississippi named Irwin Ashlock. They got into an argument, and Ashlock picked up a pinion gear and said he was going to smash Scott's brains out. Scott complained to his steward, and the union took it up with the company. Well, Chrysler came up with the claim that Scott had taken a knife from his pocket—you know, like all blacks carry knives. They claimed Ashlock had a right to protect himself, and rather than discipline Ashlock, they were going to fire Scott. This sparked a wildcat strike which shut the place down for the whole weekend. That was a beautifully successful strike. It had an old-fashioned unity—young and old, black and white, men and women. Everyone was militant. The skilled tradesmen went out, too. At a union meeting, a white worker named John Felicia, who had seen the whole thing, spoke from the stage at the hall. There were maybe a thousand people there. Felicia said there were white workers at Eldon and black workers at Eldon, but the main thing was that they were all workers and that he had seen the whole thing and that John Scott was telling the absolute truth and was totally in the right. The company needed our gears for those Valiants, so they backed down.

Everyone thought we had won, but then, after a couple of weeks, the company started acting up. They threatened to discipline the second-shift stewards who had led the walkout. They began to have foremen follow these guys around, and then, on May 1, they were told toward the end of the shift that they were all going to be suspended for an unauthorized work stoppage in violation of the no-strike clause of the contract. They were shown the door leading to the street. What happened was that a guy named Clarence Thornton shoved the plant guards out of the way and led everyone back into the plant. This was shift time. I remember meeting a steward, and he said, "We're shutting her down. Go home." By midnight, the factory was shut down. Chrysler went for an injunction and got it. The union lawyer from Solidarity House refused to defend Local 961 on the grounds it might bring legal action against the whole union. They sold out the strike. They advised us to go back to work without our stewards. We worked most of that summer without any stewards. Both Jordan Sims and Frank McKinnon were fired in this action.

In response to those firings, a grouping called the Eldon Safety Committee was formed which included myself, some members of ELRUM, and the fired stewards led by Jordan Sims. Our program was to research and document the issue of safety in the plant. We got advised by lawyers Ron Glotta and Mike Adleman that we had the right to refuse to work under abnormally dangerous conditions. That would not constitute a strike, and the company could not get an injunction. We saw that we had an umbrella for closing down Eldon. We were so naive we thought words meant what they said. When you look at our leaflets of that period, you will see that we quote the law and all that stuff. We put out a few leaflets, but events overtook us. The plant was indeed abnormally dangerous. On May 26, 1970, this was proven when a man named Gary Thompson was buried under five tons of steel when his faulty jitney tipped over. Thompson was a black Vietnam veteran about 22 years old. The jitney he was running was full of safety flaws. On May 27, we set up picket lines. By "we," I mean the Eldon Safety Committee and the League of Revolutionary Black Workers. This was not as successful as the first strike, but it cost them 2,174 axles over two days. We're proud of each and every one of them. The three wildcats within a month and a half cost them 22,000 axles during a period when they desperately needed them for their Valiants. Chrysler immediately fired me and three members of the League: James Edwards, Alonzo Chandler, and Rob McKee.

I need to backtrack here to tell something about ELRUM. Like I said before, they had started on November 10, 1968. My first awareness of them was when they began to put out leaflets. There was an immediate response, about 50 percent positive and 50 percent negative. The negative response came from the older black workers and of course from white workers, mainly because the ELRUM language was harsh. They called people "Toms," "Molly-Toms," "honkie dogs," "pigs," etc. No one seemed to have trouble with calling the supervision those names, but this was something different. The older people definitely had a lot of trouble with their whole tone. In early 1970, there was an election for convention delegates. That was just before the Scott-Ashlock Incident. Given their numerical superiority in that plant, black workers could have elected an all-black slate. There were like 33 separate black candidates, and ELRUM put out a leaflet calling them "Molly-Toms" and all that. That divided the black vote.

ELRUM was already in bad shape by that time. In January of 1969, there was a lot of complaining about the coldness in the plant and about union discrimination against blacks. Chrysler disciplined some ELRUM people who had lost time from their jobs to do an action against the union. A wildcat followed, and after that 22 ELRUM people were fired. I think that broke the back of ELRUM right there. I think those actions were premature. There was no way to logistically support that strike. They had no outside mobilization. It was just premature. Still, everything we ever did at the plant was premature. Maybe it was vanguard activity, and they just didn't have any choice. Anyway, through 1969, the *Inner City Voice*, the League paper, was sold at the plant. I had no personal contact until early 1970, about the time of the convention.

At that time, I was still mainly involved in the bylaws struggle and troubles in my own department. Still, I used to see their leaflets and groups of us would discuss them, blacks and whites. I would say that we might not be able to relate to the rhetoric, but what they were saying was true. That was the position Jordan Sims took, too. A lot of his enemies said he was the secret leader of ELRUM, in an attempt to erode his base among black and white workers. Sims said their language was crude but they were telling the truth. He would defend them as aggressively as he would any militant. That was a position of principle. I should say that I wasn't all that aware of all they were doing. I can say that the young white workers didn't like them. They could relate to what I said, but they had a hard time with ELRUM.

What really turned people off was this one leaflet they put out on the union secretaries. There was an old retiree named Butch and several white secretaries in the office. ELRUM put out a leaflet running that these white women were prostitutes for Elroy Richardson, the black president of the local. They ran all kinds of vicious stuff that people could not relate to. We knew these women and did not perceive them in that fashion. People were really put off by that issue. Another thing is that some of those young black workers who were enthusiastic about the leaflets never joined ELRUM, and some of them crossed the Safety Committee picket line. So there was this mixed response to ELRUM as we went into 1970.

Things were very complicated by 1970. Local 961 had its first black president. This was before the Scott-Ashlock Incident. ELRUM had supported the black slate in 1969, but now it had become critical and was calling Elroy a "Tom," a "fat-belly faggot," etc. When the wildcat came, ELRUM dropped that and supported him again. You can say that Richardson had a united plant behind him, but he was too incompetent and inept to be a leader. He had it all in his hands at the time of the wildcat following the Scott-Ashlock thing, but he blew it.

After the wildcat, the ELRUM cadre and myself worked on the Safety Committee. I did most of the research and writing because that was an area I had expertise in. They did most of the organizing for the strike. We met at League headquarters on Cortland Street. People ask if I felt any nationalism or reverse racism, and I can say I did not. I had a lot of basic respect for what they were trying to do. When they said, "Come on over; it's all right," I did and it was. I also had a nodding acquaintance with Ken Cockrel from law school. That may have helped, but our main contact with the League was General Baker. We had lots of contact with him and also with Chuck Wooten. They both came on the picket line with us, even though they didn't work at the plant. I would say the performance of the ELRUM people around the safety strike was exemplary.

I need to backtrack again. By early 1970, I had come to realize that I had to get beyond Departments 74 and 75. I knew you had to have an organ of some kind, a mimeoed sheet. I think that came from seeing the ELRUM example. I thought it was correct when they said whites should work with whites, which was what I was trying to do, even though I was doing it on my own from what I see now [in 1972] as correct instincts. A little earlier, a paper called *Wildcat* had been given out. People in my department had picked it up and read it. Then, early in 1970, they began to put out the *Eldon Wildcat*, a mimeoed plant newsletter. At that point, I was ready to leap out. I waited until they were at the gate, and I told them I worked in the factory and wanted to do some articles for them. We set up a meeting. Those people were experts at plant newsletters. I became identified with them immediately because people spotted my writing style.

The *Wildcat* people were Old Left. They were so secretive they had crossed over to paranoia. They used false names and all that stuff. They didn't want to expose their shit to open struggle. My opinion, then and now, is that that is an incorrect way to work. They strongly advised me not to distribute *Wildcat*. It was their policy that outsiders distributed. My opinion was that the paper had to get into the plant. We were only covering one gate. One morning, I went out and took some papers and gave them out at another gate. It soon got around the plant that I was the publisher of *Wildcat*, which was a mistruth. I was only a junior member of that circle. They would edit the shit out of my articles. They would change the content and the style. Sometimes we did this together, but sometimes they said there wasn't time. I usually didn't mind, but they would put in bad stuff sometimes without consulting me, which put me into a trick as I was identified with the paper. Other workers held me responsible. I found out later that two people in the group took the position that I was only a contact and had brought my troubles upon myself by identifying with the paper in an overt way. You must remember that ELRUM was open with their thing. I thought that was correct, and I was open with mine. That made it easier to trust each other.

What we did during that period was have ELRUM put something out one day, *Wildcat* the next, and the Safety Committee the third. Then we would start the cycle going again so that there was a steady stream of information and agitation. It was like a united front. People knew I was associated with the Safety Committee, and stewards would take me off on the side to show me violations. Management tried to keep me from going out of my department on my break. They got a guy to pick a fight with me so we both could get fired. They tried all that shit.

ELRUM did not participate as fully as it could have in gathering information, and on the day of the strike, they tried to stop distribution of the *Wildcat*. My brother was giving them out, and they said this was basically a black action and he should get out. Anyway, he didn't move. I don't think that was correct, but overall ELRUM was very good. The trouble was that after Rob, Alonzo, and James were fired, they had no one else to carry on. That was after the other 22 had been fired. Their thing was just ripped. Then they made a bad mistake, which may have been unavoidable given problems within the wider context of the League. That summer and fall they only put out one leaflet. They lost their visibility. They could have had workers from other plants distribute. They could have gone to union meetings, which was something I did. They went sometimes, but they were into a program of disruption. I didn't think that was correct, and I couldn't work with them on that. I thought it was insulting to those workers who had come to the hall in good faith to take care of whatever business they thought important. I thought it was disrespectful.

I think it would be fair to say that they were not good at dealing with people within the class who did not agree with them but who were not enemies either. I don't know what internal education the League was giving them on this. I don't know what kind of instructions they were getting. If there is no structure by which people's actions can be criticized and reviewed, you get into this kind of situation.

ELRUM still had a few people inside, but they were essentially not doing much. Now, in 1971, union officials came up for election. ELRUM ran a candidate named Eric Edwards, a guy who I have a lot of respect for. He ran a strong third as a straight ELRUM candidate, getting 342 out of about 1,000 votes. That indicated a residue of support. The company and the union were running a heavy organized barrage against Jordan Sims, who was running against Frank McKinnon for president. Sims could have won with the solid help of older workers, but they were turned off by his association with ELRUM. Jordan and I went over to the Cortland offices and talked with Baker, Wooten, and a whole bunch of them. They had always seen Sims as a sell-out and right-wing opportunist. I don't think that was correct. Anyway, he told them he didn't want their endorsement, which would be a kiss of death. The first day of the election, ELRUM did not come out in favor of Sims, and Jordan was ahead. The second day, they endorsed him, and the vote turned away. I believe that was an indication of how negative the older folks had become to ELRUM. That was one factor in his defeat. It would be interesting to know who made the decision to endorse him.

The union ran its usual shit on us. They challenged 284 ballots because of dues default, which is strange because you have [dues] check-offs at Chrysler, so if someone is behind, it is not their fault but the union's and the company's. I analyzed those ballots, and 90 percent of them were in black production units and I think they would have gone to Sims. They would have put him over as president of the local.

The administration, the international, and the company had sold this program that we were all violent individuals. They even said I was a member of ELRUM! They said I was a violent motherfucker. We got into a situation in the hall the night we were tabulating. We were there as challengers, and they brought in armed guards with shotguns, carbines, and pistols. They were provocative as hell, trying to get us into a fight. I'm convinced they wanted to gun us down. We took our time real easy. I even took my shirt off so people couldn't claim I was strapped [carrying a gun]. There was one argument which was really hot where James Edwards raised his voice, and the whole table got surrounded by those guards. These black guards were hired under the instructions of George Merrelli, the regional director. I got into a hot dispute with Russell Thompson, who was solid with the administration. Some ELRUM people came over, and Thompson reached into his shirt for a piece. I saw the guards starting over, so we just split, me and the guys from ELRUM. We were not prepared to handle that shit. What is interesting is that most of the people counting the ballots were older black women, and they were physically afraid of ELRUM people. They thought ELRUM people had guns and were going to go berserk. I knew right then that there had been a tremendous failure of ELRUM. You can't have people in the plant afraid of you in that way. Also, the same women who were afraid of ELRUM were not afraid of me. Several of them went out of their way to say this.

A similar incident occurred around the safety strike. It happened at the East Gate, which is a principal gate for the second shift coming in. The second shift is basically black and young, with little seniority. This is the 2:30 to 10:30 [p.m.] shift. James Edwards was on the gate, and at one point, James grabbed a white worker and slapped him around. Now, we had agreed there would be no violence, on advice of our attorneys, so that we could preserve the strike's legality. James violated our organizational decision. That hurt us. When people heard about that, they turned against us. They even cut a hole in the parking lot fence so they could get in easier.

I almost did a similar thing myself. I grabbed this one dude I had a thing on. He had caught me outside on the street one day and slugged me on my blind side. I had this plan for getting him that day, but I didn't. Maybe a policy of violence would have been better. Slapping some of those fuckers around might have made a difference. I don't know . . . but we had decided not to, and I stuck to that decision. We sure as hell moved too fast. We hadn't organized our base correctly. We weren't ready for that strike hit. We should have agitated more around the issue of Gary Thompson and on safety in general. We could really have made it hot, but as a result we had a not totally successful strike for which we got fired. You must understand we were genuinely angry at the death of Thompson. It verified everything we had been saying. We got self-righteous. In our arrogance, we failed to note that Memorial Day was on Friday. The people were getting triple pay for working. We couldn't have picked a worse day for a strike. It's just incredible that we didn't consider that factor. We were wrong and stupid.

These events took place in May 1970. On July 15, James Johnson entered the factory and blew away two foremen and a job setter. He was looking for his shop steward, Clarence Thornton. That was the same guy who had led the fired stewards back into the plant by shoving the guards aside. That was exemplary because Clarence was an older dude, about 46 years old, with 23 years' seniority. He was considered a good steward. Clarence was one of those sold out by the union. They left the stewards in the street for a time, and when Clarence came back, he had to sign a statement that if there was any further trouble he would get permanently fired. When Johnson first approached Clarence about his grievances, Clarence told him, "I can't do much for you because I just got back myself." Clarence had been intimidated and sold out to the point where it was no longer safe for him to fight for his membership. Johnson saw his union could not function for him and decided to deal with it himself. Those connections are important. The whole preceding set of events was to break down the stewards so they wouldn't defend their people. The company refused to deal with safety and other legitimate grievances. That's why we say Chrysler pulled the trigger. Chrysler caused those deaths. Yes, indeed, James Johnson was just an instrumentality.

It's important to note how ELRUM related to white people. The first thing is around the distribution of their leaflets. They would always refuse to give those leaflets to white workers. It wasn't until around March of 1970 that they could respect my practice enough to give them to me. Then James Edwards would go through changes about that. He would wad them up in his hand and sort of pass them to me surreptitiously so none of the black workers could see him giving a leaflet to a white. When ELRUM had its wildcat in January 1969, there was no attempt to relate to white workers about their demands. Consequently, many white workers crossed their lines, and many black workers who had close friends in the white force took the same position. They could not relate to the strike because they perceived ELRUM as having taken a racist position. One of the interesting aspects of the safety strike was that the Eldon Safety Committee was a coalition of trade unionists, ELRUM black revolutionaries, and white revolutionaries, mainly myself.

What happened to the Safety Committee is instructive. There was a steady process of attrition among the trade unionists, one of whom was a white named George Bauer, another of whom was Frank McKinnon. Some dropped out early. Some stuck right up to the strike. At the end, we had only Jordan Sims, J.C. Thomas, and a couple of others. During the strike, the trade unionists stayed for the first-shift picketing and then, except for Jordan Sims, were never seen again. The revolutionaries stayed with it to the bitter end because they had more than trade union reform to fight about. That may be a clumsy formulation, but the point is they were going to fight as long as they could. George Bauer, a skilled trades steward whom I have a lot of respect for, was fired with the other second-shift stewards. He participated actively in giving us safety information, but he never took part in picketing or in various confrontations with the union. George Bauer was not and is not a racist, and he has encountered a lot of opposition with his own skilled tradesmen. They call him a "nigger-lover." George has a quick temper. He used to be a professional boxer. He got into an argument outside the plant with an individual who had scabbed during the wildcat, and George decked him. This was outside the plant. Management moved to fire him, and the union wouldn't write a discharge grievance for weeks. Eventually, George got back in there, but he understood that he had better be careful.

Our first confrontations with the union brought a reduction in the ranks of the Safety Committee. Reuther had been killed, and the international was using that as an excuse to keep the hall closed. We insisted on the right to use our own hall. We were using the conference room to get information, write leaflets, discuss strategy, etc. Elroy Richardson came in and told us to leave. We stood up and confronted him, saying he would have to throw us out. He said he'd call the police. We said, "Fine, Elroy, you want to call the police, call the police." He went away and left us alone. The next day, when we came back, the conference room was locked. Some of the unionists felt uneasy and talked about going to lunch. James Edwards and I went over to the door. I tried to pick the door with my knife, and we put our shoulders to it. Then we went outside and found a window. We got screwdrivers and got the conference room window open. We had to actually break into our own hall. We got in and opened the conference room door. As soon as they saw this, some of them went to lunch and never came back. We started having the meeting, and another of the stewards got more and more agitated. He got on the verge of physically attacking me because I had broken into the hall. He had a very heavy thing on how Walter Reuther had been the black man's friend and ally. He was very insulted that I, a white man, had desecrated the memory of Reuther's death. He went into this thing with me and left and never came back. That was another contradiction in our ranks.

The reaction of the people in my own department to the strike bothered me. I was on the West Gate, where most of my department comes in. I'll never forget this. Almost unanimously, the people in my department and people I knew did not go in when they saw me picketing. They talked to me, and some of them even gave out leaflets. What a lot did, though, was go to another gate. I couldn't understand that for a long time. What it meant was that they could relate to me as a person, but not to the politics of the situation. There was the additional problem of how they related to the ELRUM people who were on the gate with me. This reinforced my assessment that we moved too fast. We had to do more agitation. We cost Chrysler 2,174 axles, but we could have done more. We also succeeded in exposing the Chrysler-union cooperation to the workers in the plant. That is, we produced the documentation on all the safety violations the union wouldn't deal with. This was dramaticized by the death of Gary Thompson. Even the UAW couldn't ignore that. Our strike lifted the consciousness of everybody. It used to be that workers wouldn't take the leaflets or would throw them away. Now, people at the plant almost always take the leaflet, put it in their pocket, and read it inside. That is very positive and indicates a level of consciousness higher than in most plants and higher than it had been in their plant.

How workers relate to material given at the gate isn't understood by most people in the movement. When *Wildcat* first appeared, ELRUM tried to front them off by physical threats. The *Wildcat* people came back, and ELRUM backed off. ELRUM remained extremely hostile to the *Wildcat*, even after it became known I was associated with it. ELRUM had the opinion that the *Wildcat* was from the Communist Party, and they had minimal respect for the CP. They thought the *Wildcat* was racist and an outsider sheet.

I would like to say something about other radical groups which made interventions from 1970 onwards. Up front, let me say that I am presently a member of the Motor City Labor League, a Marxist-Leninist revolutionary group. Now, Progressive Labor came out to the plant in the summer of 1970 and started selling their paper, *Challenge*. I approached them at the gate one day. This was after I was fired. I looked like an ordinary worker. I was working at Budd Wheel at that time. They assumed I worked at Eldon, and I was shocked at how they related to a person whom they perceived as a typical worker. They were condescending. I ran a little bit about my involvement in the safety strike, and they were very critical of that. They said their policy was to ignore the unions. They assured me that they would be there every week and were not fly-by-night leftists. What happened was that they managed to antagonize a lot of folks, as is their fashion. This was done to the extent that one day some white workers came out and beat the shit out of them. That indicated a failure of sorts. They told me the same thing had happened at Cadillac. That physical assault was the end of their presence, and they haven't been seen since.

The reaction of the Socialist Workers Party is interesting because I'm not aware they had any reaction at all to what was going on at Eldon. They never contacted Sims, myself, or anyone in ELRUM to speak at a forum or do any internal education for them. I want to say something about their Detroit activities in the late 1960s. At that time, I was working for the Better Business Bureau, and I used to go to their Friday night socialist forums at the Debs Hall. I went pretty regularly for almost a year. Not once did anyone ever approach me politically or be even minimally friendly. I was like a fixture for a year, but they just ignored me. Maybe they thought I was an agent or something, but that has always struck me as a totally ripped practice. You have to be blind or myopic to ignore what was happening at Eldon, and I have never seen them relate in any way out there. If they have worker cadre, they sure as hell aren't at Eldon, Budd Wheel, or Dodge Main.

The only other groups to do any work are the Motor City Labor League, Revolutionary Union, and International Socialists. Revolutionary Union has mainly tried to get on with some stewards at Eldon, but they haven't distributed leaflets or done any public work. International Socialists have been extremely interested in Jordan Sims. They wanted to do a national campaign around his discharge in pretty much the way the Angela Davis thing worked for the CP. The Motor City Labor League has had a public presence in the form of leaflets, and we have been working with the various people and with Jordan Sims.

It's a truism that struggle creates strength. It is also true that you have to find issues that affect people's lives and that you agitate and organize around those issues with the point of view of making some gains and of exposing the concrete contradictions. The aftermath of our strike was that Jordan Sims ran for president of that local [Local 961]. He maintained his membership and was narrowly defeated by Frank McKinnon, the white steward. The election was literally stolen from Jordan. Now there is a scandal about the embezzlement of funds by McKinnon and other officials. Very large sums have disappeared for over ten years, and apparently George Merrelli, the regional director, knew about it. That would make it reach right into Solidarity House. People in the plant have gotten a pretty high consciousness about this whole set-up. We managed to get the Department of Labor into the process. We showed we were correct on the statutes and the contract. They had to expose their hand in a situation affecting the health and lives of those workers. We have developed a hard core of people at Eldon who go to union meetings. There's 60-70 people who know how to function. The company and union could just give up, but they can't do that because of the key nature of Eldon. The stakes are too high. But the company, union, and Labor Department continue to shit on people, which just creates more strength for us. Eventually, they'll have to move the factory out of Detroit or let us have it.

3

In the stamping plant, which we know is a hazardous area anyway, I got my fingertip severed off in a press. They sewed it back on. . . . But that isn't as serious as some of the other things that have happened in the Rouge area in the past. Six men in a basic-oxygen plant were killed, and there wasn't enough left of those men to put in a decent shopping bag.

—Wesley Johns, in a statement to a People's Court convened by the Motor City Labor League, April 3, 1973

John Taylor's recounting of the struggle at Eldon points up some of the problems facing the militants who wanted to carry out the RUM strategy. Many nationalist-minded blacks were attracted to the RUMS. Although very militant and vocal, the RUMs often held back the development of class consciousness among other workers attracted to the wider League program. This gap between secondary and primary leadership grew wider after the strike of January 1969. All the members of the League executive would have curbed some of the more counterproductive language in ELRUM leaflets, but there were occasions when Baker and Wooten sanctioned approaches some of the other League leaders would not have approved of. Excessive emphasis on the contradictions between workers not only alienated whites who might have been neutral or sympathetic, it turned away many blacks. Older workers, who had a large stake in improving working conditions, especially disliked the wholesale attacks on "honkies" and "Toms," considering them incorrect ways to get sustained and positive action. ELRUM's attitude toward individuals such as Jordan Sims and supporters of *Wildcat* posed another kind of problem. ELRUM was somewhat sectarian toward them and judged that Sims, at best, was an honest reformist stuck in trade union attitudes, and, at worst, could turn out to be another of those "traitors from within" that the League warned about. The consequence of ELRUM's attitude was that the organization drew too rigid a line of demarcation between itself and other forces in the plant. Ken Cockrel voiced the additional criticism that the ELRUM workers fired in January had failed to build a defense committee in the plant and in the neighborhoods. He believed that the hostile ELRUM attitude toward white participation and working with nonrevolutionary blacks was retarding rather than building their struggle.

ELRUM clearly failed to rally women to its ranks. Two of the workers killed at the plant during this period were women, and their deaths were an indication of the harassment and poor working conditions women faced. It was an open secret that dating foremen had its rewards, just as refusing them had its punishments. One young black woman who suffered from drowsiness caused by excessive noise got a job classification which would take her away from moving machinery, but she could not get it acted upon because of union indifference and the hostility of her foremen. In well-known incidents on the shop floor, several other women were forced to tell off supervisers and union representatives after they became tired of fending off constant sexual advances. ELRUM bulletins spoke of the special problems facing the "sisters" in the plant, but ELRUM never developed a concrete program for dealing with such problems.

ELRUM activists generally bypassed the UAW altogether once they were out of the plant. This caused a gradual breakdown of ties with some of the more militant workers in the factory. Jordan Sims, even after being fired in 1970, went to union meetings regularly and organized his forces as he might have had he been still working inside the plant. Sims continued to contend for power in the union, and on May 23, 1973, after several highly questionable elections, he defeated Frank McKinnon 1599-735 to become president of Local 961. As an elected union official and still co-chairman of the United National Caucus, Sims was now able to carry on his fight from within the UAW hierarchy. He demonstrated an honest and aggressive unionist stance during his first year in office.

Citing shortcomings in the ELRUM performance in no way diminishes the importance of the work it carried out over a two-year period. A handful of revolutionary minded production line workers had set themselves against the company and the union, and against the timidity and weariness of many workers. Taylor, a white Appalachian, called them exemplary; and their nationalism notwithstanding, he considered them the best leadership to have emerged in the plant. Many who criticized ELRUM for making mistakes retained their jobs and continued to keep their mouths shut while the ELRUM activists were fired and often blacklisted from the industry. Students and teachers at universities who didn't put in eight to ten hours a day at Eldon did not always comprehend that the clumsiness of some phrasing or tactical action was as much a product of fatigue as of poorly developed political skills. The League leadership itself was concerned with arriving at a proper evaluation of the Eldon experience. From the summer of 1970 onward, the League began a serious rethinking of its tactics, strategies, and personnel.

4

I don't own anything. I'm about $1,000 in debt. I work at Dodge Truck. . . . I started on the afternoon shift, working ten hours a day, six days a week. I punched in at 4:30 and punched out at 3:00 in the morning. I slept the rest of the day and then got up and went back to work. I work in the paint department, which is on the second floor, and during the summer the temperature is about 130-150 degrees.

—Richard Wieske, in a statement to a People's Court convened by the Motor City Labor League, April 3, 1973

No plant seemed more different from Eldon than General Motor's much-vaunted Lordstown Vega factory in Ohio. Constructed in a farming area adjacent to steel-mill towns, Lordstown was technologically the most ambitious factory in the auto industry. Lordstown was operated by the GM Assembly Division (GMAD), which engineered jobs to a fraction of a second and weighed paint wasted in the dye vats by the ounce. Lordstown bragged of the fastest assembly line in the world! It produced 103 cars per hour. Dodge Main officially turned out only 64 cars an hour, although workers said production often went up to 76. At Ford's Mahwah plant, the official speed was 52 cars an hour. The Lordstown "miracle," according to GMAD, was due to mechanization of jobs, robots, and sophisticated computer controls: in short, automation. Twenty-six Unimate robots did most of the welding. The Assembly

Line Production and Control Activity (ALPACA) was the main computer control, while Product Assurance Control (PAC) supervised actual production. Best of all, most of the 8,000 workers at Lordstown were young and so anxious to work that a trailer-camp city opened right across the turnpike from the factory. There were no large minority groups in the factory, and the workforce had no known old-time radicals or hardcore unionists. The only problem with Lordstown was that it didn't work. The Vega turned out to be one of the worst-built cars in America, and two years after GMAD took over, 97 percent of the workers voted to strike over working conditions. The three-week Lordstown strike of 1972 destroyed the automation myth. Unable to explain the strike in realistic terms, the media called it an "industrial Woodstock." The simple truth was that the list of Lordstown complaints could have been written by any worker at Eldon or Dodge Main. If the streamlined production of a highly automated plant at Lordstown was in any way significantly different from what transpired at older plants, the difference was not evident either to the average worker on the line or in the quality of the final product.

Emma Rothschild devoted a chapter to Lordstown in her perceptive book, *Paradise Lost: The Decline of the Auto Industrial Age.* Her conclusion was: "The major principle of Lordstown production is the speedup, as developed in the 1910's." The line moved so rapidly that workers could not keep up with it and often did their jobs improperly. The quality-control supervisers, not wanting to increase costs in their departments, let the defective parts pass, hoping they would be caught somewhere down the line. Some 23,000 Vegas had to be recalled for defective parts in 1970, vindicating anew Ralph Nader's evaluation of Detroit cars as "unsafe at any speed." The workers at Lordstown complained of the dreadful monotony of the work, as well as the speed. They complained of capricious layoffs and disciplinary crackdowns. Many of them voiced hatred of the assembly line itself and questioned the necessity of capitalist division of work. Almost all the workers stated that they were not going to put in 30 or 40 years in the plants the way their parents had. They wanted more from life and were willing to do more than just talk about it. Absenteeism, especially on Mondays and Fridays, soared. Management complained of chronic and wholesale tardiness, sabotage on the line, and "unreasonable" worker attitudes.

GM complained about its workers; but like Chrysler, it refused to improve the conditions of work or real wages. True to their hard-headed, tough traditions, GM executives said that whenever there was a reorganization and consolidation in the plants, there would be strikes. Ten reorganizations by GMAD had produced eight strikes. That was how it was in the auto industry. The quality problem was overblown, according to the executives, and would be corrected through managerial adjustments. Joseph Godfrey, the head of GMAD, told *Automotive News* in October 1971, "The workers may complain about monotony, but years spent in the factories leads me to believe that they like to do their jobs semi-automatically. If you interject new things, you spoil the rhythm of the job, and work gets fouled up."

As workers were killed and maimed in the plants, and as they challenged the necessity of the assembly line system itself, top executives painted pastels of happy and affluent workers. In early 1972, George B. Morris, Jr., vice-president of General Motors and director of labor relations, gave this impression of how a $10,000-a-year worker lived to Haynes Johnson and Nick Kotz of the *Washington Post*, who included it in their book, *The Unions:*

> [H]e lives in Flint, or one of the communities around Flint, he's got a hell of a nice home, two-car garage. He has two cars.
>
> He's got a trailer that he hooks on the back of one of those cars and he hauls his boat up north and he's got a hell of a big outboard motor on the back of that and does that on the weekend in the summer. And he probably has a summer place up north, too, on one of the fine lakes in northern Michigan.
>
> In the wintertime, he puts a couple of snowmobiles on that trailer and hauls them up there. He leaves Friday night while you and I work.
>
> I guess I'm not affluent by my definitions here. But this fellow has everything you could aspire to. You come to our plants and look in our parking lots on Friday and see how many of them—even second shift people—will be there with their trailers and their campers and have them all loaded. . . .
>
> Do you think all the people that are driving up I-75 are corporation presidents and bankers and stock brokers and lawyers? The hell they are. They're hourly rated people that work in those plants. What more do you want? If affluence is too strong a word, this is certainly not a pauper society we're talking about. This is a fellow who has aspired to material things and has them.

Chapter Six

Finally Got the News

Many music lovers don't know that nearly a whole generation of original and highly talented musicians in Detroit were either snuffed out or forced to flee Detroit to keep their music careers alive. You'd come into a studio, cut a record, and they'd pay you maybe $20 and a bottle of whiskey. It didn't matter if the records sold ten copies or if they sold ten thousand.

—Eddie "Guitar" Burns, interview in *Fifth Estate*, September 5, 1973

In Detroit, more than anywhere else in America, popular culture and the political rebellions of the 1960s were interwoven. An early sequence in *Finally Got the News*, a film the League of Revolutionary Black Workers made about its activities in 1969-1970, shows one auto worker picking up another in front of his house. They are first-shift workers, and as they drive down one of the expressways named after an auto industrialist, the only commentary is an urban blues song:

> Please, Mr. Foreman, slow down your assembly line.
> Please, Mr. Foreman, slow down your assembly line.
> No, I don't mind workin', but I do mind dyin'.
> Workin' twelve hours a day,
> Seven long days a week,
> I lie down and try to rest, but, Lord knows, I'm too tired to sleep.
> Lord knows, I'm too tired to sleep.
> Please, Mr. Foreman, slow down your assembly line.
> I said, Lord, why don't you slow down that assembly line?
> No, I don't mind workin', but I do mind dyin'.

The song was written and recorded by Joe L. Carter in 1965 when he was a production line worker at Ford Rouge. Like most of the Detroit blues singers, Joe L., as he billed himself, had been born in the South, worked regular jobs during the day, and played mostly on weekends. The Detroit blues sound had never had much of a mass audience. Other than brief spots on some black radio stations, its exposure was mainly limited to the red-light district around Hastings Street which began to be torn down in the late 1950s in the name of urban renewal. The blues singers often had colorful names and played unusual instruments. The only one to achieve national fame was John Lee Hooker, but there were many others, including Washboard Willie, One-String Sam, Doc Ross, Faye Thompson, Eddie Kirkland, and Bobo Jenkins. They played a down-and-dirty urban blues that spoke of the agony of everyday industrial life. John Lee Hooker worked in a steel mill. Doc Ross worked for GM. Bobo Jenkins pumped gas at a filling station, and he worked for 24 years for Chrysler. Roselyn, a folk singer who made her appearance in the 1970s, told *Fifth Estate* reporter Pat Halley in September 1973: "Anybody who plays music in Detroit plays the blues sometimes." Halley commented, "Anybody who lives in Detroit lives the blues sometimes, if not all the time."

During the 1960s, groups began substituting vocals for instrumental lines and mixing in gospel elements. Berry Gordy, an auto worker, founded Motown Records, and soon the entire country was listening to a new "soul" sound. The most famous Motown group was Diana Ross and the Supremes, a group of women who began as a teenage trio trying to sing their way free from the poverty of one of the city's most dangerous housing projects. Most of the other Motown singers had similar backgrounds. Small groups all over the city practiced faithfully and performed whenever possible in hope of making it to the super big time, which, for Diana Ross, the girl next door, meant million-plus album sales, appearances on network television, and a starring role in Hollywood's *Lady Sings the Blues*. For every Marvin Gaye and Mary Wells, for every Aretha Franklin (Reverend Franklin's daughter) and Della Reese, there were hundreds of unknowns singing, writing, and performing all over the city.

The music of the white population of the city had not fared nearly so well. The 1950s and 1960s all but wiped out public performances.

The gypsy violins of Del Ray were ignored to death. The music of Eastern Europe was forgotten, transformed into the champagne froth of a Lawrence Welk, or reduced to the polkas played at Polish weddings. The Greek music which had thrived around Monroe Street for decades underwent flagrant commercialization following the success of the films *Never on Sunday* and *Zorba the Greek*. The old-timers who played mountain tunes on folk instruments disappeared as electric bouzoukis took over with tunes bearing little relationship to the bouzouki music of Greece, which had clearly political lyrics and a waterfront origin. Most Arabic music degenerated into mere accompaniment for belly dancers, who sometimes were the same gyrators who used to perform at the Empress Burlesk. Aside from the music of groups building on black musical traditions, the only white music that prospered was the country-western style transported north by migrating Appalachians. On Detroit bandstands such as those along Jefferson Avenue, Third Avenue, and around the ballpark, small groups mixed traditional country favorites with new and original compositions. Eventually the style broke out of its characterization as "Nashville" sound in much the same way black music had broken out of the "race" music category.

The inclusion of Detroit music in the League film was not accidental. The League people had always been supportive of the popular and fine arts, and their ranks included painters and poets. *ICV* gave lavish space to original artwork, poetry, cartoons, and photography. The *South End* carried on this policy to such a degree that Sam Cohen, an anarcho-Reichian playwright who made Wayne one of his foci, stated that the Watson regime at the *South End* was more friendly to him than any other regime in the decade. RUM leaflets and newsletters featured original drawings and poetry. One anonymous mock-heroic poem which came out of the Dodge Main struggles became an organizational trademark, with the words FRUM, CADRUM, JARUM, and so on substituted for DRUM.

> Deep in the gloom
> of the oil-filled pit
> where the engine rolls down the line,
> we challenge the doom
> of dying in shit
> while strangled by a swine. . . . . .
> . . . . . . For hours and years

we've sweated tears
trying to break our chain. . . . . .
But we broke our backs
and died in packs
to find our manhood slain. . . . . .
But now we stand
for DRUM's at hand
to lead our Freedom fight,
and now 'til then
we'll unite like men. . . . . .
For now we know our might,
and damn the plantation
and the whole Chrysler nation
for DRUM has dried our tears,
and now as we die
we've a different cry
for now we hold our spears!
U.A.W. is scum
OUR THING IS DRUM! ! ! !

Other popular and fine arts were part of the Detroit scene of the 1960s. At one time, there were six independent theater groups performing on proscenium stages, in coffeehouses, and in church basements. All of them had substantial black participation, and the Concept East was founded to stage plays written by blacks and performed mainly by blacks. The most ambitious of the theater groups was the Unstabled Coffeehouse, an enterprise run by Edith Carroll Cantor, a socialist. The Unstabled featured poetry, chess, and dance some weeknights; and on weekends, plays early in the evening, folksinging later on, and jazz after hours. The Unstabled produced works by Detroiter Ron Milner and Reverend Malcolm Boyd, who was then based in Detroit, as well as a rich selection of plays by Jean Genet, Le Roi Jones (Imamu Amiri Baraka), William Saroyan, Tennessee Williams, Edward Albee, Jack Gelber, and Samuel Beckett. One original play called *Sitdown '37* was created for the UAW and was presented in Flint on the 25th anniversary of the Flint sitdown strikes which unionized GM. The play was well received by the workers, the majority of whom had participated in the struggle. Many wept openly, and there was wild cheering at the closing scenes of triumph.

Two quite different publishing experiments aimed at mass audiences appeared at the same time as the theater groups. One was a magazine called *On the Town* that was black-owned but interracially staffed. It was published from 1963-1964 and tried to combine bar listings and humor with serious commentary on music, the new Detroit theater, and politics. It circulated approximately 10,000 copies of each issue, almost entirely within the center city. A more aesthetically oriented venture that continued to thrive in the 1970s was Broadside Press, founded by librarian and poet Dudley Randall. Begun with private savings, Broadside became one of the most important black poetry publishers in the United States. Randall introduced poets such as Sonia Sanchez, Don Lee, Nikki Giovanni, and Etheridge Knight. Broadside published a book which honored Malcolm X with poetry by black and white writers, and it published many established writers such as Gwendolyn Brooks and Le Roi Jones.

Detroiters have always complained about the neglect of the arts in their city, but virtually every schoolchild in the city has been taken to see the Diego Rivera murals in the Detroit Institute of Arts. Covering four immense walls, the frescos depict automaking at Ford's River Rouge plant. The main panels are montages in which machines hover like robot monsters, spewing forth flames and poisonous gases, as workers with glaring eyes, and curses under their breath, labor before hostile foremen and plant visitors. Sharp, almost cartoon-like insets ridicule Henry Ford, while small details such as red stars on a glove and a handwritten WE WANT on a workman's paper cap emphasize Rivera's revolutionary perspective. The murals are capped by an homage to the four races of mankind and the natural abundance of the earth. The renowned Mexican muralist completed his nine months' work in 1933, and many city leaders wanted the walls whitewashed as soon as the scaffolding came down. The *Detroit News* and the Catholic Archdiocese were particularly incensed, but the work was spared the destruction accorded the Rivera murals done for New York's Rockefeller Center, which were demolished by the same people who had commissioned them. The Rivera frescos became familiar to the people of the Motor City through the years, and radicals were especially fond of using them in their literature. Sections of the murals appear in *Finally Got the News* and on the cover of a 1973 publication of the Motor City Labor League.

The Rivera murals at the Detroit Institute were matched by street developments in 1968. On a building on Mack Avenue, under the supervision of artists who had done similar work in Chicago, black Detroiters painted a Wall of Dignity. Some of the scenes depicted the glories of ancient Africa, but most were a litany of black struggles in America. The figures of Marcus Garvey and Malcolm X were prominent, yet most of the work focused on anonymous and angry blacks smoldering with rebellion. Across the street from the Wall, the facade of St. Bernard's Church was decorated with similar work. The huge center facade depicted a black Pharaoh, while side panels emphasized mass struggle and contemporary leaders such as Martin Luther King, Elijah Muhammad, Adam Clayton Powell, and Malcolm X. Most of the work was done by Eugene Eda and Bill Walker, the artists who also did much of the work on the Wall of Dignity.

Diego Rivera himself could not have wished for a more popular or public art. Bill Walker was quoted in a September 1971 *Liberation* article written by John Weber as saying, "In questioning myself as to how I could best give my art to Black people, I came to the realization that art must belong to ALL people. That is when I first began to think of public art." John Weber, a white associate of Walker's, wrote that more than 30 such projects had been done in Chicago, and that by 1969 they had begun to involve white and Latin artists as well as blacks. Like most revolutionary and mass art, the muralist movement was little discussed in aesthetic journals. Needless to say, no funds were available for keeping Detroit's Wall of Dignity in a state of good repair.

As always in the Motor City, traces of the history of the working class, of racial conflict, and of the popular arts mingled on the same neglected corners. One block west of the Wall of Dignity was an Arab community center where authentic Middle Eastern music was sometimes performed, and several blocks beyond the Arab center were blues bars. On nearby Garland Street, there was the now-forgotten house which had been the scene of a race riot in 1924 when it was purchased by Dr. Ossian Sweet, the area's first black homeowner. Several blocks to the east of the Wall were the Mack stamping plant and the former Briggs plant, two Chrysler factories with long histories of radical worker organizations. A mile to the south, in another decaying neighborhood, a string of hillbilly music bars was adjacent to more factories owned by Chrysler. In the midst of all this stood the building on which the murals were painted. It had been burnt out during the Great Rebellion. Formerly, it had been called Fairview Gardens and had been used as a roller-skating rink and a wrestling emporium. On the bricks upon which the Wall of Dignity was painted, there had been wrestling posters advertising various ethnic heroes and villains such as Killer Kowalski, The Sheik, Chief Don Eagle, Mr. Togo, Man Mountain Dean, and Lou Klein.

2

I think Finally Got the News represents both a breaking of new ground and simultaneously an endpost of some kind. At the same time it signals the end of white filmmakers making films about other people's struggles, it re-opens a whole area and direction long ignored by the New Left—that of the lives and importance of ordinary working people in this country.

—Peter Gessner, filmmaker, in a letter to Dan Georgakas, July 1, 1972

Finally Got the News, the League's most ambitious art project, began in the spring of 1969. A group of whites working in New York Newsreel, a radical filmmakers' collective, had the idea of making a film about DRUM in much the same style as the ones they had done on the Black Panthers. Although most of the Newsreel group of that period favored the Black Panther-Weatherman thesis that the revolution would be led by a relatively small group of elite professionals with a mass following based in the lumpen proletariat, the group that wanted to do the Detroit film had a worker orientation. In June 1969, Jim Morrison headed a small Newsreel delegation to Detroit, where they collected more than 20 hours of taped conversations and gathered various League documents. Most of the help given to them was from Cockrel, Hamlin, and Watson.

The raw material gathered by the Morrison group was favorably received by New York Newsreel, but there was some hesitation about providing funds for an actual film. An exasperated Morrison took fund-raising into his own hands by undertaking an ill-fated hashish-smuggling scheme that netted him a 10-year prison sentence when he was caught at the Canadian border. Morrison served more than three years before escaping from an honor farm when he realized he was not going to be paroled. He remained at large as of 1974 and was given a screen credit on the final film, although he did not do much work on the actual production.

Shortly after Morrison's venture, the main body of Newsreel came up with funds, and a Newsreel unit was sent to Detroit. From the beginning, the group had two factions. Stewart Bird, René Lichtman, and Peter Gessner saw their task as one of making a film which accurately presented the strategy and activities of the League. The others had a grander objective. They felt that both the white and the black movements in Detroit needed to be updated by an injection of Weatherman and Panther thinking. Rather than making films, this faction, headed by George de Pue, set about making an ideological intervention into the local political structure.

One of the first problems confronted by Newsreel was the attitude of the League itself. A majority of the leadership believed in keeping a low public profile. Many of them did not want any filmmakers, much less white filmmakers, covering meetings, demonstrations, and factory agitation. They thought workers who were moving toward them might be frightened off. They also feared that the film would ultimately be useful to the companies, police, and union for gathering intelligence about League activities. John Watson had a much different vision of what the film could be. He saw the tremendous outreach a movie would provide both in educating and in organizing. Watson took personal responsibility for the film and secured League approval for the project.

The division of opinion over the film was a precursor of the issues that would cause a split within the League ranks in 1971. Those who were most dubious about the film were the people most concerned about the dangers of premature national exposure, of coalitions with whites, and of the use of mass media. They expressed their uneasiness in many ways. During the early stages of shooting, they did not stop nationalistically oriented workers from running off white camera crews, and they often failed to inform the filmmakers about key public events. Many of the League units under their personal supervision never appeared in the film. Their hostile attitude eased as the filmmaking proceeded, but it was never totally erased.

The reluctance of these League members to have a film made about them was in marked contrast to the attitude of many radicals in the 1960s, who often seemed to measure their success by the number of times they appeared on television. The League rejected such a publicity-conscious approach and was very concerned with the image the Newsreel film might project. The League definitely wanted the usual "by any means necessary" rhetoric omitted or curtailed. Watson insisted that the film be conceived within a teaching rather than a reporting framework. He knew that Newsreel's audiences were primarily the white college students who made up the bulk of the "movement," but he wanted this film's explicit Marxist message to be directed toward an audience of black workers. Although the typical Newsreel audience would benefit from the film, their needs would be secondary to those of black workers. Bird, Lichtman, and Gessner were more pleased than upset by his orientation, but many difficult meetings were required to hammer out specific methods.

Watson's first notion was to use a lot of heavy Marxist terminology and quotations. He was soon persuaded that it would be more effective to have different League leaders speak informally in the same way they would speak to a group of workers. The title of the film, *Finally Got the News,* was taken from the words chanted by General Baker to workers during the 1970 elections at Dodge Main:

> Finally got the news
> How your dues are being used.
> Be bad, be bad, be bad, be bad, be bad!
> Can't do nothing if you ain't bad!

The approach ultimately adopted was to give a theoretical view of how the working class, led by black workers, could make a revolution, with most of the actual footage showing how the League handled concrete problems arising from its revolutionary perspective. The effective montage history of American labor which opens the film was primarily the idea of Stewart Bird, who saw it as a way of covering a complex subject with images rather than words. The ultimate decisions about this and other sequences were worked out in joint meetings. Watson generally indicated the overall direction, while the Newsreel team solved the technical problems. Both groups agreed that League people should be trained in technical skills. This training did not work out as well as it could have, but toward the end of the collaboration League members were doing some of the camera work and other technical tasks.

The first half of *Finally Got the News* presents a clear exposition of the idea that black people in the United States have been and continue to be exploited primarily because they are workers. In an opening sequence, Watson says:

> You get a lot of arguments that black people are not numerous enough in America to revolt, that they will be wiped out. This neglects our economic position. . . . There are groups that can make the whole system cease functioning. These are auto workers, bus drivers, postal workers, steel workers, and others who play a crucial role in the money flow, the flow of materials, the creation of production. By and large, black people are overwhelmingly in those kinds of jobs.

Scenes within the Detroit factories and interviews with local leaders such as Ron March and Chuck Wooten supplement the more general approach of Watson with specific details. These sequences emphasize the deteriorating work and safety conditions within the factories. They reach an artistic peak when the off-camera voice of Ken Cockrel denounces capitalism in a long tirade that can only be described as a prose poem. Against placid scenes of executives "working" at their desks, a "voice from the ghetto" says:

> They give you little bullshit amounts of money—wages and so forth—and then they steal all that shit back from you in terms of the way they have their other thing set up, that old credit-stick-'em-up gimmick society—consumer credit—buy shit, buy shit—on credit. He gives you a little bit of money to cool your ass and then steals it all back with shit called interest, which is the price of money. They are mother-fucking, non-producing, non-existing bastards dealing with paper. . . .
> He is in mining! He went to Exeter. He went to Harvard. He went to Yale. He went to the Wharton School of Business. And he is in "mining"! It is these mother-fuckers who deal with intangibles who are rewarded by this society. The more abstract and intangible your service, the bigger the reward.
> What are stocks? A stock certificate is evidence of something which is real. A stock is evidence of *ownership*. He who owns and controls receives—profit!
> This man is fucking with shit in Bolivia. He is fucking with shit in Chile. He is Kennicott. He is Anaconda. He is United Fruit. He is in mining! He's in what? He ain't never produced anything his whole

life. Investment banker. Stockbroker. Insurance man. He don't do
nothing.

We see that this whole society exists and rests upon workers and
this whole mother-fucking society is controlled by this little clique
which is parasitic, vulturistic, cannibalistic, and is sucking and destroy-
ing the life of workers everywhere; and we must stop it because it is—
evil!

Another telling sequence in this part of the film deals with two
Ford executives, one black and one white. Only the black executive
speaks; but like some two-bit actor from a vulgar Marxist playlet, his
white superior chews on a cigar and leers approvingly at every word.
The black explains how company and union come together to work for
the benefit of the "greater society." This ventriloquist act would have
been farcical in a fiction film, but it succeeds admirably as a real-life interview.

The first section of the film concludes with the 1970 plant election at
Dodge Main. Rather than lock-stepped, black-bereted, leather-jacketed
Panther units, the film shows rather ordinary people becoming very angry
with the system. Workers by the busloads arrive waving clenched fists
and shouting, "DRUM-DRUM-DRUM-DRUM." General Baker is
heard over the megaphone directing the chanting as the workers, young
and old, men and women, enter the union hall. They have to pass other
workers, many of whom are black. These men wear union caps and
stare at the DRUM forces in the way police stare at peace marchers.
The class line is drawn very sharply in terms of psychological identifica-
tion, as well as economics. Some workers have identified with the master, and some with the revolution.

What is most striking in these emotionally charged scenes is that
the struggle transcends a simple plant election. The people who are politically in motion are people who work on the line every day, people
who drive their own cars, people who own homes, people who have
families, people who may even own the proverbial color television set.
These same people are very obviously and very enthusiastically supporting an anti-capitalist revolutionary organization. Workers viewing
such footage can identify with the kind of people participating and
with the kind of action being taken. They can see that being a radical
does not require becoming an incredible, gun-slinging hero who defies
the police with every breath. A union election is one of the lowest levels

of mass action, but it is mass action nonetheless, and not elite action, just as the strike and the boycott are mass actions in which the people serve themselves rather than relying upon a group of elite warriors.

The second half of the film never regains the sharp ideological and artistic focus of the part which ends with the Dodge election. There is a valiant attempt to deal with the relationship of white workers to revolutionary black workers that might have been the subject of an entire second film. Retired Appalachian-born white workers are shown sitting on the porches of their frame houses. They drink beer and play guitars as they put forth a very heavy anti-company line that comes near to matching the RUM positions until an old man concludes, "Everyone in this country is almost in revolt. We want to get more money. Everyone else is getting their share. Certain groups are doing good—the colored and the mothers on welfare." Watson's voice cuts into explain the paradox created by racism: "The white workers face the same contradictions in production and life as blacks do. If they work harder, they think the enemy is 'the nigger.' If life is worse, the problem is 'crime in the streets.' . . . [George] Wallace raps the 'money barons' and 'the niggers'; and these white workers love to hear it. . . . Many white workers end up being counter-revolutionary in the face of a daily oppression which should make them the staunchest of revolutionaries. . . . We are calling for the uplifting of the working class as a whole."

Watson's analysis is sound, but he offers no solutions, not even a transition strategy. His lack of program in this area reflects the League's indecision on the matter. Filmed interviews with white working-class students pick up the problem from another angle. The students speak poignantly of the alienation felt by their fathers and mothers. They argue for an alliance with the League, but it is clear that they speak as individuals. The scenes are a kind of brave hope in the future that only succeeds in revealing the enormous problem racism presents to those who would unite the working class.

Similar problems surround the treatment of black working women and the role of community organizing. Hurried sequences do little more than register the filmmakers' awareness that such topics need further investigation. Again, the film reflects the League's poorly thought-out positions on these vital questions. Some footage showing the funeral of a ten-year-old boy accidentally shot by the police is decidedly out of rhythm with the rest of the film, in spite of its attempt to link the life of the factory with the violence of everyday life. Ken Cockrel's summation interview is less effective than it might have been because it follows these disconnected and only partially thought-out sections.

The erratic second half of the film is partly the result of problems that nearly destroyed the film completely. While the three Newsreel filmmakers already mentioned were working on making a film, the rest of the Newsreel group in Detroit was involved in politics. As part of their program of intervention, the Newsreel people organized an anti-repression conference to which they invited Robert Williams, recently returned from exile in China, Emory Douglas of the Black Panthers, and Ken Cockrel. The ideological tensions between the Panthers and the League had become public knowledge. Cockrel emphasized that, as of that time (January 1970), no one in the League's orbit had been killed by police or had been sentenced to a jail term. His tone made it clear that he thought the League's tactics were the major reason for this fact, and that Panther tactics were not needed or wanted in the city of Detroit.

In spite of its lack of a single black member, the Detroit Newsreel group continued to push the Panther line, as well as maintain pressure for a Weatherman approach among whites. The radical forces within the city became increasingly annoyed that a small outside group with no local membership base and no local work continued to advocate projects contrary to the wishes and detrimental to the safety of local activists. The League, for its part, became indignant when it learned fees and expense money were paid to the Panthers by a group that always claimed poverty when approached for funds needed by local people. The mounting pressure on Newsreel caused an internal collapse, and the group decided to give its equipment to a cultural group in Ann Arbor and to leave the city. The League responded by seizing the Newsreel equipment on the revolutionary ground that the group had raised money for the purpose of making radical films, which was what the League proposed to continue doing, and on the legal ground that the seizure was in lieu of unpaid speakers' fees. Bird, Gessner, and Lichtman did not approve of the manner in which the League took the equipment, but they agreed to continue working on the film as individuals, even though the Detroit Newsreel group had ceased to exist.

3

Near the freeway
you stop and wonder what came off,
recall the snowstorm where you lost it all,
the wolverine, the northern bear, the wolf
caught out, ice and steel raining
from the foundries in a shower
of human breath. . . .
—Philip Levine, "Coming Home, Detroit, 1968"

Shortly after the seizure of the Newsreel equipment, John Watson founded Black Star Productions. A fund-raising letter of late 1970, addressed to the general public and signed by Rachel Bishop, described Black Star's objective: "to produce and distribute films dealing with the most crucial social and political issues of our times." John Watson, in a similar fund-raising letter dated May 5, 1971, said Black Star films would serve "as a means of political education and as a real alternative to the current lack of such films." Black Star was organized as a component of the League, yet its haphazard staff, at one time or another, included the three former Newsreel people, Nick Medvecky, and an Italian with experience making revolutionary films. The immediate goal of Black Star was to arrange for the widest possible distribution of *Finally Got the News* and to use that film as a basis for soliciting funds for future films.

Watson made a trip to Europe in the spring of 1970 to promote Black Star. He was interested in selling copies of *Finally Got the News* to European distributors, and he wanted to secure additional filmmaking equipment, which was cheaper to purchase in Europe. He visited Scandinavia, England, Germany, France, and Italy. His greatest success came in Italy, where a segment of the film was sold to Italian television and copies were acquired by extra-parliamentary groups and the Italian Communist Party for distribution to their members and supporters. The film was also shown as one of the supplementary films at the 1970 Pesaro Film Festival.

Watson's efforts in England, France, and Germany were not as successful, although he did make some minor sales. Many Europeans found it hard to relate to a film dealing with blacks as workers, especially a film without the flamboyance the films about the Panthers had made them accustomed to. They were impressed that the League itself had made the film, rather than being merely the subject of someone else's production. Although distribution of *Finally Got the News* was generally limited to a few politically motivated fringe groups, many contacts expressed an interest in seeing whatever future films Black Star made.

Watson's first stop in Europe was Sweden, where he visited Glanton Dowdell, a League exile with an unusual personal history. Dowdell was 47 at the time of Watson's visit and had fled the United States after being charged with forging $65,000 worth of government bonds. One of his co-defendants had been murdered in Detroit, others had pleaded guilty, and there had been attempts on Dowdell's life. Like Malcolm X, Martin Sostre, and Eldridge Cleaver, Dowdell had a criminal background. His specialty had been armed robbery, and much of his political career involved being in charge of security. Dowdell was also a gifted artist and an articulate politician. In the mid-1960s, he had taken part in a variety of united front activities which had generated funds for radical organizations. He had operated a small art gallery, helped organize the Detroit Black Art Conference, and painted a famous *Black Madonna* portrait in a short-lived alliance with Reverend Albert Cleage, with whom other League people had worked in the Freedom Now Party. Dowdell had been active in physically removing drug pushers from around some black high schools, and he was rumored to have been an inspiration for the armed robbers who preyed on after-hours clubs owned by the mafia and black racketeers. In 1966, he, General Baker, and Rufus Griffin were charged with trying to start a riot on Detroit's east side, and he received a suspended sentence. During the Great Rebellion, the police destroyed his art gallery, and he was shot at several times. Dowdell established a Solidarity Committee for the League when he settled in Sweden, and after receiving official status as a political refugee, he brought his wife and five children to live with him in exile.

The film was important in establishing Dowdell as a genuine political figure, and it aided him in his struggle with the Panther committee in Sweden. The tensions which had been growing between the Panthers and the League in the United States had spilled over to Europe. Dowdell had been treated by the Panthers as an interloper and a dangerous rival. The resourceful Dowdell eventually made significant contacts with prominent politicians in Sweden, and he organized a conference for the League in which major Swedish and Finnish labor organizations participated. Ken Cockrel and Luke Tripp also visited Dowdell during 1970 to bring him up to date on the defense work being done in his behalf and to elaborate on new League plans.

The potential represented by Dowdell, the Italians, and the various European contacts never materialized into the kind of network Watson had in mind, but his partial success indicated that his international plans for Black Star Productions were not without substance. Upon his return to the United States, Watson explored other possibilities. One of the most promising of these was a projected film about drug addiction. Carolyn Ramsey, who had met Watson through the West Central Organization, worked on a script and did some work with Wayne's television station to pick up technical skills. Other activities included agreements with various Arab sources to circulate Palestinian films in the United States. One about Al Fatah was secured and distributed. The activity of Black Star Productions and the existence of *Finally Got the News* brought Watson into contact with film stars Jane Fonda and Donald Sutherland. In early 1971, he advanced the idea to them of doing a feature-length film about the life of Rosa Luxemburg, a leader of the German Communist Party who was arrested and murdered in 1919. Paula Hankins, who had been working with Watson since the first issues of *ICV*, got together a first draft of a script.

The more time Watson devoted to Black Star Productions, the more criticism he accumulated from the factory-oriented leadership. Luke Tripp approved of *Finally Got the News,* but thought the Rosa Luxemburg film was pure escapism. People like Baker and Wooten felt that Watson was retreating from the League's work in the factories and becoming dazzled with the notion of film success. They noted that he often got carried away by specific projects and they joked about the rare breed of Belgian dogs Watson had long raised and sold for side income. They said Watson was getting his priorities mixed up. Hamlin and Cockrel generally backed Watson because they saw *Finally Got the News* and future productions within the BEDC context. Watson's own view was that films could be a tremendous source of revenue, while giving the League ideological clout the mimeograph-minded activists had never conceived of. Jane Fonda wanted to help Black Star and offered to use her influence at Warner's to get apprentice training for League people; but in a letter to Watson written on April 16, 1971, she touched on doubts similar to those advanced by the in-plant organizers:

> The main questions asked are why do a film that would require so much money to portray a revolutionary heroine that the masses of Americans would have difficulty relating to when the time, energies, and resources could be spent to make several movies about our own rich history of struggle? Why, if one is intending to make a revolutionary film that will move people in America, go outside of America when we have our own culture, heroines, and heroes that need to be portrayed for us to develop a sense of our past so we can have a vision of our own, unique future?

Eventually, the various projects of Black Star Productions fell victim to the general collapse of the League, but the film *Finally Got the News* remained a solid contribution to radical filmmaking, able to survive the organization it was made to promote. Some film critics considered it a radical classic comparable to the memorable *Salt of the Earth*, made in the 1950s. *Finally Got the News* had spoken of a specific time and a specific experience in cinematic and ideological terms that would remain relevant as long as working people were not able to control their own lives.

4

"It seems to me," said Booker T.,
"That all you folks have missed the boat
Who shout about the right to vote
And spend vain days and fruitless nights
In uproar over civil rights. . . ."

"I don't agree," said W.E.B.
"For what can property avail
If dignity and justice fail? . . ."

"It seems to me," said Booker T.—

"I don't agree,"
Said W.E.B.

—Dudley Randall, "Booker T. and W.E.B."

While Watson was busy developing Black Star Productions, Mike Hamlin was opening another cultural front. Hamlin had become concerned about the relationship between progressive whites and the League, as well as the general lack of a League public education program. Meeting with several white and black activists, Hamlin developed the concept of a book club discussion forum. Perhaps 100 people might be persuaded to attend monthly sessions to hear a radical speaker analyze a book dealing with problems the League considered relevant. The device was aimed openly at whites and middle-class blacks. Hamlin hoped to develop their revolutionary consciousness and to provide a middle-class cushion against possible media and police attacks upon the League. The speeches at the book club could be mimeographed and made available for those unable to attend the actual discussions.

An initial sample mailing to gauge interest brought an astounding 400 positive responses, and membership in the club grew to more than 800 during the first year of operation. The very success of the idea soon proved to be another point of contention within the League leadership. The in-plant leadership perceived the book club as one more diversion of funds, personnel, and interest from the problems of black workers. They believed that the black middle class was virtually useless and that, if the League was going to spend any energy on whites, it should be with white workers. Hamlin's response was that the League needed a working relationship with the black middle class, progressive whites, and various community organizations to avoid isolation and defeat. If anything, he thought the in-plant leaders should encourage the rank and file to take part in the book club to deepen their comprehension of complex social and economic issues.

The book club also advanced another Hamlin project. White individuals and white organizations such as Ad Hoc, People Against Racism, and the Detroit Organizing Committee had worked with the League on different projects. Hamlin wanted to see these forces forged into a white umbrella group that could be some kind of rough counterpart to the League. Jim Jacobs, one of the most effective Detroit Organizing Committee members and a frequent writer on working-class struggle in Detroit, believed that Hamlin had what amounted to an infatuation with the idea of getting groups together and consequently minimized important ideological differences. Generally, however, Hamlin's effort was greeted enthusiastically as a direct attempt by the League to link up white and black militants in a structured rather than a personal system of contacts.

The fruit of Hamlin's initiative was the creation of the Motor City Labor Coalition, which soon became the Motor City Labor League (MCLL), a group which at one time or another in its development contained almost all the active indigenous white radicals in the city. The two key organizations in putting MCLL together were Ad Hoc and People Against Racism. Ad Hoc was led by Sheila Murphy, a young woman with a reputation as one of the most militant, committed, and diligent Detroit activists. Her Irish-American father had been the distributor of the anarchist-oriented *Catholic Worker* in Detroit. He believed in voluntary poverty, pacifism, and a fundamental reordering of church priorities. Sheila Murphy had grown up in tough neighborhoods and had developed the kind of personality stereotyped by the image of a scrappy Irish redhead. She had worked as a secretary for the West Central Organization. According to her own account, WCO had the only stencil-maker available to radicals in the city, and she got to know almost everyone engaged in mass agitation. These people included John Watson, Ken Cockrel, and Justin Ravitz. In time, Murphy began to take a leadership role in different groups which used church financing for radical projects. Her groups usually had loosely defined memberships organized around specific issues.

People Against Racism was primarily the creation of Frank Joyce, a radical with a substantial history of trying to organize white people to fight racism within their own communities. Joyce's groups tended to be tightly knit operations with broad programs and demands. He was born in Royal Oak, a Detroit suburb, and he had been a boyhood friend of Tom Hayden, one of the founders of SDS and an anti-Vietnam War organizer. Joyce's personal style was very much in the mode of SDS-type radicals of the 1960s. He participated in many national conferences, traveled to North Vietnam, and worked in Chicago as a staff member of the defense committee of the Chicago Seven (Tom Hayden, Dave Dellinger, Rennie Davis, Abbie Hoffman, Jerry Rubin, John Froines, and Lee Weiner), who were accused of conspiring to disrupt the 1968 Democratic convention. Joyce was frequently consulted by forces outside Detroit regarding national mobilizations around one issue or another. He was the major Detroit link to the national white movement and was acquainted with almost everyone who was politically active in the Detroit area.

MCLL had many women in leadership roles and tried drawing in individuals with long-time radical experience in the city, as well as recruiting new activists. One of the major MCLL thrusts was the book club; and even after the League split in 1971, the book club sessions continued. The format for the sessions was for the audience to be grouped at tables, each with a discussion leader. After the featured presentation, there was discussion at the tables in which everyone was urged to participate; and later, there were questions from the tables to the speakers.

MCLL had a split of its own in 1972, but the concept of the book club forum had taken root. The group which continued with the MCLL name began to focus its book club topics more sharply on problems related to local radical history, mass culture, and the use of media. A separate series of programs for women dealt with cultural, as well as purely political, questions. The MCLL newspaper, the *Journey*, published poetry and fiction and devoted half a page of each issue to the writing of children. One of the more ambitious MCLL cultural projects was a plan to stage a play based on Harriette Arnow's novel *The Dollmaker*, which had a Detroit setting.

The group which broke away from MCLL took the name From The Ground Up, and it, too, developed book club forums involving hundreds of people. Aside from their inherent intellectual value, the book club forums of both organizations served as devices for bringing guest speakers to Detroit from all parts of the country. These speakers included prominent attorneys, labor organizers, poets, historians, and activists who related their own experiences of struggle to the local scene. From The Ground Up also set up a complete printing center to back up its activities. This center was designed to do commercial work so that it might become self-sustaining, as well as to prepare leaflets, booklets, posters, and other agitational material. The organization also established the From The Ground Up Bookstore.

The bookstore was yet another expression of the Detroit movement's intense seriousness about mass education. The League had set up a Black Star Bookstore in 1970 on a stretch of Linwood Avenue which included Muslim Mosque No. 1, the Shrine of the Black Madonna, and Central High School. Ernie Mkalimoto, an able militant who had met Baker and Tripp on the Cuba journey of 1964, had come from New York to run the bookstore. Originally thought to have an almost unlimited funding base in the Black Economic Development Conference, the operation eventually fell apart from lack of the capital needed to provide a wide selection of books. In 1972, a China-Albania bookstore was opened across the street from the old Black Star Bookstore, but it sold only Peking publications and served more as an organizational headquarters for the Baker forces than as a real bookshop. MCLL had a similar set-up, with a small bookstore in the front of its offices. The From The Ground Up Bookstore had a different character. Under the management of Jack Russell, the husband of League activist Michelle Russell, the store was considered a prime financial and ideological resource. Instead of restricting itself to a narrow range of "approved" material, the bookstore stocked an assortment of diverse radical literature which might be of interest to the city's militants.

5

And you the audience of indifference
in the bleachers of your set up judgeship
will have no choice.
The war will be brought into the stands.

—C.G. Johnson, untitled poem

The underground press and counter-culture of the 1960s sought to destroy the straight, materialistic, unfulfilling world of Middle America through a nonviolent and beautiful revolution shorn of the ugliness of politics and ideology. First by winning over America's youth, then by taking over all cultural and social institutions, the counter-culture hoped to accomplish even more than the political revolutionaries of the 1930s had advocated. Those who pursued this course in a sincere effort to bring change to America were soon crushed by capitalist realities. Stripped of the political sensibilities it consciously rejected, the counter-culture, like the Motown sound, was easy prey for the money boys of Broadway, the ad agencies, organized crime, Hollywood, and the recording industry. Its music, health foods, drugs, hairstyles, mysticism, and colorful clothing were transformed into new commodities to be sold in the American marketplace.

Exactly where the counter-culture left off and hardcore revolutionary culture began was not always clear in the 1960s. Mammoth antiwar events reflected both. The counter-culturalist of one summer might be the political activist of the next, and vice versa. Those who regarded themselves as primarily political activists, especially those in SDS, were often enthusiastic about the spirit of the counter-culture and the beauty of its artistic efforts while remaining uneasy about drugs, nonviolence, and the notion that youth could be regarded as a revolutionary social class or category. They realized that the counter-culture challenged the authority of the state, the nuclear family, and the traditional political party by raising searching questions about the quality and purpose of everyday life in much the same manner as what they called the New Left. Despite these similarities, the frivolous and self-destructive nature of many counter-culture activities repelled many political activists and the working people they were trying to reach. The huge outdoor concert at Woodstock, New York, was followed by another at Altamont, California, where all the ugliest aspects of the counter-culture asserted themselves before film cameras, which even recorded "live" a murder by the Hell's Angels motorcycle gang hired to protect the Rolling Stones rock group. Advocacy of the drug culture ultimately posed an irresolvable contradiction to the political necessity of cleansing the cities, especially the ghettos, of the heroin, cocaine, and pill traffic which bred street violence and indirectly paralyzed social movements.

The counter-culture succeeded in generating a new feeling of liberation which came to characterize much of the 1960s. To develop and sustain the proposed cultural revolution, it was necessary to integrate that revolution into the everyday lives and politics of ordinary people and to keep it beyond the grasp of capitalist co-optation and commoditization. Political focus and organizational structure were crucial to maintaining the momentum and integrity of the counter-culture, and only the political revolutionaries sought to provide that focus and structure. For them, a successful cultural revolution could only come upward from the people within the context of an overall social, economic, and political revolution.

In Detroit, the relations between the counter-culture and the political revolutionaries became especially strained and guarded. The erratic poet John Sinclair, with his Artists' Workshop just off the Wayne campus, was the most visible example of the counter-culture. Sinclair wrote a regular column for the *Fifth Estate* in which he espoused music and drugs as viable revolutionary weapons of a youth insurgency. Originally hostile to talk of violent revolution, Sinclair had a change of heart in the midst of the Great Rebellion and hoisted a huge "Burn Baby Burn" sign on top of his home overlooking the Lodge Expressway. The police promptly shot up the sign and the house. Some time later, Sinclair formed a White Panther Party whose first programmatic demand was "Full endorsement and support of the Black Panther Party's 10 point program and platform." Many of Detroit's revolutionaries regarded that idea as dubious in itself; the second demand was simply ridiculous: "Total assault on the culture by any means necessary, including rock and roll, dope, and fucking in the streets." In the next years, Sinclair's closest associates would be convicted on bombing charges and Sinclair himself would be sentenced to ten years in prison in a celebrated marijuana case. In his 360-page memoir of the period, published in 1972 and titled *Guitar Army*, Sinclair exposed the gap between himself and the Detroit revolutionaries by simply avoiding all mention of the politics and views of the League of Revolutionary Black Workers or those of the people who flowed into and out of groups such as the Motor City Labor League. His omissions included Justin Ravitz, the attorney who did the legal work leading to Sinclair's own release from prison. Sinclair's path after getting out of prison in 1971 took him out of Detroit to the nearby university town of Ann Arbor, home of the University of Michigan, where his major activity was organizing musical concerts.

Rather than depending on the outside ranks of the counter-culture, the political revolutionaries in Detroit drew on their own ranks for artistic and cultural work. Besides filmmaking and the book club forums and the bookstores, the revolutionaries encouraged the use of original artwork and writing in all their publications. One of the most original and distinctive artists to emerge from the revolutionary cauldron was b.p. Flanigan (who capitalized only his last name in order to draw attention to the importance of the collective clan name and to minimize the importance of the individual personal name). Flanigan came from a working-class background. He had served in Vietnam, had been addicted to heroin, and had been seriously injured while working at Ford Rouge. Flanigan had a vision of a cultural renaissance in which murals, poetry, and other art forms would be a major revolutionary tool for expressing anti-capitalist and anti-elitist views. Stylistically more complex than most writers in political circles, Flanigan employed the latest literary and artistic techniques in work that focused on his personal experiences. He encouraged others to talk about their lives in the same way, shunning current artistic or movement fads in favor of a personal style. He hoped that, one day, there would be no more artists, only humans with their individual and communal songs to sing. He published a wall-poster poem called "The Ceremony" in 1972 that had the power of an ideological manifesto while sticking close to the particulars of the Detroit experience:

"dearly beloved,
we are gathered
here today in . . .

. . . detroit, michigan: home of the "motown sound"/gm/ford/chrysler/rats in the kitchen and roaches in the bathroom/no heat in winter & nothing cool when the summer comes/pistons pounding out a DRUM beat . . . "do you take" . . . "to love and cherish" . . . woodward avenue/junkies, whores & little kids on the way up to take their places/a dime bag to get the day over with . . . "and do you take" . . . "to have and to hold" . . . the day shift, afternoons, midnights—at least 8 hrs. with the devil in hell/rouge, chevy, fisherbody (makes dead bodies), budd, eldon gear & axle, dodge main, jefferson, iron foundries & specialty forge foundries/monsters that eat alive & spit out bloody hands/feet pieces of skin and bone/& with regularity—A DEAD BODY!!! . . . friday nite . . . get that check/carry it on home to the crib (with wife and kids), then get out on the street: get fucked up/(reefer, jones, coke, ups & downs, johnnie walker black & red) try to freeze your head/can't think about the shit starting all over again on monday./. . . "and now a message from our sponsor" watch tv/listen to the radio/read papers/they all say: "buy this, get that & YOU TWO can be a success."/damn, brother, sister, a success in this motorized, computerized, iron & steel jungle is just staying alive!!!

"in sickness and in health"   detroit, michigan/any city
"for better or for worse"   my/our home

"until DEATH

do us part."

Chapter Seven

Black Workers Congress

1

Our objectives: 1. Workers' control of their places of work—the factories, mines, fields, offices, transportation services and communication facilities—so that the exploitation of labor will cease and no person or corporation will get rich off the labor of another person, but all people will work for the collective benefit of humanity.

—Black Workers Congress manifesto, 1971

From the first days of DRUM, workers and activists from every part of the United States had communicated with the Detroit group to learn how to set up similar organizations. The League of Revolutionary Black Workers had been developed to weld the Detroit RUMs into a single political unit, and many League members were interested in finding the best method of expanding the League and the RUM idea into every major city in the nation. Some of the people in the League believed it was sufficient to set an outstanding example in Detroit and let others imitate that model independently. Others thought such an approach was too haphazard and that the League should create a national organization, just as DRUM had created the League. The name "Black Workers Congress" was adopted for the projected organization, and at one time the BWC concept had the support of the League's entire Executive Committee.

The decision to form a separate organization with a new name rather than franchise League chapters in other cities reflected a close reading of the history of other black organizations which had recently tried to organize nationally. Police infiltration, financial stresses, and the problems of limited personnel had crippled RAM, Malcolm X's organization, and the Black Panther Party. The Detroiters did not want to find themselves in a position where one or more of their key leaders was indicted for something done in the name of the League in places where the League could not exercise daily supervision over activities.

The Black Economic Development Conference of April 1969 gave the League its first major national podium and deepened some of its contacts with groups in other parts of the country. The League soon drew up a manifesto and a call for a Black Workers Congress founding convention. The 32 objectives of the manifesto mostly concerned workers' demands, the elimination of racism, the liberation of women, and foreign policy questions. The workers' demands were for what amounted to workers' control of production, leading to the formation of a socialist state. The question of racism was dealt with by calling for the granting of strong cultural autonomy to all minorities who wished it, for dismantling of the police apparatus, and for specific programs to combat racism wherever and in whatever form it existed. The demands regarding women dealt both with sexism on a strictly sexual level and with its manifestation in the workplace. The foreign policy items supported various national liberation movements, called for an immediate end to the war in Vietnam, and advocated diplomatic recognition of China and Cuba. The principal vehicle for bringing BWC into existence was to be a series of black united fronts and third-world alliances backed by a complex network of printing shops, neighborhood service centers, student organizations, and economic cooperatives. The manifesto's final demand was for the eventual creation of a black revolutionary political party, although little was said about its specific nature or precise ideological orientation.

The manifesto received an excellent response, yet the in-plant League leadership began to cool toward the whole idea. They felt that continued success in the factories had a higher priority than organizational ties with like-minded people in other cities. They were concerned that many of the Detroit RUM units were beginning to run out of steam. In February 1969, Chuck Wooten had been fired from Dodge Main after striking a superviser, and Sidney Lewis, an incorporator of the League, had been fired in August for striking a foreman. Other organizers and sympathizers were being eliminated from the plants as a result of similar incidents or disciplinary actions by the company with the collusion of the union. By the summer of 1970, ELRUM had nearly ceased to exist as an open organization, and in other plants the local RUMs had to remain semi-clandestine to preserve themselves. The in-plant leadership argued that the League was in no position to launch a national drive because it had to tend to its withering base. These leaders wanted the resources, energy, and personnel being expended on book clubs, filmmaking, printing, BWC matters, and community work to go into direct plant operations. They asked Ken Cockrel, Mike Hamlin, and John Watson to spend more time with workers and their immediate problems.

The BWC advocates replied that the League could not advance secretively, worker by worker, plant by plant, but must leap forward, making massive and simultaneous gains in various sectors of public work. The operations being criticized as diversionary were, they argued, essential to maintaining organizational momentum. Dismissed workers would never be rehired unless there were strong defense committees with popular bases able to apply mass pressure. The same kind of mass pressure was crucial to discouraging, exposing, and defeating the provocations of company, union, and police. Films and publications were central to educating the worker base and spreading the League program to the general public. One film like *Finally Got the News* was more valuable in teaching and inspiring workers than many hours of discussion and study.

The political disagreements between the League leaders began to feed personal antagonisms. The in-plant people charged that the BWC wing liked to be with "bourgeois" people and with white folks more than they liked to be with black workers. Cockrel was cited for having what was termed an arrogant and authoritarian attitude toward comrades. Watson was charged with having become a dreamer who let transoceanic trips and filmmaking fantasies replace his former vision of a worker-led American revolution. Hamlin was said to be so enamored of the idea of a national organization that he had lost his common sense. As for James Forman, who had entered the League through BEDC and was one of the strongest advocates of BWC, he was the wrecker and splitter Baker had suspected him of being all along.

The BWC supporters had countercharges. They said that the Cortland office, Baker's personal headquarters, had become a disgrace to the League. Visitors and members alike complained of its inhospitable atmosphere and its generally cluttered, dirty, and rag-tag appearance. Women said they were afraid to go there for fear of verbal and even physical assault. The BWC wing charged that some of the so-called plant organizers were just hangers-on who lived in League facilities and took League salaries but who did more drinking than organizing. Many of them were simple-minded black nationalists or had a street-gang mentality, and this outlook had pervaded the workers' ranks to such a degree that only a stiff internal education program could rectify the situation. Baker and Wooten were said to be paternalistic to workers, accepting and sometimes lauding their low level of ideology simply because they were "basic brothers off the street." John Williams and Luke Tripp were criticized for lacking the imagination to see that the BWC approach would revitalize the organization and that the media materials being prepared would do quickly the educational work they thought must be done on a laborious one-to-one basis. Cockrel complained that some of the League "organizers" were involved in petty crimes that had nothing to do with the organization and constituted an unwarranted drain on its legal resources. The BWC people underscored their arguments by saying that they had been largely responsible for gathering most of the resources which made the League possible and that every time they proposed a new step forward, the others invariably resisted them.

The internal quarrels continued for more than a year. There was a purge of some members in late 1970, including Ernie Mkalimoto and others who might have become the core of a competent secondary leadership. Cockrel, Hamlin, and Watson seemed harder and harder to get hold of and were often absent from the city on one project or another. In the early part of 1971, pursuing leads for Black Star Productions, Watson took a trip to the Middle East, where he received a commendation from Arab guerrilla organizations for his work in publicizing their views in the United States. Cockrel traveled to the West Coast several times. While there, he tried to convince Angela Davis to entrust her defense to an all-black united front, instead of relying exclusively upon the Communist Party, of which she was a member. (Davis had been accused of abetting an escape attempt by black prisoners, a charge she was later acquitted of.) Hamlin spent more and more time in the company of Forman. Personal ill feeling intensified, and much of the organizing work within the city continued to wind down.

The situation reached a decisive phase when Cockrel, Hamlin, and Watson issued what amounted to an ultimatum to the rest of the Executive Committee. They demanded an internal education program frankly aimed at thinning out the ranks. All cadres and members of the organization must agree to support fully all the published objectives of the League. There would be no more backroom mutterings from nationalists about "white journalism" or that "Marx was a honkie." Certain members of the central staff would be purged, and there would be a reshuffling of responsibilities based on the outcome of the internal education.

The BWC advocates were not interested in just winning a vote of confidence in the Executive Committee by a 4-3 or 5-2 margin. They wanted to convince the others that their policies were the only ones that would lead to growth and that, without unity of purpose within the executive, votes and programs were relatively meaningless. When their views were rejected, Ken Cockrel, Mike Hamlin, and John Watson formally resigned from the organization, ending political and personal friendships that in some cases had involved their entire adult lives. They stated that they would devote their full time to building a BWC that was totally independent of the League. Although many activists involved in the League components under their personal direction went with them into the new organization, most of the League's members and sympathizers were unprepared for a split among the top leadership. Through their inaction, they supported neither side. The resignations became public on June 12, 1971. By the first of the year, those who remained in the League were making plans to affiliate what was left of the organization with a group called the Communist League. The League of Revolutionary Black Workers had become history.

2

Above all, I will wage the ideological struggle—the drive for political education. I will continue this work that I have tried to do most of my adult life with vigor. For it is my duty to help make black revolutionaries.

—James Forman, *The Making of Black Revolutionaries*, 1972

James Forman was a key figure in the split between the League and BWC. He had been instrumental in organizing BEDC and would play a similar role in setting up the machinery for BWC outside of Detroit. The funds generated by Forman and BEDC had allowed Cockrel, Hamlin, and Watson to put some of their out-of-plant projects into practice. Forman viewed the League as subordinate to BWC, a position in sharp contrast to the League belief that BWC would be a creature of the League. Willingly or not, by intensifying frictions caused by the internal weaknesses of the League strategies, organizational structure, and personnel, Forman served as a major catalyst in dividing the League against itself.

Forman's background was impressive. A good ten years older than most of the League leaders, he had been raised in a working-class section of Chicago's South Side and, like Mike Hamlin, had served in the Korean War. He had gone to the South in 1958 as a reporter for the *Chicago Defender* and soon found himself drawn to activism. He became part of the newly formed SNCC in 1960, and from 1961-1966 was the organization's executive secretary. Stokely Carmichael and H. Rap Brown gained more fame than Forman, but many people in the movement regarded him as the "brains" of SNCC. In 1967, designated the International Affairs Director of SNCC, he traveled throughout Africa and represented SNCC at an important UN meeting in Zambia. Following this trip, Forman played a central role in winning 50 percent participation for blacks in the National Conference for New Politics founding convention in Chicago. He scared a lot of whites into voting for this arrangement, but this victory in what was billed as a new party and a new politics proved to be short-lived since the conference never got off the ground. In February 1968, Forman took the post of Minister of Foreign Affairs of the Black Panther Party, but fierce personal and political disagreements led to his resignation in July of the same year. He then began developing BEDC, and by the spring of 1969 had joined the central staff of the League. In addition to his political work, Forman had written a book, attended most national black conferences of importance, and lectured extensively, building up a reputation as one of the leading black revolutionary organizers and theorists.

When Forman arrived on the Detroit scene, he brought along his national prestige, large-scale financial resources, and solid contacts throughout the country. Forman considered Detroit to be a launching pad for a new national organization. BEDC would be used to attract initial funding and publicity for an organization that would be larger and more effective than even SNCC had been. The League would serve as the model for many leagues in urban, rural, and academic settings. Forman's approach was tied to his own personal style. He was the perpetual traveler, wheeler-dealer, organizer, and thinker who supposedly knew what was happening at the base. He was the revolutionary connection bringing local groups the latest news and plans of the "brothers and sisters" in other places. BEDC was a typical Forman production in that it brought together hundreds of people who spoke in the name of America's black population, yet who were not themselves unified in any significant manner and who often represented only themselves or paper organizations. Forman meant BWC to be something quite different.

BWC would complete a personal and historical transformation in the black movement by linking the Southern and rural experience of struggle to the Northern and urban experience. It would link the vital poor people's movement of one region to the new working-class movement of the other, using some of the personnel of SNCC and the League, the highest expressions of each of those struggles, to begin its work. This vision reflected important insights into the developments of the late 1960s; yet BWC eventually failed in its goal of reproducing DRUM and League organizations on a national scale. From the start, BWC suffered from excessive personalism, theoretical simplification, and lack of a solid center of organized mass support.

BWC was built from the top down, and the top of the pyramid was occupied by James Forman, the titular national leader. He traveled almost continually, linking up former SNCC contacts, new workers' groups, and local black militants. Forman spoke with the authority of his own long experience and with the authority of his connection with the League. The forces which had come with him into BWC were soon getting directives on how to proceed with national, regional, and local projects. When they asked Forman to take on the editorship of the BWC paper, however, he refused on the grounds that to do so would mean becoming stationary in the city of Detroit, a condition he could

not accept. What Forman did want to do was make 16 educational
films of one-to-two-hours duration. They would feature himself as the
speaker and his writings as the subject matter. Letters to John Watson
gave instructions on how the films could be made in a single whirlwind
week. Forman's projected films were not to be real cinema in the way
Finally Got the News had been, but simply filmed lectures. These films
would be used in the Frantz Fanon Institutes Forman planned to create
in every large city. The institutes were conceived as revolutionary training centers which would teach the thought of Fanon as interpreted by
Forman and grafted onto the organizational approach of Forman. This
organizational approach, in turn, was outlined in a series of pamphlet
essays which were collected under the title *The Political Thought of James
Forman*. The 200-page paperback was printed for BWC use by Black
Star Publishing, mainly through the efforts of Helen Jones and Fredy
Perlman.

Forman's political thought was less a system of ideas than a series
of demands sprinkled with organizing suggestions. It was primarily an
attack on existing oppression rather than a proposal for a new system.
Forman's organizational speeches and public writings were often at
variance. While speaking, he hailed the League as the most advanced
black organization to appear in the United States and the first black organization to try seriously to apply Marxism to American conditions;
yet in his 550-page book, *The Making of Black Revolutionaries*, he devoted
less than a page to it. The League was stuck into a chapter titled "The
Black Manifesto"; and in a chronologically incorrect sequence, only
Mike Hamlin and John Watson were mentioned by name. Hamlin
wrote a preface to *The Political Thought of James Forman* in which he
pledged Black Star Publishing to publicizing ideas that would help the
formation of a political party capable of leading the American revolution. Forman's own introduction was far less precise and used loose na-
tionalistic phrasing to make its points:

> I am extremely elated that Black Star Publishing is printing as its first
> book this collection of speeches and writings that are all geared to
> helping to make revolutionaries of black people in the United States.
> There is a great deal of—but not enough—descriptive literature on Af-
> rican people wherever they exist. Much of this literature does not ad-
> dress itself to capitalism and imperialism as being integral to the cause
> of racism, and certainly does not hold high the banner of armed strug-

gle by All-African People as the only ultimate solution to ending these destroyers of humanity, to the establishment of a new and just society capable of ending all forms of human exploitation.

The Forman idea of revolutionary theory and practice, "Formanism," reflected a precise, if restricted, sense of organization and an amalgam of popularized theoretical tendencies of the 1960s. The major organizational form was the umbrella group operating with a popular front strategy. The organizations had plans for becoming mass-membership groups; but more important than gaining members were the immediate goals of organizing conferences, workshops, and lectures and producing documents. This procedure would attract outside funding and prepare the ground for political education classes. The end product of this program was supposed to be the creation of Frantz Fanon Institutes. In effect, Formanism substituted ideological struggle for struggle over material conditions. The focus had to remain ideological because people were recruited into study groups and organizing commissions rather than action groups prepared to deal with immediate issues. Reduced to study groups and organizing commissions, politics was effectively separated from the problems of work and daily life. The education itself was anticolonial, anti-racist, and anti-imperialist, but ideas were not presented in the context of a serious class analysis of the roles blacks play in America or of the state of mid-twentieth-century capitalism. Unlike the economically grounded and disciplined organizational approach of Marxism-Leninism, the approach of Fanon-Formanism was exemplified by loosely structured groups stressing psychological interpretations of social reality and the accumulation of technical skills. Formanism was less a program for moving toward power than a defensive tactic for dealing with oppression.

3

I don't have skills like a secretary or something. I went into the factory because it was the only place where I could get a job making decent money, but if you stay a lady, you don't make it out there. They all put the pressure on you.

—Carla Cook, a production line worker at the Eldon Avenue Gear and Axle plant, in an interview with the authors on August 19, 1972

The founding convention for BWC was more than a year in the making. It took place in Gary, Indiana, in September 1971, shortly after James Forman, Muhammad Kenyatta (a Philadelphia-based black activist), and Helen Jones returned from a trip to China and Vietnam. More than 400 delegates from all parts of the country participated. Many of them were disheartened to hear of the Detroit schism, for Detroit was to be the headquarters of BWC and the League membership was to have been its first mass base. The ultimate consequence of the split was that the League would be one of the few black worker groups specifically excluded from possible membership. In spite of this situation, the convention sessions were lively and the atmosphere optimistic.

At least one-third of the delegates to the founding convention were women, and there was significant participation by third-world groups that were not of African heritage. Both of these facts were related to a conscious attempt of BWC to have a wider active base than the League had enjoyed. BWC membership was open to all third-world people: Asian Americans, Native Americans, Arab Americans, and Latin Americans. The BWC manifesto included many specific items important to women, such as a commitment to daycare centers, equal pay for equal work, and paid vacations for housewives. The keynote speech was given by John Watson, who reiterated the importance of seeing third-world people as workers:

> Since slavery, black labor has continued to assume particular importance in the development of both domestic capital and international imperialism, primarily because the black female and male workers are the final prop, the ultimate mainstay, onto which capitalism shifts its weight in order to survive.
>
> Black workers have remained a source of the cheapest, most productive labor. First as agriculture labor, then as miners, merchant seamen, government transport and service workers, dock and warehouse workers, etc., and finally as the most exploited section of the proletariat in light and heavy industry. Today, black and other third-world workers are still solidly entrenched at the base of the proletariat.

The delegates to the Gary convention had gathered to discuss plans of action. Some of the representatives from the South had already begun RUM groups in Atlanta and Birmingham, but their hopes for a national workers' organization were never to be fulfilled. Most of the convention's time was spent in setting up a national newspaper and an elaborate commission structure to investigate and advance various areas of work. The manifesto spoke boldly of people learning many skills and of those with skills sharing them. Like most BWC ideas, these remained real only on paper. From the convention onward, the organization bogged down in endless discussions on how to proceed, whom to charter, whom to place in positions of authority, and a multitude of bureaucratic questions. The printing apparatus of BWC churned out more materials for internal organizational affairs than for agitation at the factory gates or in the streets.

BWC proved to be a particular disappointment for the women who had belonged to the League. Even though many women had worked hard for the League and had positions of secondary responsibility, the League had never allowed a strong woman leader to emerge, and few women had been on the central staff. Its materials gave little emphasis to the strategic role of women in making the American revolution. Early in the League's history, Edna Watson, Paula Hankins, and Rachel Bishop had initiated an organizing drive among hospital workers, partly to give female leadership to one area of work. They were not supported by the rest of the organization in the manner they expected, and the work had to be abandoned. DRUM had only one woman, Betty Griffen, on its election slates, and ELRUM had none. Most women in the League had strong personalities and were hard workers; but they invariably found themselves under male supervision, whether they were involved in printing, organizing, or writing.

The League's Executive Committee was openly hostile to the women's liberation movement, which it generally referred to as the "white woman's liberation movement." Most of the male cadre proudly expressed chauvinistic attitudes, and some members of the workers' components were charged with physically abusing women. The League considered women's liberation as it was then being discussed a divisive issue; and although at times there were women's committees, the League never drew up a program for women. For all their gruffness, the League males were not nearly so reactionary as some of their enemies liked to paint them. Some of the roughest talkers were the men most likely to help out with babysitting, cleaning, shopping, or cooking. Helen Jones and Mabel Turner were key personnel at Black Star Publishing, and women were also central to the operations at Black Star Productions. The Executive Committee, in the person of Mike Hamlin, also went out of its way to contact Michelle Russell, a board member of Resist, an anti-war organization, and an Executive Committee member of New University Conference, an organization of radical college teachers. Russell was persuaded to move to Detroit, where she became a member of the League on the eve of the split. She served as an important member of BWC and local Detroit groups working against police repression.

More than anyone else associated with the League, James Forman had been an open advocate of the women's liberation movement. Some of the women considered this position an indication of Forman's great sophistication and genuine understanding of the revolutionary process, while others became suspicious that it was a device to increase his narrow power base in the League. When BWC was formed, many women had hopes that Forman's leadership would result in women having more responsibility than they had enjoyed in the League. These hopes went unfulfilled.

The tensions over women's liberation were complicated by what Detroiters called "the white wife question." Both Mike Hamlin and Ken Cockrel began living with white women after the League was formed. Some of the black women in the organization took that as a kind of rebuff to black women, and some workers cited it as another aspect of Hamlin and Cockrel's growing alienation from the black base. The people who formed BWC felt that the matter had been dealt with many times in the past and did not need a new airing. Watson reminded his old associates of the internal havoc the white wife question had caused in UHURU; Charles "Mao" Johnson had withdrawn from activism partly because he refused to defend himself constantly for having a white wife. James Forman, whose wife was also white, figured in the controversy as well. Despite Watson's warning, the issue disturbed BWC, as it had disturbed the League. The tragedy of the whole discussion of white wives was that, justified or not, it often divided many of the black women in the League and in BWC from the most flexible and innovative leaders while reinforcing vague nationalist feelings in others.

BWC's position on women, like its positions on most questions, was more or less irrelevant in the long run, since the organization never really came to life. An early BWC announcement spoke of the two main pillars of the organization as being the League in Detroit and the black workers' group at Ford's Mahwah plant in New Jersey; but the Mahwah group, like the League, never became part of BWC. As much as Forman and others traveled from city to city, the BWC skeleton could not put on flesh. BWC remained a scheme for possible unification, a promise without fulfillment. The problems in each region were different, but one constant was that too few people were attempting an immense work with too limited resources. With no strong base to build on, BWC could establish no centers to which people could be brought for training and inspiration. There were no real-life models to be studied. Government, unions, companies, and rival political groups chewed at the edges of each local. BWC produced reams of proposals and organizational manuals, but no real organization—lots of ideology, but limited political practice. By its own estimates, BWC never had a formal membership above 500—little more than the number that attended the founding convention.

The organization was top-heavy, and the only real links between the units were the thought and person of James Forman. This personalism proved catastrophic, for in spite of his vast experience, his organizational skills, his ideas, and his pronouncements, Forman could not get BWC moving. Detroit was the national center of BWC; Mike Hamlin was its official chairman and John Watson its major thinker, aside from Forman. Even so, as late as January 1972, or almost three years after BEDC, Forman had not yet sunk any roots in the city. He wrote the central committee of BWC, stating, "For more than two weeks I have been in Detroit, Michigan, trying to arrange my life so I could work out of Detroit as a home base. . . . I have never spent much time in Detroit in the technical study of our work here and sharing experiences. My trips have usually been of short duration and my conversations limited to a few people."

These tenuous ties between Forman and the ostensible center of the organization were indicative of the quality of his BWC contacts throughout the nation; and, as Forman himself stated in his report of January 17, 1972, "I was in closer contact with the realities of the national situation than probably anyone else in the organization." BWC developed major problems of credibility when people discovered that things often moved because of a show, a bluff, or white guilt, rather than because of a solid organizational push. Forman was constantly moving himself around and urging others to do the same, but the BWC "work" he was engaged in invariably turned out to be just another meeting. The numerous directives and reports written by Forman were indicative of the organization's style. Unlike the vivid, well-thought-out language of Cockrel and Watson, or the spirited language of the RUM writers and General Baker, Forman's writing was dull, bureaucratic prose, complete with points and subpoints occasionally spiced with a slogan or revolutionary jargon. Elaborate agendas, tedious meetings, and internal debate were the hallmarks of life in BWC. In this sense, Formanism came more and more to represent the antithesis of the League, which had always been more concerned with workers' action and power than with ideological talk. BWC was increasingly caught in the trap of Formanism. People became weary of attending one conference after another only to discover that it was still the next city which had the mass base or was about to launch the organizing drive that would put BWC on the map. Demoralization led to attacks on the leadership of James Forman. People began to comment openly that he did all of his writing in the first person.

4

Point of information: what is the executive secretary's practice in terms of organizing industrial workers?

—Bill Thomas, speaking at a February 1972 meeting of BWC's Detroit branch

The first substantial attack on Forman's hegemony came from Ken Cockrel, who charged him with incompetence and egotism. Cockrel described Forman's reports as vague, programless, and individualistic. Cockrel wanted to know why the central committee had never received a full report on what was accomplished in China and North Vietnam or on how people were being selected for subsequent trips. Cockrel called Forman "an American Airlines revolutionary" who junketed around the country trying to build organizations through deception and intrigue, a person more interested in personal power than in the organization's welfare.

A BWC commission met in Detroit in February 1972 to investigate Cockrel's charges. After two days of almost continuous meetings, the commission voted against Cockrel. Few of its members supported Forman outright, but the majority felt that Cockrel had not proved his charges and that the organization's problems could not be blamed on one individual. Cockrel, Michelle Russell, Ted Spearman (one of Cockrel's law partners), and Gregory Hicks, who had been active in *Black Student Voice*, left BWC. Over the next year, the Detroit chapter all but melted away. John Watson took a "leave of absence" to return to Wayne State University and finally get a degree. Fred Holsey, who had been a leader in ELRUM, Chuck Wilson, who had represented the League at an international conference in Italy, Paula Hankins, who had been active since the founding of *ICV*, Carolyn Ramsey, who had worked at Black Star Productions, and Larry Nevels, who had headed UNICOM, were among those who resigned, decimating the Detroit chapter to the point of not even having a staff around which to build a base. The same process occurred in BWC chapters all over the country.

Throughout this difficult time, Mike Hamlin retained his position as national chairman, but by April 1973 he and the other central committee members had had enough of Forman and Formanism. In a 43-page paper, the surviving BWC, headed by Hamlin, expelled Forman for his role in the League split and the failure of BWC. The paper was extraordinarily candid and was virulently anti-Forman. It stated that the early critiques of Forman voiced by John Williams, speaking for the League, and later repeated by Cockrel were essentially correct. Neither Williams nor Cockrel was spared personal attack, but the dispersed former League executive was united, two years after its fatal split, regarding the role of Forman in its disintegration.

The BWC paper stated that "James Forman was in search of a base and the League represented the future." It described Forman as "secretive, paranoid, furtive, and individualistic to the bone. Commanding large sums of money, sections of the [League] leadership drew closer [to him] and sections of the leadership pulled away." Briefly, the paper stated how Forman had failed to win leadership posts in the League. John Williams had replaced Forman as head of International Black Appeal, and Ernie Mkalimoto had been voted into an educational position Forman had specifically asked for. As plans for BWC began to develop, Forman had made it a practice to bring his supporters into Detroit, where they came into verbal and physical conflict with many League members working in the factories. Forman had held meetings all over the country tacking together students and "movement" activists. At those meetings, he had told people that, with some bright exceptions, there was a "cancer" of reactionary nationalism, male chauvinism, and lack of political education in Detroit. The in-plant leadership of the League had correctly perceived, the paper went on, that BWC leadership was being transferred out of Detroit hands. As one of many components, the League would be ruled by BWC policy decisions, which would, by and large, be James Forman's decisions. The BWC paper stated in capital letters: "OUR CONCLUSION IS OBVIOUS. JAMES FORMAN OPPORTUNISTICALLY DESTROYED THE LEAGUE, DOING THE WORK OF THE BOURGEOISIE."

Forman's response was that he was being made the scapegoat for the failure of first the League, then BWC. People did not understand that his "getting acquainted" sessions and his "sharing of experiences" approach was as political as more programmatic aspects of work. He felt that the personal attacks on him were evidence of how much educational work had *not* been done and that his ability to raise money was an indication of how much better he understood political processes than his facile critics did. He defended his style of work as necessary because of the personal dangers inherent in his vanguard role and the vanguard role projected for BWC. Lacking any home base in BWC, however, he could not muster the votes to prevent his expulsion.

Even before the move against Forman, BWC had begun looking for a new strategy. By the autumn of 1972, BWC was a public participant in a movement to create a new American communist party. The organizations involved in this movement included Puerto Rican groups, Chicano groups, Asian-American groups, and primarily white groups with origins in the old SDS. The New York-based *Guardian*, a newspaper with a posted circulation of more than 25,000, was involved in the unity effort and sponsored a series of forums to air theoretical differences. These forums had an average attendance of 500 persons, and one which included Mike Hamlin among its four speakers drew an audience of 1,200. All of the participating groups emphasized work among the industrial working class. Their Marxism tended to rigid orthodoxy which had more in common with the ideological theories of the 1930s than with the evolution of Marxist thinking in the post-war decades. The groups demonstrated nearly uncritical acceptance of the theories of Joseph Stalin and Mao Tse-tung. The Communist Party U.S.A. was seen as a major enemy of the American working class, and people who challenged Stalinism or Maoism were denounced as Trotskyists, anarchists, and petty bourgeois intellectuals. The single major difference from the 1930s was that the genuine participation of blacks and other third-world people in leadership roles was central to the strategy of the proposed new party.

5

General Baker had good rapport with the gut-bucket element in the plants, but he wasn't sure he trusted those intellectuals. Gen would run his thing on you, but you could deal with Gen. I never had any trouble with Gen.

—Jordan Sims, in an interview with the authors, August 19, 1972

By late 1971, the League of Revolutionary Black Workers had begun a transformation of its own. Originally, the League wanted to continue its struggle with Formanism from within BWC. John Williams and other representatives attended a Baltimore conference and other meetings, but they soon concluded that the exclusion of the League was final and irrevocable. They continued with their plan for International Black Appeal; but it began to flounder and like BWC remained more of a plan than a reality. Within a short time, the League ceased public activity and began a startling change in style and theory. Chuck Wooten had come into contact with members of the California-based Communist League, a small organization which espoused a rigid Marxist approach emphasizing heavy reading and memorization of the works of Mao and Stalin. Robert Williams (no relation to the Robert Williams who had been in exile in Cuba and China) moved from California to Detroit, where he became the theoretical leader of the individuals remaining in the League. Intense self-criticism sessions and study groups became the prerequisites for continuing membership. Most of the students dropped away, and many individuals, including Luke Tripp, became inactive. The worker components which had been physically the most sloppy and ideologically the most casual sections of the old League became highly structured, disciplined, immaculately clean, and ideologically dogmatic.

The secretiveness which had characterized the Baker approach became more pronounced than ever. The China-Albania Bookstore was opened, but there were few public meetings and almost no publications. Some members of the League holding professional jobs were ordered to give them up to work in the factories or to serve the organization. This proletarianization of the ranks was the most rigid and crudest possible application of Lenin's dictum of "fewer but better" revolutionaries. When the organization resurfaced, it had become the Detroit branch of the Communist League. Baker remained one of its principal leaders.

Knowledge of precisely what the Communist League was doing remained sparse until the spring of 1973. Most of the former League sympathizers were put off by the heavy Marxist terminology, the Maoist paraphernalia, and the whole sectarian environment of the Communist League. That spring, however, members of the Communist League began to attend social functions given by other groups, called on former League members, and showed visible work in the factories. Their personal attitudes had undergone an astonishing shift. They were extremely polite to whites and seemed eager to form alliances with similarly oriented groups. The line of the Communist League was very much like that of the groups with which BWC was working. The Communist League advocated a new multinational (interracial) communist party based on Marxism-Leninism. The organization accepted whites and all third-world people as members. Just how much of the old RUM membership the Communist League had managed to keep in contact with and how many new recruits it had gained was a matter known only to the organization, but obviously some kind of continuity existed. At least 50 members of the Communist League were visible in the summer of 1973 during a series of wildcat strikes which swept the Detroit auto plants. Perhaps it was only coincidence, but each of the three Chrysler factories to suffer major wildcats in that summer had had an active RUM unit.

The Communist League's strict organization, self-discipline, and stress on Marxist ideology represented a specific set of solutions to some of the problems which had plagued the earlier League. Baker's RUM strategy had often seemed more dependent on spontaneous mass action than on the work of pre-existing organizations. At other times, his groups seemed like industrial guerrillas whose unrelenting attacks would eventually spark a general uprising. The freewheeling style of the old League had been compared by some Detroiters to that of the Industrial Workers of the World or "Wobblies," an anarcho-syndicalist formation that had a mass following in the first decades of the twentieth century. The League idea that one vast general strike could end wars and abolish capitalism itself suggested even programmatic parallels with the IWW. For the League activist, like the convinced Wobbly, each battle over wages, hours, or conditions was only so much preparation for the final struggle to abolish the master class. The daily fights with the boss were the furnaces in which revolutionary fighters were forged. The *Industrial Worker* of June 3, 1909, had stated: "The very fights themselves, like the drill of an army, prepare the worker for even greater tasks and victories." In summing up the contradictions faced by the IWW in his *We Shall Be All*, published in 1969, historian Melvin Dubofsky could almost have been writing about the contradictions which faced the League of Revolutionary Black Workers:

> The organization's refusal to sign contracts raised problems that the IWW never resolved. American employers were never particularly happy dealing with labor unions, and certainly under no circumstances would negotiate with a labor organization that refused to sign contracts and insisted that capitalists had no rights worthy of respect. Hence, employers constantly used the IWW's no-contract principle to rationalize their own resistance to any form of collective bargaining. If the IWW could not negotiate with employers, how could it raise wages and improve working conditions? If it could offer the members nothing but perpetual industrial warfare, how could it maintain its membership, let alone increase its ranks? On the other hand, if the IWW did sanction contracts, win recognition, and improve its members' lives, what would keep them from forsaking revolutionary goals and adhering to the well-established AFL pattern? If the IWW began to declare truces in the class war, how could it bring about the ultimate revolution? In the end, IWW leaders usually subordinated reform opportunities to revolutionary necessities, while the rank-and-file, when it could, took the reforms and neglected the revolution.

The Black Workers Congress and the Communist League rejected both the reformist ideas associated with traditional trade unionism and the freewheeling, libertarian ideas associated with the IWW. Like many white radicals who had belonged to the organizations collectively called the New Left in the 1960s, the black revolutionaries of BWC and CL were seeking organizational and ideoiogical theories that emphasized the role of industrial workers and professional revolutionaries. The disappointments, frustrations, and failures of the 1960s when the movement had been infused with an anti-authoritarian and egalitarian spirit often led to sectarianism and to rigid notions of hierarchy and centralism in the 1970s. One of the distinctions of the League of Revolutionary Black Workers had been that it had tried to combine its developing Marxist perspective with a structure that allowed considerable independence to its various units and individual members.

Ken Cockrel and his associates in Detroit considered the politics of the Black Workers Congress and the Communist League to be "playing in the sandbox." They felt that both BWC and the Communist League were organizational retreats to old forms which had failed in the past and would fail in the future. Cockrel believed that rigid cadre groups dealing with ideological subtleties were not essential to making a bid for power either within the factories or outside. He advocated building mass movements around immediate and pressing social issues. As an attorney, Cockrel had immediate familiarity with the manner in which judges and city officials won elections. He thought a radical thrust in that area would be profitable. Partly through accident and partly through a deliberate selection of cases, Cockrel had become a major adversary of the Detroit Police Department. From the time of New Bethel onward, Cockrel had risen steadily to become Detroit's most well-known and influential radical. More than any other single individual, he was identified in the popular mind and in the mass media as the personification of a serious black revolutionary. By the autumn of 1972, one of his white law partners had won an important judgeship in the local criminal court system, and Cockrel himself began to speak seriously of making a bid to become the mayor of America's fifth-largest city.

Chapter Eight

Stop the Robberies, Enjoy Safe Streets: STRESS

1

I am not saying that the white people of Detroit are different from the white people of any other city. I know what has been done in Chicago, I know what prejudice growing out of race and religion has done the world over, and all through time. I am not blaming Detroit. I am stating what has happened, that is all.

—Clarence Darrow, in a speech to the Ossian Sweet jury in 1925

In 1967, during the height of the Great Rebellion, three white police officers killed three unarmed blacks at the Algiers Motel, located on Detroit's main avenue. The shots were fired by David Senak, Robert Paille, and Ronald August. The victims were Auburey Pollard, Fred Temple, and Carl Cooper.

Senak's grandparents on both sides were Czechoslovakian immigrants. His father worked for Holley Carburetor and his mother was a keypunch operator for Chrysler. Before joining the Detroit Police Department, Senak did a four-month hitch with the Air National Guard. At the time of the Great Rebellion, he was 23.

Auburey Pollard's parents had come from the South in 1943, the year of the race riot. His mother was a laundress and housekeeper for white families; and his father, who had spent some years in the Navy, worked in Chrysler plants. Pollard had gotten work as an arc welder at Ford in October 1966, but he was soon demoted to laborer and left his job in March 1967. The 18-year-old Pollard had done 15 days in the Detroit House of Correction for striking one of his high school teachers. One of his brothers, Chaney Pollard, 21, was in the U.S. Marine Corps at the time of the Great Rebellion; the other, Robert Pollard, 17, was in the Michigan Reformatory at Ionia doing a three-to-ten-year sentence for having robbed a newsboy of $7.

Ronald August, 28, had enlisted in the Navy and had been proud to be on the ship that had picked up astronaut Scott Carpenter. His father was a tool grinder. August had joined the Police Department in 1963, when he found all skilled job opportunities closed to him.

Fred Temple, 17, had quit school in the 11th grade and had gone to work at Ford. His father had worked as a machine operator at Thompson Products for 24 years.

Robert Paille, 31, was of French Canadian background and had served in the Air Force. His father had been a lumberjack.

Carl Cooper, 17, had been in trouble with the police since he was 13. His mother worked as a power sewer at Walker Crouse Enterprises, and Cooper began hanging around the motel after he was laid off from his job at Chrysler.

The events which brought these six Detroiters into a deadly confrontation have been exhaustively and sensitively recorded in John Hersey's *Algiers Motel Incident*. Shorn of its particulars, the story is typical of police-black confrontations in the city. People of the same class origins, people sharing many similar problems, came face to face at gunpoint as problems of race negated their commonality. Those who held power in American cities had historically manipulated racial differences and violence to divide their opposition, to limit criticism, and to maintain control, even though things sometimes got out of hand. The Great Rebellion was only the most destructive among hundreds of rebellions during the period, and it fit into a historic pattern as old as the United States.

Slavery had never existed in Michigan because the state was part of the slave-free Northwest Territory, and blacks had worked and lived as free people since the days of the earliest settlements. Detroit, the last station on the underground railroad, had been a frequent meeting place for militant abolitionists. A plaque just off the Fisher Expressway a few blocks from the city's courthouses marks the site where John Brown, Frederick Douglass, and a group of Detroit abolitionists had a historic meeting some eight months before the raid on Harper's Ferry. Fifty miles northwest of Detroit, the Republican Party had been formed by people with strong anti-slavery sentiments.

Racism also had a long history in the city of Detroit. A serious race riot had taken place in 1833 and another in 1863, in the midst of the Civil War. In the second instance, white workers had burnt out the black section of town after the newspapers fed their fears that freed black slaves would flock northward and take away all their jobs. A few years later, the first national organization of American workers, the National Labor Union, established its headquarters in Detroit. One of its two major leaders, Welsh-born Richard Trevellick, argued unsuccessfully that the union should accept blacks as members. As a compromise, he urged the National Labor Union to take the position that blacks and convicts should receive equal wages for doing the same work as free whites. He was again defeated. Trevellick and other labor spokesmen continued the unsuccessful fight against racism in the Greenback Labor Party and the Knights of Labor. Lily-white unionism became entrenched with the rise of the American Federation of Labor, and immigrant workers coming into cities like Detroit were taught that if they were white, no matter how difficult circumstances were for them, life for their children would be "all right." Racism grew so virulent that, by 1924, the Ku Klux Klan's influence in Detroit enabled its write-in candidate for mayor to win the election with 123,679 votes. He was prevented from taking office only when 17,000 of his votes were taken away on technicalities, allowing the otherwise runner-up to become mayor on the basis of 116,807 votes. A state proposal to outlaw parochial schools during the same period was defeated 2-1, but it garnered 353,817 votes. Fiery crosses and men in white hoods were no novelty in the Detroit streets of the 1920s. On July 11, 1925, 10,000 people cheered KKK delegates as they flayed at "Catholics, Jews, and niggers." On September 9 of the same year, hundreds of whites, led by the KKK, attacked the home of Ossian Sweet, a black doctor who had recently moved into an all-white neighborhood. The Sweet family was armed and fired upon the mob in self-defense, killing one white. Dr. Sweet, rather than the rioters, was put on trial, and it took all the legal and oratorical skills of Clarence Darrow to gain an acquittal. Mob at-

tacks on black families daring to move into previously all-white neighborhoods remained a constant problem through the 1970s.

The KKK remained 200,000 strong during most of the 1920s and
1930s, and it bred an even more extreme organization called the Black
Legion. From 1933-1936, the Black Legion was involved in some 50
murders in the state of Michigan. The Legion's enemies were not only
blacks, Jews, and Catholics, but communists and union organizers.
During the same decade, Father Charles E. Coughlin, a Catholic priest
advocating a mixture of racism and populism, won an enthusiastic mass
following in the region through his radio programs and publications.
Coughlin's anti-Semitism became so outrageous that he openly defended the Nazi regime in Germany and had to be silenced by the
Catholic hierarchy when the United States entered World War II.

All these forms of bigotry were cleverly manipulated by Detroit
corporations. Each new white immigrant group had to fight its way into
the good jobs and better neighborhoods. The corporations consciously
pitted the groups against one another, being most blatant with regard
to blacks, who at one time were used exclusively as strike-breakers.
Henry Ford elevated the divide-and-rule principle to a full-blown racial
strategy, and one of his payoffs came when 800 black workers at the
Rouge plant were the only rank-and-file group to put up a physical
fight against the UAW during its final organizing drive in April 1941.
The vigilante and lynching tradition had corporate counterparts, too.
All the major firms hired private detectives and did surveillance on employees as a matter of routine. Again, it was Henry Ford who led the
way. He hired ex-prizefighter Harry Bennett to organize a private Ford
army of 3,000 men who were primarily ex-cons, prizefighters, wrestlers,
football players, and other "tough guys."

The race riot of 1943 was one of the consequences of institutionalized racism in the city and the auto industry. The labor shortage
caused by World War II brought black workers into the city by the
tens of thousands, but they remained locked in narrowly defined ghettos and found social and economic progress virtually nil. Tens of thousands of white Appalachians came into the city at about the same time.
The old generation of mainly immigrant workers looked upon both
newcomer groups with distaste, but found it easier to accept a white
hillbilly accent next door than a black skin. The violence which ensued,
fed by the tensions of the war years, was strictly racial: whites against

blacks, with the whites led by a nearly all-white Detroit Police Department. Thirty-four people died, hundreds were injured, and millions of dollars were lost through property damage and lost work hours. The riot was the most violent in American civil history, though it was to pale before the Watts uprising of 1964, just as Watts would be only a prelude to Newark and then to the most violent rebellion of all—the Great Rebellion of 1967.

The violence of 1967 was significantly different from that of the earlier Detroit explosions. The riots of 1833, 1863, and 1943 had been conflicts between the races. The 1967 Rebellion was a conflict between blacks and state power. In 1943, whites were on the offensive and rode around town in cars looking for easy black targets. In 1967, blacks were on the offensive and their major target was property. In some neighborhoods, Appalachians, students, and other whites took part in the action alongside blacks as their partners. Numerous photos show systematic and integrated looting, which the rebels called "shopping for free." Even so, the Rebellion was entirely a product of the black movement of the 1960s, and that in turn had been a direct consequence of the frustrations and unkept promises of the post-war era.

However people defined it, the Great Rebellion struck fear into the white population of the city of Detroit. The National Guard and police used to quell the fighting were nearly all white. Many of these men undoubtedly had fathers and mothers who had been in the plants during the 1930s when blacks were used as scabs and when the police and the National Guard were used against the unions. Now, they had become the guardians of legitimacy. Their gut fear of black liberation, combined with the long tradition of racism, was to increase in the following years. Instead of a private army like Henry Ford's or a clandestine Black Legion, white Detroiters put their faith in these men, the armed power of the state. The Detroit Police Department in particular became the front-line force against black liberation.

2

I wanted to start in an apprenticeship in electrical work, or plumbing, or carpentry. Any apprenticeship. But the doors were closed then, it seemed to me, because every place I went they just weren't hiring. . . . [T]he Police Department had always had a recruitment drive, so to speak. . . . I went down there and

put in the application, and within a few weeks I had heard that I was accepted.
I learned about it a month before we were married.

—Ronald August, Detroit police officer, quoted in John Hersey's
Algiers Motel Incident, 1968

The Detroit Police Department of 1967 in no way represented the
estimated 35 percent of the population which was black. First, there
were only 217 black officers in a force of 4,709. These blacks held only
nine of the 560 posts of sergeant or higher, only three of the 220 posts
of lieutenant or higher, and only one of the 65 posts of inspector or
higher. During this same period, 35 percent of the city's civil service
employees were black, as were 35 percent of the public school teachers.

Following the Great Rebellion, the Police Department received a
$15,000 grant to bring up the number of black officers. Despite 1,700
written inquiries and 375 formal applications, only several dozen
blacks were hired in the course of a year. The slowness in hiring blacks
was matched by an intense interest in not losing any whites. The city's
total population had declined by 100,000 in the decade of the 1960s,
while the surrounding metropolitan area was zooming from 2.4 million
to 4.2 million. Ninety percent of the increase in the metropolitan area
was accounted for by whites, while the city's white population declined
by 20 percent. The median age for the whites who remained within the
city limits was 36, compared to a national median age for urban dwellers of 28. The *Washington Post* of February 20, 1973, summarized the
population shifts by calling Detroit a city which was getting "blacker,
older, and poorer." The white exodus had involved the working class as
fully as the middle class. Policemen wanted to move their families out
of the city, too, but Detroit had a rule that its police must live within
the city. False addresses and other ways of evading this provision became common and were winked at when they involved whites. The department also allowed an officer a one-year grace period to find a
Detroit address after being hired, and in a key ruling the department
permanently exempted 400 officers from having to comply with the
rule at all. A Police Community Relations Sub-Committee staff memo
of March 25, 1968, described the situation as intolerable: "The people
in the black community see this move as one allowing an occupation

army to occupy the city during the day and return safely to their homes in the white suburbs at night."

The *Detroit Free Press* undertook a survey in 1968 of attitudes within the Police Department. The gap between the black and white officers shown by the survey reflected the polarization within the city. More than 50 percent of the white police thought that housing opportunities were equal for both races, that job opportunities were equal, and that blacks were favored in the schools. Among blacks, 8 percent thought that job opportunities were equal and only 3 percent thought that housing opportunities were equal or that blacks were favored in school. Seventy-two percent of the detectives and 50 percent of all the white police believed that the police treated blacks fairly. Eighty-seven percent of the blacks thought otherwise, 56 percent saying that blacks were treated very unfairly and 31 percent saying that blacks were treated slightly unfairly. Forty-seven percent of the white police thought the Great Rebellion had had obvious long-term negative effects, while almost the same percentage of blacks believed the opposite. Sixty-four percent of the white patrolmen thought that the Great Rebellion had been planned in advance, while 72 percent of the blacks in all ranks thought it had been spontaneous.

The Detroit of 1968 was deceptive. Liberal Mayor Cavanagh, the candidate of the Trade Union Leadership Conference, was still in city hall. The highest officers of the largest corporations in the city had rallied behind the New Detroit Committee, which had pledged millions of dollars to rebuild the city in a fresh outburst of racial cooperation. The UAW, the most liberal of all the major trade unions, stood ready to do its share, just as reliable Wayne State University, under the leadership of liberal President Keast, was prepared to hold its doors open round the clock, 12 months a year. In spite of these good intentions of the liberals, conditions of life, work, and education were so harsh for black people that *ICV*, DRUM, Watson's *South End*, and the League of Revolutionary Black Workers found a ready audience for their revolutionary ideas. The city was growing physically and spiritually uglier all the time. Its violence was so intense that it became the national leader in murders. Detroit had called itself "the Arsenal of Democracy" during World War II. Jerry Cavanagh had referred to it as "the All-American City." Now, the newspapers dubbed Detroit "Murder City, U.S.A." Again and again, as the policies of liberalism failed in the schools, in the factories, and in the streets, the guns and nightsticks of the Detroit Police Department were the reality Detroit blacks and their allies had to face.

3

The DPOA believes . . . the charges of police brutality are part of a ne-farious plot by those who would like our form of government overthrown. The blueprint for anarchy calls for the destruction of the effectiveness of the police. Certainly, it must be obvious that every incident is magnified and exploited with only one purpose. A lot of well-meaning people, without realizing their real role, are doing the job for the anarchists.

—Carl Parsell, president of the Detroit Police Officers Association, in *Tuebor*, December 1968

During 1968, the Detroit Police Department became involved in a series of incidents in which the racism of its officers was the major factor. The first incident occurred on May 3, 1968, during the Poor People's Campaign led by Reverend Ralph Abernathy. A rally had been scheduled to be held at Cobo Hall, Detroit's convention center near the City-County Building, the Ford Auditorium, the Veterans Memorial Building, and other structures of the attempted waterfront resurrection begun in the 1950s. The demonstration, which was being telecast over a local channel, was peaceful and orderly until a car stalled. At that point, the police suddenly became extremely agitated and, almost without warning, mounted a cavalry-style charge upon the demonstrators. Nineteen people were seriously injured in the action. Phillip Mason and Sam Dennis, officials of the U.S. Department of Justice, observed the melee and were quoted in an article about the incident published in the November 13 edition of the *Detroit Free Press*. Mason stated, "I saw old ladies being pushed and manhandled, grabbed by the collar and pushed out doors. I saw young men being beaten with billy clubs." Dennis added, "I saw officers ride horses into a crowd which I judged to be under control. In addition, I saw officers strike individuals in that crowd for no apparent reason. . . . I asked several command officers to pull other officers back. They attempted to but were unsuccessful. In fact, one command officer was knocked down by a patrolman. . . .

All of this was over a stalled car well out of any traffic. Police were insensitive."

Black and liberal spokesmen denounced the actions of the police. State Senator Coleman Young told the *Michigan Chronicle* on June 1, "If the mayor is afraid to take on the DPOA [Detroit Police Officers Association] then we will do it for him. Otherwise this city is headed for a bloodbath." This and other protests led to some face-saving gestures from the mayor's office, but little else. The furor over what came to be called Cobo Hall I had barely quieted down when a new incident occurred in the same area on the occasion of a rally for George Wallace's presidential campaign.

Cobo Hall II involved more than 1,000 black and white demonstrators who gathered on October 29 to express their displeasure with Wallace's candidacy. Some Wallace backers came to Cobo Hall carrying aerosol spray cans with incapacitating chemicals similar to the Mace used by police. When one of these cans was used on a black demonstrator, fistfights broke out and the police flew into action. Their pro-Wallace sympathies were obvious. They made virtually no attacks on Wallace people and seemed to single out white anti-Wallace demonstrators for the roughest treatment. The idea of containing the violence seemed to have no priority at all. The police violence was more flagrant than during Cobo Hall I. Bystanders, reporters, and photographers were beaten. Even James Herman, a field investigator for Mayor Cavanagh's Community Relations Commission who was specifically assigned to observe the event, was injured by the police. In a typical incident, a busload of Wallace supporters threw hunks of scrap iron at a group struggling with a Wallace-ite. The people hit by the iron were attacked by the police, while no action was directed toward the bus. Numerous individuals complained of being beaten at the rally and at police headquarters afterwards. Sheila Murphy, then 20 and a staff organizer for Ad Hoc, which had raised money to assist Detroiters involved in earlier conflicts with the police, told news reporters shortly afterwards that the police warned her that they would kill her if they got her alone.

An even uglier incident followed a few days later at the nearby Veterans Memorial. On the night of November 1, an organization of police officers' wives was giving a dance in the first-floor ballroom. More than 100 couples were in attendance, enjoying some ten kegs of

beer and the quiet sounds of the Ron Ross Quartet. On the sixth floor
of the same building, the black Ebenezer A.M.E. Church was holding a
teen dance featuring the hard-driving contemporary rhythms of the
Seven Sounds. The two parties had no reason to interact and might not
even have known about each other's presence except for inadequate facilities. The Veterans Memorial was so poorly planned that people had
to take elevators to free floors because the ballroom floors didn't have a
sufficient number of toilets.

As the evening progressed, word began to circulate among the policemen that black hooligans were causing trouble in the elevators.
Women, in particular, complained of obscene gestures and sexual
threats. In a sequence of events that was not entirely clear, several Detroit police stopped two separate groups of black teenagers outside the
building. The teenagers were beaten and kicked, and at least one shot
was fired.

The incident was like many a Detroit catch-you-in-the-parking-lot
brawl, except for the participants. On one side were armed white police
officers, and on the other, some of the sons and daughters of Detroit's
black elite. James Evans, 17, who was hospitalized overnight because of
the beating given to him, was the son of the director of the Fisher
YMCA. Another hospitalized teenager, Derrick Tabor, 17, was the son
of a minister, and he managed to get a call through to his father, who
got to the scene while the beatings were still in progress. The 15-year-
old son of Reverend Nicholas Hood, Detroit's only black councilman at
the time, was not personally injured but was an eyewitness to the
whole affair.

Black pressure for a full investigation soon ran into what was
termed a "blue curtain of silence." DPOA President Carl Parsell said
that his men had been taunted and harassed to the breaking point by
"Negroes," but he admitted he wasn't sure if they were the same "Negroes" who were at the church dance. A security guard reported that
three black teenage stragglers in the elevators who were not connected
with the dance left after he confronted them. James Heaney, 60, an attorney and realtor who had run for mayor in 1965 as a candidate from
the ultraconservative Greater Detroit Home-Owners Council, backed up
the police and the security guard. He said that he had been in the building late that evening and had been threatened by some black teenagers.

Whatever substance there was to the allegation that some anony-mous black youths had threatened people in the elevator, it soon be-came clear that the two separate groups of teenagers attacked by the off-duty police had not done any taunting. In addition to the beatings, kickings, and shooting, a car had been hauled away, and when it was returned, its owner found it plastered with George Wallace stickers. Many officers who had not taken part in the actual violence had not taken any steps to stop the beatings, a sworn duty they were required to carry out by the same laws which required them to carry their guns. Eventually nine men were suspended because of the incident. James H. Brickley, a white assistant Wayne County prosecutor, made a public statement on November 16 in which he declared that the attacks had been unprovoked and that there was no evidence that the police or their wives had been abused or insulted by the youths who were at-tacked. Brickley added that, even if they had been, the action taken was totally illegal: "The policemen, with varying degrees of participa-tion, threatened and assaulted the Negro youths without provocation or justification. At no time did any of the police officers identify them-selves, make any arrests, or make any report of the incident."

Four months later, when one policeman was killed and another se-riously wounded during the New Bethel incident, the events of 1968 were invoked by all sides in the dispute. To the black community, New Bethel was another indication of the vigilante mentality of the police and its over-reliance on force. Only Judge Crockett's intervention had saved an ugly situation from exploding into a major racial confronta-tion. On the other side, the DPOA took out a full-page ad calling for Crockett's removal. Carl Parsell complained that the blue-blood New Detroit Committee was trying to use the police as a scapegoat. The tone of his speeches and his general attitude were the same as they had been the previous December in his editorial for *Tuebor*, the DPOA newsletter, when he wrote: "In the 1967 riot when police were re-stricted in the beginning from exercising their legal powers, the situ-ation got out of hand. When proper force was used in the Cobo Hall [incidents] peace and order was restored." Parsell's editorial had also denounced the Michigan Civil Rights Commission: "We charge the civil rights commission with denying constitutional rights to police offi-cers and denying them due process of law."

The DPOA failed in its attempt to remove Crockett from the bench, and an April 16 report of the Detroit Commission on Community Relations was highly critical of the police department. The report noted that the *Detroit Free Press* had publicly apologized for reporting inaccurate information to the public about New Bethel and that a letter written by a black Detroiter had characterized the slain Officer Czapski as a fair-minded and decent man. The report criticized the police reaction as a tragic mistake that was "part of the inheritance of the ghetto rebellion in the summer of '67 in which issues of community policy and response were never properly resolved. Nor were they clarified in April of '68, the Martin Luther King assassination aftermath with its curfew and police mobilization. . . . The DPOA promises of 'support law and order and remove George Crockett' have merged to symbolize the specter of the police state and paramilitary government of a colonial people."

The Community Relations Commission report had just started to circulate when a new flare-up occurred over the New Bethel case. This time, the trouble involved Recorder's Court Judge Joseph E. Maher and Kenneth Cockrel, who was the attorney for Alfred Hibbit, one of the men accused of killing Czapski. During the pretrial hearings, Maher abruptly interrupted Cockrel's presentation and ended the proceedings, after doubling Hibbit's bail to $50,000, even though Hibbit had turned himself in as soon as a warrant was issued for him. An infuriated Cockrel stormed from the courtroom and was quoted by the media as calling Judge Maher "a racist monkey, a honkie dog fool, and a thieving pirate."

Cockrel's words were barely out of his mouth before Judge Maher was calling for Cockrel's disbarment on the grounds of contempt and general unprofessional conduct. Cockrel shot back that he was expressing the sentiments of the black population of the city of Detroit in language congenial to them. The disbarment attempt moved rapidly, and the case was heard in late May. Cockrel's chief counsel was Sheldon Otis, and the Detroit Recorder's Court bench was represented by Michael O'Hara, a former state Supreme Court justice. Wayne County Circuit Court Judge Joseph Sullivan heard the case, since Judge Robert Colombo had disqualified all the Recorder's Court judges from hearing the case. Harry Philo and Justin Ravitz, two of Cockrel's law partners, assisted with the defense. His legal team also included Howard Moore of Atlanta, who had defended Stokely Carmichael and Julian Bond on similar charges, Dennis James of the National Lawyers Guild, Ed Bell of Detroit, who would soon become a judge himself, and Myron Wahls, the president of the Wolverine Bar Association, the professional organization for Michigan's black lawyers.

The first day of the trial, more than 75 sheriff's deputies patrolled the court and hallways as hundreds of people tried to get into the courtroom. Eventually, a door was broken down, a court reporter fainted, and the court had to be adjourned for one day. The following morning, to the astonishment of the media, the defense said that psychiatrists, psychologists, attorneys, and semanticists would prove that Cockrel's accusations were true. Nationally famous attorneys such as F. Lee Bailey were prepared to fly to Detroit to testify on Cockrel's behalf. Harry Philo indicated the uncompromising view of the defense by stating that the $50,000 bail was "thievery and piracy"; the defense believed that Maher "violated two different statutes several times, that he did it knowingly and that therefore he is a criminal . . . a despicable incompetent who is white." Thus, Cockrel's term "honkie dog fool" was correct in a colloquial sense. Sheldon Otis declared, "It is bad enough that our society has made Mr. Cockrel a second-class citizen because of his color. To make him a third- or fourth-class citizen because he is a lawyer would seem to me to be tearing the guts out of the Constitution. Attorneys . . . are obliged *not* to remain silent. It is their obligation to inform the public. Mr. Cockrel would be derelict in his duty if he did not do so." To make it clear that the case could not be hushed up, Cockrel said that he would make daily reports to the public at Detroit's Kennedy Square each day the trial lasted.

In early June, following a six-day recess, the charges against Cockrel were dropped. Judge Maher agreed to reduce Hibbit's bond to $10,000, and Cockrel issued a statement that saved some face for Maher: "I do not retreat from public statements I have made. I must add I regret that the choice of language employed by me is so widely misunderstood by such a large segment of our population. I have spoken and I shall always speak in the language, colloquial or otherwise, which I believe is understood by the persons to whom I address myself." He told reporters, "This is a vindication of the position we took. I have no regrets for what I said. I think my characterizations were accurate."

4

In each case, Cockrel—dramatic and persuasive—argued to juries well-populated with the kind of persons he designs his people's party for—blacks and workers, the little people he regards as oppressed.

—*Detroit News Sunday Magazine*, October 14, 1973

Cockrel's ability to turn a defense into an offense and to capture favorable publicity in the process was demonstrated over and over again in his struggles with the Detroit police and judicial system. His struggle with Judge Maher proved to be a worthy prelude to his actual defense of Hibbit before Judge Colombo. Assisted by Justin Ravitz, Sheldon Halpern, and Milton Henry, Cockrel took the offensive with a sensational run-around, left-end play by attacking the entire jury-selection system. He charged that in a city which was predominantly working class and in which the population was approaching a black majority, there could be no justice from a jury-selection system that produced only two black jurors and almost no young people or members of the working class. In a series of spectacular and effective legal moves, Cockrel and Ravitz demonstrated that the jury-selection rolls were not fair. Districts with heavy black or working-class populations were slighted in favor of areas with exclusively or predominantly white voters of middle-class background. Young people considered mature enough to vote and to serve in the armed forces were being scratched from lists as immature. One Wayne State University instructor had been disqualified simply because he wore a beard.

The outcome of the Cockrel-Ravitz maneuver was that the original Hibbit jury was thrown out and a new jury, which was predominantly black, was selected. Hibbit and the other defendants were exonerated at the trial and other subsequent trials. Even more significantly, the challenge to jury-selection procedures made appeals possible for thousands of Michigan prisoners, and it helped establish new ground rules for Michigan jury selection. The attorneys were pleased with their work, but they did not consider it revolutionary in a pure sense. It was merely a step toward re-establishing basic Bill of Rights guarantees. They felt that ultimately the system would revolt against its own rules rather than allow black and working-class juries to sit in judgment on cases involving laws based primarily on property rights. This revolt would bring about a situation in which class interests would be clearly defined on a mass scale.

The James Johnson case, which came up a year after New Bethel, was a further opportunity for application of the "jury of your peers" strategy. This time, rather than emphasizing race, the defense team led by Cockrel emphasized class. They wanted as many people on the jury with direct work experience in the city as they could get. Their "expert" witnesses included production line workers who could talk about the dehumanizing effects of working at the Eldon plant. The defense argued that the irrationality which had caused the crime was not a result of some flaw in James Johnson's brain or personality, but of the policies of the Chrysler Corporation. In the contempt case, the judge had been put on trial; in the New Bethel case, the jury-selection system had been put on trial; and in the Johnson case, the Chrysler Corporation was put on trial. In each instance, eloquent and brilliant legal work brought victory in cases which seemed all but hopeless on the surface.

Cockrel had more than the "gift of gab" or "charisma" going for him. His court defenses were meticulously planned and fit into a wider political movement. In each of the celebrated cases, Cockrel broke the bonds limiting the trial to one individual in a specific situation defined by a set of precise circumstances. He enlarged the scope of the cases to involve the interests of a whole community or class, which in turn lent its strength to the particular defendant. As the police continued to gear up their repressive machinery, Cockrel elaborated an anti-repression strategy which became the line of the League of Revolutionary Black Workers. At a January 30, 1970, anti-repression conference organized by the Detroit Newsreel organization, Cockrel said that all revolutionary organizations which find themselves in numerous conspiracy trials should look to their own structures, because that should not be happening at all, and never on a wholesale basis, if the organizations were properly set up. He noted how grand juries and police had failed to jail people like Mike Hamlin, Chuck Wooten, John Williams, Luke Tripp, Ron March, and Fred Holsey. The attempt to dislodge Watson from the *South End* and the attempt to disbar Cockrel himself had also failed, as had attempts to expel high school supporters of the League. All this and more had been accomplished because local people had been engaged in a local mass struggle. They had not been obliged to call on national celebrities to defend them. Their tactic of defense had not been to complain or moralize but to take the offensive in court and out of court. The ultimate goal was to control the court and police completely. Thus Cockrel declared, "You do not circulate petitions, write letters to attorney generals, meet with black police assistants, etc. You take over the Police Department, and you take over the city. This is not reformist. Reformism is what is counter-revolutionary. The content of the particular movement is critical—the overall perspective."

Cockrel severely criticized many of the participants in the anti-repression conference. In an open attack on the Panthers, he stated that a political organization must do everything in its power to avoid being transformed into defense committees solely concerned with keeping its leadership out of jail. Cockrel may well have had the murder charges leveled against Bobby Seale in mind. Seale's chief accuser was George Sams, a member of the national Black Panther Party who had once been a black gang leader in Highland Park. The League people had considered Sams to be so irresponsible and irrational that they wouldn't even let him be around them, much less be a member of their organization. A related point concerned the uncritical attitude many radical whites had toward blacks. Cockrel attacked the white chairman of the meeting: "Is it [your] position that any utterance that is ever made by any blood at any time is profoundly revolutionary in content and should not be in any way stifled, stymied, ordered, directed, or organized? We [the League] regard that as being a wholesale abdication of the responsibility to use one's time efficiently and to use the time of other people efficiently." Cockrel went on to say that much of the work done on "big" national cases was relatively meaningless because it did not and could not involve the large mass of working people, who had enormous problems of their own to deal with. One thread that ran throughout Cockrel's thinking was the need to concentrate mass power on a weak point in the system: "We say that the point of greatest vulnerability . . . is the point of production in the economic infrastructure of the system. We say it makes sense to organize workers inside of plants to precipitate the maximum dislocation and maximum paralysis of the operation of the capitalist-imperialist system. We say that all people who don't own, rule, and benefit from decisions which are made by those who own and rule are workers." In these remarks, in his practice of law, and in the projects he foresaw for the League, Cockrel was moving toward building a black and worker base for a bid for elective office. His main target was the repressive mechanisms of the state. Cockrel believed that control of the factories and control of the streets needed to go hand in hand with control of the courts and the police.

5

We know that today we have the highly sophisticated Green Beret STRESS unit roaming our city at will and killing on whim. . . . It promises to get even better. General John Nichols is in Germany tonight, studying police procedures in Munich, Frankfurt, and Berlin. Maybe he'll have ovens for the survivors and witnesses of STRESS murder. Nichols said he'd tattoo STRESS on his chest to prove it was staying.

—Sheila Murphy, in a From The Ground Up Book Club seminar, March 21, 1973

Detroit had always been known as a violent city, but by 1970 the situation was clearly out of hand. There were more than 23,000 reported robberies, which meant that at least one out of every 65 Detroiters had been a victim. An army of drug addicts lived in the remains of 15,000 inner-city houses abandoned for an urban renewal program which never materialized. More than 1 million guns were in the hands of the population, and union officials estimated that half the workers came to the plants armed with one weapon or another. The celebrated police-riot cases of 1968 followed the pattern of the Algiers Motel case: no cops were convicted. By January 1971, the atmosphere of permissiveness regarding police misconduct and the growing chaos in the streets had prepared the way for a new police unit called STRESS (Stop the Robberies, Enjoy Safe Streets). This unit was a secret, elite section of Detroit's undercover assault squads.

The Detroit Police Department never released information on exactly how many men were involved in STRESS or on their exact duties, but the unit was estimated to have no more than 100 men. The favorite STRESS method was the "decoy" operation in which one police officer acted as a potential victim in some area where a crime was likely to occur. As the decoy was attacked, other STRESS officers moved in for the arrest. STRESS operated in "high-crime" areas, which invariably turned out to be areas with overwhelmingly black populations. The difference between STRESS's decoying tactic and patently illegal "entrapment" was soon washed away in a floodtide of blood. During the first year of STRESS's operation, the Detroit Police Department chalked up the highest number of civilian killings per capita of any American police department. The Detroit police killed civilians at the rate of 7.17 per 1,000 officers in 1971. The five closest rivals in killings by police were Houston (5 per 1,000 officers), Baltimore (2.93), Chicago (2.54), New York City (1.84), and Philadelphia (1.28). More than one-third of the killings in Detroit were done by STRESS, which represented, at most, 2 percent of the department. The police regarded STRESS as a tough-fisted sheriff's posse dealing with saloon toughs and desperados; but to the citizens who suffered an estimated 500 raids without search warrants and 20 deaths by police bullets within 30 months, STRESS seemed more like Billy the Kid run amuck behind the protection of a badge.

The STRESS officers stated that there were more shootings and killings involving their unit because they were doing dangerous work. They were fighting crime in the streets on the only terms criminals understood. They felt that they should be commended for bravery rather than criticized. STRESS Commander James Bannon took a gruff attitude toward the complaints of citizens' committees. He was quoted in *Ramparts* in December 1973 as saying, "No god-damned bunch of intellectual eunuchs is going to tell professional policemen how to do their job."

Bannon's tough talk could not mask obvious problems regarding his men. Critics pointed out that Raymond Peterson had 21 citizen injury complaints lodged against him even before he became a STRESS officer and that Michael Ziolkowski was under trial board investigation for mistreatment of a black prisoner at the very time of his appointment to STRESS. The critics wanted to know by what standard these men were picked for jobs which brought them constantly into situations in which their judgments could mean life or death for a citizen. Peterson came to be known as "Mr. STRESS." He was involved in nine killings and three nonfatal shootings during the first two years of STRESS's existence.

Most STRESS killings took place under street circumstances which made judgment in any one case a matter of believing either a policeman sworn to uphold the law or a person accused of perpetrating a street crime. Pressure against STRESS built up through 1971, especially among blacks, but it was not until March 9, 1972, in an affair called the Rochester Street Massacre, that the description of STRESS as a bunch of trigger-happy cops became incontestable. The Rochester Street shooting differed from others because this time the victims of STRESS were not civilians, but other law-enforcement officers!

The incident began when three black STRESS officers observed a man later identified as a Wayne County sheriff's deputy walk into a building at 3210 Rochester with what appeared to be a gun. The STRESS squad called other police and entered the apartment with guns blazing. Wayne County Sheriff's Deputy Henry Henderson was killed, and three other deputies were seriously wounded. According to subsequent court testimony, all the deputies might have been killed if Patrolman Richard Herold had not arrived on the scene and put a stop to the carnage.

Exactly what transpired at Rochester Street was never made clear. A popular rumor held that the police were "battling for drug turf." Patrolman Herold proved to be a pivotal figure. He had reputedly fought with other police over which heroin dealer worked for which officer. One point beyond rumor was that on January 8, 1973, he was suspended from the force after being arrested in Toronto, Canada, for possession of and dealing in cocaine. This charge was soon followed by a Detroit indictment on similar charges. During the Rochester Street incident, 44 shots were fired by the Detroit police, 41 of them by STRESS officers. Deputy Henderson sustained six gunshot wounds as he stood with his back to the wall, hands in the air, and ID badge in hand. Three officers were eventually brought to trial, but all were acquitted. On this occasion, Prosecutor Cahalan refrained from making a public statement that black jurors would not convict blacks, as he had after the New Bethel case. What was clear now to everyone was that STRESS could be counted upon to shoot before asking any questions. Constitutional guarantees against illegal search and seizure and police violence were absolutely meaningless should STRESS decide it was a "kill" situation. The Detroit Police Department learned nothing from the Rochester Street Massacre, for in April 1973, Police Commissioner John Nichols took Ronald Martin, one of the defendants in the case, to Washington, where Martin informed a House Select Committee on

Crime that STRESS was like the United States Marine Corps, "only better."

Even before the Rochester Street Massacre, blacks felt that they were in a virtual state of siege. If STRESS cops could kill sheriff's deputies and get away with it, the average citizen didn't have a chance. STRESS's tactics were like the Army's "search and destroy" policy in Vietnam. Eleven deaths occurred between April and August of 1971, and all but one of the victims were black. Cockrel and other radicals working as members of the Black Workers Congress, the Labor Defense Coalition, and the State of Emergency Committee took a leading role in attacking STRESS. On September 23, 1971, more than 5,000 people were mobilized by the State of Emergency Committee to demand the abolition of STRESS. The Detroit Commission on Community Relations stated that a broadly based multiracial opposition to STRESS clearly existed. Two more STRESS killings took place in November and December of 1971, bringing the year's total to 13. The Michigan Civil Rights Commission was moved to attack STRESS's methods, and urged elimination of the decoy technique and better screening and supervision of personnel. The Rochester Street Massacre occurred on March 9 of the following year, and on March 17 Mayor Roman Gribbs and Commissioner Nichols announced "reforms." The death toll had now reached 16, but decoy operations were not reduced and lethal force was still justified as long as "reasonable" grounds existed for believing a felony had been committed. The "reform" move was countered on March 26 by a rally of more than 2,000 people at the University of Detroit stadium in support of a petition campaign to abolish STRESS and a lawsuit against Mayor Gribbs, Commissioner Nichols, and Prosecutor Cahalan. The petition campaign was to gain more than 40,000 signatures, and on April 6 the anti-STRESS suit, prepared by Cockrel, Ravitz, and others, was filed in Wayne County Circuit Court. The plaintiffs included the NAACP, Local 600 of the UAW, relatives of STRESS victims, and Local 26 of the Detroit Public Workers union. Judge John O'Hair, who had served as a representative of the Police Department when he was assistant corporate counsel, placed the case on the regular docket rather than grant an immediate hearing.

STRESS burst back into the headlines on December 4, 1972, when four STRESS men were involved in a shootout with three armed blacks: Mark Bethune, John Percy Boyd, and Hayward Brown. The three young men had been waging a private war against big-time heroin dealers in their neighborhoods. STRESS had staked out one of the dope houses that the three vigilantes attacked. Instead of pursuing the dope dealers, STRESS chased Bethune, Boyd, and Brown. A shootout followed which resulted in the four STRESS officers being wounded, while their prey escaped. Three weeks later, in a second shootout with the vigilantes, STRESS officer Robert Bradford was slain and another officer wounded. The vigilantes escaped once more, and Commissioner Nichols went on television describing them as "mad-dog killers." In the weeks which followed, STRESS put the black neighborhoods under martial law in the most massive and ruthless police manhunt in Detroit history. Hundreds of black families had their doors literally broken down and their lives threatened by groups of white men in plain clothes who had no search warrants and often did not bother to identify themselves as police. Eventually, 56 fully documented cases of illegal procedure were brought against the department. One totally innocent man, Durwood Forshee, could make no complaint because he was dead. This 57-year-old unemployed security guard was killed when he fired his shotgun at STRESS invaders whom he believed to be a gang of robbers. On January 12, 1973, Hayward Brown was finally captured. Bethune and Boyd, disguised as a priest and a nun, got out of the city safely but were killed a month and a half later in a shootout with the Atlanta police.

Hayward Brown chose Ken Cockrel to be his attorney, and, employing his usual tactic of turning a defense into an offensive, Cockrel decided to put STRESS on trial. In defending his client's participation in one killing and several woundings, Cockrel invoked the Algiers Motel, Cobo Hall I, Cobo Hall II, Veterans Memorial, New Bethel, the Rochester Street Massacre, and the whole record of STRESS and the Detroit Police Department. In three bitter and hotly fought trials, Cockrel won total acquittal for his client. The 18-year-old Brown, who was an ex-junkie, came to be a kind of folk hero. He and his two comrades had taken on a job that the STRESS squad, for all its bloody fingers, had not been able to handle. Brown spoke on the radio, on television, and at public meetings and called for the abolition of STRESS. The From The Ground Up organization circulated 8,000 copies of an attractively designed 60-page booklet which gave details on various STRESS killings and pinpointed the political forces supporting and opposing STRESS. During the same period, Raymond Peterson, "Mr. STRESS," was charged with murder when his description of a killing did not hold up against laboratory evidence. The victim in this case was a worker stopped on an expressway by Peterson, who was supposedly on his way to his suburban home. The knife which the worker allegedly used to threaten Peterson turned out under examination to belong to Peterson. Citizens clamored for an investigation of other STRESS killings, but Prosecutor Cahalan seized all the pertinent homicide files and kept them from public view.

The acquittal of Hayward Brown and the charges against "Mr. STRESS" were an indication of a new view of the police forming in the minds of many Detroiters. Originally, STRESS had been accepted by the inner city as a possible solution to the cycle of violence of which it was the principal victim. The record of STRESS soon proved that the unit meant only an increase in violence. STRESS was a new lethal weapon in the hands of a government which had driven local blacks to violent rebellion twice in 30 years. Black veterans who had banded together to demand jobs and other benefits were victims of midnight STRESS raids. Paroled prisoners working for penal reform reported being followed and threatened by STRESS. Workers said STRESS men had infiltrated the auto plants in order to spy on worker organizations.

The Brown verdicts proved that jurors of all colors were no longer accepting police testimony as automatically more honest than that of ordinary citizens. Jurors were concerned that law officers now viewed themselves as above the law. STRESS obviously regarded itself as a judge, jury, and executioner mandated to deal out instant "justice." Despite the change in public opinion, the Detroit Police Department remained unmoved in its support of STRESS. Police officers rallied around Peterson, saying that he must not be made a sacrificial lamb to a public willing to make a hero out of a "cop-killer" like Hayward Brown. STRESS was renamed the Felony Prevention Squad, and additional "reforms" were made; but to take no chances of having their real power curbed, the police were ready to make a bid for control of the city government itself by running Police Commissioner John Nichols for mayor. The Detroit Police Officers Association was so sure of itself that it made a thinly veiled threat on the lives of Cockrel and Brown by offering them "one-way tickets to Atlanta."

The prospect of the man ultimately responsible for STRESS becoming mayor of Detroit unsettled all the forces within the city that wanted to end racial polarization and that were worried about new civil disturbances. Nichols was part of a nebulous hard-line political group which included Prosecutor Cahalan, several former FBI men, and Roman Gribbs, who had been Wayne County sheriff before becoming mayor. Nichols was the toughest of the lot. His politics were pure "law-and-orderism," which in Detroit meant, among other things, "keeping the niggers in their place." Nichols, like Frank Rizzo, the Philadelphia police commissioner turned mayor, and other police officials seeking elective office around the country, was trying to ride a tide of white fear to political power. In Detroit, a vote for John Nichols meant a vote for STRESS.

Chapter Nine

Mr. Justin Ravitz, Marxist Judge of Recorder's Court

1

Building the kind of power necessary to making more fundamental changes requires the organized activity of large numbers of people willing to struggle for that change. Engaging in the electoral process can be one way to develop such an organization.

—Committee to Elect Ravitz Recorder's Court Judge, *The Mini-Manual of Criminal Justice*, 1972

In 1972, Justin Ravitz was elected to a ten-year term as judge of Recorder's Court. The *Detroit Free Press* ran a story on the election headlined "Radical Judge-Elect Ravitz Plans To Shake Up Court"; this was restated on a follow-up page: "New Judge Is A Marxist Who Plans To Shake Up Court." The Ravitz victory was the first materialization of the election strategy advocated by Cockrel and the forces around him. This group was convinced that the electoral process was a viable means of educating the public on issues, of propagandizing wider solutions, and of winning some limited power. It was a process that could enable them to control some of the weakest links in the power chain of capitalism: its elective officers, its courts, and its legal system. Winning limited power would afford radicals positions from which to launch or to protect future assaults on the strongest links of the system. Elections

were not to be substituted for other more radical activities, but to aug-
ment those activities with an attack from within basic American institutions.

In an article titled "Toward Our Own Courts . . . & Beyond" published in abridged form in the *Guardian* newsweekly of November 14,
1972, Margaret Borys, one of the principal coordinators on Ravitz's
campaign staff, underscored the long-range strategy involved. She
noted that the campaign focused on the real causes of violence in Detroit—the disparity between the lifestyles projected on television and
the reality of life as lived in Detroit, the desperation of the 200,000
chronically unemployed Detroiters, the heroin problem that caused $1
million worth of property to be stolen every day by Detroit's junkies,
and police officers who behaved like an occupying army rather than a
part of the community. She described the basic goals of the campaign
in this way:

> The Ravitz Campaign understood that we can neither litigate nor elect
> our way to liberation, but selective and serious entries into each arena
> can advance the building of a socialist society. An aggressive, honest,
> and persuasive campaign helped promote the reality that "radical prob-
> lems" do indeed "require radical solutions." . . . The political objectives
> of the Ravitz Campaign are continuing ones: (1) to build class solidarity
> by organizing a self-conscious and anti-racist white movement (2) to
> take leadership in the implementation of transitional reforms and de-
> mands (3) to achieve a mass multi-racial, independent, radical people's
> political movement—a movement conscious of the need and value of
> victories, unafraid and relentless in its pursuit of power.

The campaign emphasized Ravitz's record as a radical attorney. In
addition to his role in the New Bethel case, the James Johnson case,
and the anti-STRESS suit, Ravitz had many other impressive court victories to his credit. He had successfully defended welfare mothers arrested for demonstrating at the Bureau of Social Services; he had
successfully defended anti-war demonstrators who were arrested for
protesting the bombing of Hanoi and the mining of Haiphong harbor;
and he had successfully challenged the Michigan anti-marijuana law,
freeing 130 people from prison. He had also led the litigation against
city and county officials responsible for the inhuman and barbaric conditions in the Wayne County Jail, litigation that brought about a 50
percent reduction in the inmate population.

Ravitz's campaign literature employed radical populist language to give a revolutionary critique of the system. The major mass-distribution brochure reprinted a *Detroit News* front-page photo story showing Ravitz and Cockrel discussing the primary election returns under a big headline: "Radical Tops Court Nominees." The brochure's own headline was "Justin Ravitz Is A Lousy Politician—and that's good." Ravitz's record was presented with emphasis on his concern for the problems of working people, and he was contrasted to the do-nothing "politicians." A more substantial piece of campaign literature was *The Mini-Manual of Criminal Justice*, a 22-page booklet that attacked the entire legal system in unmistakably radical terms. The booklet dealt with judges, the money bail system, the Wayne County Jail, the Detroit Police Department, the Wayne County Prosecutor's Office, prisons, 24-hour arraignments, the summons system, pretrial confinement, sentencing, and the heroin problem. The booklet was prefaced with a militant poem by b.p. Flanigan. A typical passage began the section "Heroin: Our Analysis":

> When we properly understand the role of money in the American capitalist economy and the dominant control of monied forces in major government policy decisions and actions, nationally and internationally, then we understand that they purposely have created and maintained conditions that keep hundreds of thousands of people existing in conditions that will force them to fall prey to heroin addiction, just as they keep at least five to six million people, at all times, unemployed.

The campaign was coordinated by a staff of half a dozen, but reached out to involve hundreds of people. On the day of the election, more than 400 unpaid volunteer poll-workers stood in the rain for as long as 13 hours passing out literature. Several dozen others were organized into support teams that delivered hot food and beverages throughout the day. Almost everyone connected with the organization had little or no previous electoral experience, yet Ravitz finished second among the seven judges elected, with 130,514 votes on a nonpartisan ballot. Ravitz had received endorsements from some unexpected sources: Council 77 of the AFL-CIO, the *Detroit Free Press*, the Urban Alliance, the Detroit Bar Association, all the district organizations of the Democratic Party, and the UAW. Borys characterized most of these groups as having "diminishing but real importance, [yet] they shall continue to be a factor in tactical maneuverings until the left wins the continuing allegiance of the masses of people."

Cockrel's approach had never gotten majority support within the League of Revolutionary Black Workers, and the Ravitz campaign failed to get majority support within the Motor City Labor League. The organization appeared to be solidly behind Ravitz during the primary, but his victory served to disunite rather than rally the organization. A group centered around Frank Joyce brought the whole electoral strategy into question. They felt that MCLL was being transformed into a Cockrel coattail rather than pursuing its own independent course. Bumper stickers at Ravitz campaign headquarters were pushing Cockrel for mayor in 1973, and many MCLL members questioned the viability of a white organization pushing a black candidate as one of its major activities. Beyond the specific contests, many MCLL members believed, as most radicals of the New Left did, that elections led to reformism. If Detroit's local elections had not been nonpartisan, Ravitz might have had to run as a Democrat to have a serious chance of winning. The Joyce group cited the history of the Communist Party, which had worked in the liberal wing of the Democratic Party and had been in-strumental in building the CIO only to be destroyed in the McCarthy era because of its watered-down programs and liberal rhetoric. The MCLL militants also spoke of ex-communist Jay Lovestone, who had become a key anti-communist on George Meany's central staff at the AFL-CIO; and they pointed out that Max Shachtman, once a firebrand Trotskyist, had ended his long career by supporting the war in Viet-nam. Ravitz's candidacy in the August primary had been endorsed by several ministers, a rabbi, Ernest Mazey of the American Civil Liberties Union, numerous doctors, poet John Sinclair, various attorneys, one city councilman, one state representative, and one state senator. To some people in MCLL, this was the reformist handwriting on the wall.

The differences within the organization proved irresolvable; and so, in the middle of September, a group led by Sheila Murphy with-drew from MCLL to continue with the election work. In November, they formed a new organization called From The Ground Up. Two summers after the split, it was clear that MCLL had turned decidedly against participation in elections and in favor of intensifying its work-place organizing and deepening its Marxist-Leninist ideology. Among the organization's major concerns was the possible formation of a new communist party involving fusion of various groups in the city and around the country. This was similar to the direction being taken by groups such as BWC and the Communist League.

Cockrel's colleagues and those who had resigned from MCLL were not indifferent to criticism about the dangers of electoral politics, but they were willing to stake their organizational and personal futures on a different line of reasoning. They felt that the ideological purism of many of the radical groups produced an oppositionist mentality incapable of dealing with questions of real power. The STRESS unit was terrorizing half the city of Detroit. Winning a Recorder's Court judgeship meant being able to deliver some measure of protection to the people. Mass popular support from blacks and whites alike would not be won by abstract ideological debates but by extracting concessions from the system. Radicals must head mass struggles so that demands and perspectives could be given a more revolutionary direction. Demonstrating efficient leadership and winning limited victories would strengthen and deepen the popular base. The League had been successful because it had developed many levels and types of power. Reformism was, indeed, a pitfall, but the forces around Cockrel and Ravitz were confident they would avoid it.

Cockrel was not beguiled by his local fame and popularity. The Hayward Brown case required almost all of his legal and organizational talents during most of 1973. New charges were continually brought up, and the case seemed endless. The James Johnson case was similar. Ron Glotta had won workman's compensation for Johnson early in 1973, but in the summer Johnson was charged with assault with intent to murder at the hospital where he was an inmate. Cockrel felt compelled to intervene, and he proved that Johnson had been unjustly accused. It was beginning to seem that a handful of cases could keep Cockrel tied up indefinitely. He told the *Detroit News*:

> I wonder if the time and energy spent on them [the Brown cases] means all that much in terms of furthering the Movement, educating the people, or building up an organization. Much time and energy was spent, a great deal of it to the exclusion of most other things.
>
> And you have to weigh it.
>
> It resulted in the exoneration of an individual. But what was its effect in terms of education and organization? What if the same time

and energy had been devoted toward building an organization? Would the effect have been broader and more important?

Cockrel expressed these doubts in a highly favorable seven-page feature story on him in the *Detroit News Sunday Magazine* of October 14, 1973. The magazine's front cover showed Cockrel standing before a section of the Diego Rivera murals. The headline read: "Revolutionary in a Legal Sheepskin—A Look at Kenneth Cockrel, the Radicals' Courtroom Crusader." An invitation was clearly out for Cockrel to become the black revolutionary tinsel for Detroit's power structure; yet Detroit politics were as deceptive as ever. Behind the glib facade of amity were the lightly veiled death threats delivered by the DPOA. Some people believed that the greatest danger facing the electoral strategists was not reformism but liquidation by the police or right-wing vigilantes. As pressure against STRESS mounted, individual officers were being suspended and disciplined. They and their political allies perceived Cockrel and his allies as their principal nemesis. Many people around Cockrel felt forced to carry weapons lest, in the next Algiers Motel Incident or Rochester Street Massacre, they become the victims. They knew only too well that they were actively opposing the military apparatus of the state with limited and underdeveloped forces. Cockrel spoke of cutting down on the number of criminal cases he handled and perhaps concentrating on workman's compensation or other labor-oriented aspects of the law. He also hoped to have more time to think, organize, and travel.

2

> *I will handle at most approximately 5 percent of [the] docket. They are, on the one hand, scared as hell of me coming over, and they deserve to be, because we're going to fight them like hell. But, on the other hand, there's a certain smug attitude. "Ravitz will be co-opted. . . . What can one judge do?" and so on.*
>
> —Justin C. Ravitz, speaking at the founding session of From The Ground Up, November 20, 1972

Justin Ravitz took office early in 1973. In his first year on the bench, he tried to differentiate himself from the other judges, while being sufficiently cooperative to achieve the changes he sought in fundamental practices. One innovation he instituted at once was to have the courtroom spectators and the judge stand for the jury, rather than having the spectators and the jury stand for the judge. The jurors were often visibly confused by this sudden shift in protocol. Ravitz would explain, "Excuse me; in this court we stand out of respect for the jury and what you represent. So, as soon as you wish to be seated, please do so and we'll all sit down." Ravitz did not wear a robe or display an American flag, behavior that quickly brought about a Michigan Supreme Court ruling compelling all judges to wear robes and show the flag. The Supreme Court spoke of a "proper" judicial atmosphere. Ravitz replied that he, too, was interested in a "proper" judicial atmosphere, but that his definition of what was proper was somewhat different. He did relent to the extent of putting on a robe and displaying an American flag next to the water fountain behind a partition that hid the flag from the jury, although it was in full view of anyone entering or leaving through the main doorway.

One of Ravitz's major court reforms had to do with the time people were detained before their cases were heard. The average holding time was 12-24 hours, meaning that some people were held for a much longer time and some for a shorter period. In 1972 alone, 23,070 persons had been detained and never taken to court because there were insufficient grounds. Ravitz argued that if the police were compelled to take their prisoners to court immediately, there would be many fewer false arrests and harassments without cause. He set a personal example in his own court and made a series of proposals aimed at getting other judges and the Supreme Court to speed up the system. He threw out all entrapment cases, took the civilian side whenever the situation was questionable, and refused to honor warrants with technical errors. In a move that puzzled some police, he gave them precise instructions on legal definitions of entrapment and technical training in making out proper warrants. He explained that he was not against the police carrying out their jobs but was interested in protecting people's constitutional rights. A further demonstration of his determination to live within the spirit of the Bill of Rights was his acceptance of work-release bonds instead of cash bail. Ravitz stated that the poor should not be denied bail simply because they didn't have ready cash. On one occasion, he accepted a stereo set as bail.

Ravitz did everything in his power to demystify the courtroom, to give political education where the system had miseducated, and to correct the various misconceptions about the judicial system fostered by schools, movies, television, and cheap detective stories. Sensitivity to individual needs, personal informality, and political education classes all had a role in his perception of what one judge could do. Among his initial efforts was a letter he got another judge to co-sign, which was sent to arrestees informing them that they should not waive their pretrial examinations, a right most of them were giving up, although fully one-third of those who did not had their cases dropped. Ravitz took on at least one speaking engagement a week, and he conducted a series of Saturday seminars held in his courtroom, where he explained the judicial system as it actually functioned in the city of Detroit. In all of these activities, Ravitz raised many critical questions. In an article written in 1974 and scheduled for publication by a Ralph Nader study group on judicial problems, Ravitz wrote:

> Did you ever stop to think why lawyers and judges talk in language real people cannot understand? Why nearly all people—plaintiffs, defendants, witnesses, jurors, and indeed, most lawyers—are so frightened when called upon to speak in an American courtroom? Why can't we understand what goes on in our courts, and why are we so afraid in our courts? . . .
> The rawness of white racism in this country is only a part of the real message. The law is not only not "color blind," but it more than "tolerates classes among citizens." It is designed to tolerate and perpetuate class division. The law serves the dominant class in a class society.

Ravitz tried to use his radical sensibility in handling every kind of case in order to demonstrate to one and all that a Marxist judge could administer the law more wisely, humanely, and fairly than any other kind of judge. Men convicted of rape were given a pamphlet on rape written by a women's liberation group. They were told to study the pamphlet with other men convicted of the same offense and, when they felt that they had genuinely begun to understand themselves, to contact the judge about the possibility of parole. Ravitz warned them not to "play games with me," as that would result in a closing of communications. Similar tactics were worked out with drug addicts. More overtly political cases were handled with the same tact. In one instance,

Ravitz opened his court at night to allow his former law partner Ken Cockrel to get Hayward Brown released without bail. In another case, he gave right-winger Donald Lobsinger a 45-day sentence for a political disturbance that could have netted him a full 90 days. Ravitz gave Lobsinger's supporters some leeway in the courtroom and refused to respond to Lobsinger's "red-baiting." He also transformed some apparently routine cases into political ones. One such occurrence was his handling of a case involving the Wrigley's supermarket chain. One Wrigley store had systematically overpriced its meats through false weight measurements. A check showed that 33 out of 40 packages had been priced incorrectly in favor of the store. The usual procedure in such cases was for the corporation to plead guilty and the charges against any individual to be dismissed. The corporation then paid a nominal fine because a corporation cannot be jailed. Ravitz discovered that this practice had been going on for years. Determined to set new ground rules, Ravitz stated that he was going to punish the supermarket to the maximum allowed by law and that he would hold meat clerks personally responsible for the mislabeling. He noted in court how the Wrigley chain's attorney had tried to instruct him on the "usual" procedure, forgetting who was the guardian of the public trust and who was the criminal. In a test case, Ravitz fined the supermarket $100, the statutory maximum, and ordered payment of $100 more in court costs. He gave the meat clerk one day in jail to serve notice that, in the future, the old ways could not be taken for granted.

Ravitz's performance in court generated a lot of quiet excitement in the city. His manner was unpretentious. He spoke quietly and repeated his points until his listeners understood, generating an air of mild-mannered fairness. Teachers brought their government classes to observe the radical judge. Individuals wandered into the courtroom to get a look at "the commie judge." Ravitz found that initial hostility was usually overcome when people observed his actual practice. A black worker's comment, "If he's a commie, right on, commies!" was echoed by local news broadcaster Lou Gordon, who ended a Ravitz interview by saying, "If this is a Marxist judge, we need more Marxist judges." As Ravitz told the authors in February 1974, "We're an aberration, and people want to see what is going on. People who have spent all their lives standing in line waiting to be robbed at cash registers are finding out we're on their side."

A dissident view of Ravitz was voiced by Peter Werbe, who had been a major figure at the *Fifth Estate* for years and who was doing an all-night talk show on WRIF-FM, an ABC affiliate. In August 1973, he told the authors: "Ravitz gave a guy 20 years the other day. I don't want that kind of power." Werbe was stating frankly what many of the counter-culture people of the 1960s felt. The Cockrel and Ravitz forces couldn't have disagreed more. They were willing to accept the responsibilities of power, and they were ready to struggle for it whenever they could. They anticipated stretching the political system to its limits, confident that it would ultimately unmask itself in desperate attempts to keep radicals from achieving full power. The very day after Ravitz's election, the Detroit Bar Association spoke of the advisability of having judges appointed rather than elected. Other moves were afoot in the state to limit the kinds of cases that could go before juries at all, to impanel juries of less than 12 people, and to allow majority decisions (8-4 or 9-3) to convict. These moves and others to broaden police powers by negating vital parts of the Bill of Rights could be important issues around which radicals might rally mass support. Cockrel had stated his view in the 1970 anti-repression conference: "We don't engage in bullshit arguments about 'that's reformist' or 'that's not reformist.' That which is reformist is that which is counter-revolutionary. What is not reformist or counter-revolutionary is any action that conduces to the creation of a larger propensity on the part of most people to view revolution as the only course of conduct available to end oppression. That's what we relate to—that's what we understand and see very clearly as being real."

3

I will lead a business resurgence that will produce jobs by the thousands, revitalize our downtown, and our entire city. I will move Detroit forward on a program that includes new port facilities, a stadium, rapid transit, recreational facilities, and housing.

—Coleman Young, quoted in campaign literature, autumn 1973

The election for mayor in 1973 surfaced many plans for a new Detroit. On the far right stood Police Commissioner John Nichols. The two major liberal contenders were Mel ("the Other") Ravitz, a pipe-smoking ex-Wayne State University teacher who had served on the city council for many years, and black State Senator Coleman Young. The UAW's endorsement was crucial to their respective chances for election. The Detroit UAW, which was more in touch with political realities in the city, wanted Young; the Wayne County organization, which included the Detroit organization but reflected suburban attitudes as well, wanted Ravitz. The top UAW leadership pushed through an official endorsement for Ravitz, but many powerful local units worked on behalf of Coleman Young, hoping to repeat for a black candidate what they had done for Jerome Cavanagh a decade earlier. The other major candidates were Circuit Court Judge Ed Bell, a black Republican who resigned his office to run, and John Mogk, a political unknown who waged a populist door-to-door walking campaign and ended up getting the *Detroit Free Press*'s endorsement for the primary election.

Cockrel had made it no secret that he was considering entering the race. He was not interested in running for mayor in 1973 in order to win some other office in the next election, a common practice in Detroit, and he was not interested in running only to educate the public about socialism, as the candidates of the Socialist Workers Party did. Cockrel wanted to run only if he could win. A serious race for the office required large-scale financing and, more important, a broadly based political organization. After considering all factors, the Cockrel forces decided that, in spite of the personal publicity he had received, there were too few primary or secondary leaders for the kind of campaign needed to win the major office in the city government. The pieces needed for a power play were in place, as they had been for the League of Revolutionary Black Workers in 1969; but, once again, there was a lack of the organizational momentum and personnel that could have activated them.

The primary election narrowed the field to John Nichols and Coleman Young. Few elections in modern Detroit history had offered such a clear-cut choice. Nichols was the prototype of a white conservative, complete with police credentials—the candidate of the homeowners' associations, negrophobes, and support-the-cops-at-any-cost elements in the city. Young was a black, labor-oriented liberal with a "pinko" past. His camp contained many elements, extending from black nationalists to Democratic Party hacks and UAW liberals. Its lower echelons even

included former SNCC people and former League activists such as
Larry Nevels and Althea Hankins, both of whom ran regional campaign
offices. Cockrel refused to take any active role in the election. Backing
Nichols was, of course, unthinkable, and supporting Young would
mean promoting the very coalition radicals had been trying the hardest
to dismantle. One of the internal contradictions in Cockrel's political
outlook was that he had agreed that Ravitz should accept the same sort
of coalition support in his race for a judgeship. The major difference
was that the radicals set the ground rules in the Ravitz effort, with the
liberals playing a supporting role, while with Young's campaign the opposite would be true.

In an election marked by severe racial polarization, Young won a
narrow victory. Those radicals who opposed electoral struggles believed
that this victory showed the weakness of the strategy advocated by
Cockrel and his followers. Because of that strategy, all the opposition
to STRESS had benefited not the revolutionary forces but Coleman
Young, who was just another liberal. They pointed out that, although
Young had a radical past, his present political cohorts were Leonard
Woodcock and Henry Ford II. These critics brushed aside Young's appointment of 37-year-old Larry Nevels to a $24,000-a-year job as head
of the neighborhood city halls as a case of one more black radical being
sucked in by the Democratic Party. What appeared to be a major triumph for black Detroiters and progressive forces, especially in opposition to the racist Nichols, was, they insisted, only another instance of
prolonging the existing system through liberal reformism. If the city
could prove flexible enough to elect its first black mayor, it was reasonable to assume that STRESS might be abolished and the mass discontent quelled without any real change in the power structure. The
Cockrel forces replied that they had taken the lead against STRESS to
stop police-state repression and to build a mass movement, not to win
an election. Nichols had been defeated, which was good, and the military situation was thereby more favorable; yet STRESS and the police
department remained unchanged. As long as the police ran amuck, a
mass movement would be needed to keep them in check. Nevels believed he could use his post as creatively as Ravitz had used his and was
angry that radicals had not supported his bid for a seat on the city
council. Nevels had lost the primary by only a few thousand votes, and
organized radical support could have made the difference between de-

feat and victory. For his part, Cockrel believed that he could have been elected mayor had the city's radicals rallied around him from the preceding summer. As it was, if life in the city improved to any visible degree, the liberals would be difficult to dislodge. Cockrel believed, however, that conditions would worsen and that the Young administration might prove to be only the last stand of a failed liberalism. The election proved nothing to Cockrel about the validity of electoral struggle other than that the politics of winning a ten-year judgeship were relatively easy compared to those required to elect the city's chief executive.

Chapter Ten

The 54-Hour Week

1

For the first time in the history of the UAW, the union mobilized to keep a plant open.

—Bill Bonds, WXYZ-TV News, speaking of events at the Mack stamping plant, August 16, 1973

For Chrysler Corporation, 1973 was a wildcat summer as walkouts shut down three Chrysler plants: Jefferson Assembly, Chrysler Forge, and Mack stamping. The wildcat at Chrysler Forge lasted longer and was more damaging to production than the official three-day UAW strike, which came in the autumn around model changeover time. The problems leading to the wildcats were very much like those which had led to the formation of DRUM; but this time the strikers demonstrated a much higher level of racial cooperation, and their spokesmen talked from a clear class perspective.

The first wildcat occurred at Jefferson Assembly, where 90 percent of the workers in the metal shop were black. The poor working conditions in the metal shop were aggravated by the attitude of a white superviser named Tom Woolsey. Blacks charged that he was an outright racist. A petition calling for his removal was signed by 214 of the 300 workers in the shop, but the plant management and the union disregarded the workers' petition. On July 24, Isaac Shorter, 26, and Larry Carter, 23, took direct worker action. They climbed into the electric power control cage and, by pushing one button, halted the assembly line at the start of the first shift at 6:00 a.m. Not bothering with the union hierarchy, Carter and Shorter negotiated with the company directly from the cage. They said that they would continue the occupation until Woolsey was removed and they were granted an unconditional amnesty. Workers clustered outside the cage with chains in case anyone should try to remove Shorter and Carter by force. Black, white, and Arab workers brought food or stood guard, many of them coming from other departments to demonstrate their support. Thirteen hours later, the two men were carried from the plant on the shoulders of their fellow workers. Chrysler had capitulated on all counts. Doug Fraser, the UAW director for Chrysler, wondered aloud why the company had set such a dangerous precedent, but said that the men deserved "an A for ingenuity."

The photo of Carter and Shorter being carried triumphantly out of the plant appeared in all the Detroit papers and in labor-oriented publications throughout the nation. Readers discovered that Shorter was a native of Cleveland, Mississippi, where he had been active from 1969-1970 as chairman of the local National Committee to Combat Fascism, an arm of the Black Panther Party. He later moved to Los Angeles, where he worked in a Chrysler plant until it cut back production. He arrived in Detroit in September 1971. Carter came from Pensacola, Florida, where he had been fired by a Coca-Cola Bottling firm for participating in a unionization effort. He, too, had come to Detroit in 1971. The two men shared an apartment and were good friends. In their statements to the press, they emphasized the class rather than the racial aspect of their actions. Shorter said that he had talked with Woolsey and said, "'Hey, man, me and you are in the same class. We are both workers.' But he couldn't understand. And from then on, we started getting into it." He told another reporter, "The black workers in this city could control it. But at the same time, there's no such thing as black control. Because it's not a racial thing. It's the system, which is a capitalist system. It oppresses all people. Blacks, whites, Chicanos, just name it, yellow, brown. And that's the way we should look at it as being."

A few weeks later, on August 28, an even more serious wildcat took place at Chrysler Forge. The plant employed 1,100 workers in the making of crankshafts, pinions, and torsion bars. A week before the strike, two workers were crippled by accidents. One had an arm torn off, and another had a finger crushed. Approximately 60 percent of the Forge workers had been working a nearly steady seven-day week for the past six months. The immediate trigger to the strike was the firing of 16 workers who had been vocal in exposing health and safety violations. The leadership of the strike was primarily white, but leaflets from the *People's Tribune*, the organ of the Communist League, one of the successor groups of the League of Revolutionary Black Workers, were given out the day of the shutdown. One of the wildcat leaders was soft-spoken Jerome Scott, a former member of DRUM and a current member of the Communist League.

The strike at Forge lasted six days and threatened to paralyze all Chrysler production. By August 10, a harried Doug Fraser had said that he would "legalize" the strike if Chrysler did not make concessions. Chrysler then agreed to correct 100 safety grievances immediately and to put 150 more under advisement. In a stormy meeting, more than 800 workers decided, by a narrow majority vote, to return to work. In an action not seen for many years, Doug Fraser made a personal appearance at the Forge gates the next morning to urge people to return to work. With a Channel 2 News camera going, Fraser had a verbal confrontation with John Taylor of MCLL. Fraser, a former DeSoto worker, called for a fistfight in the parking lot but backed off when Taylor proved more than happy to accept the challenge. The attempt to blame the strike on "outside agitators" and "radicals" gained momentum when Jerome Scott was charged with criminal acts and civil contempt. What the red-baiting could not cover up, however, was that working conditions were the main cause of the strikes. Anthony McJennet, a Forge worker, told the *Detroit News*, "Chrysler treats a man like a piece of meat." He might have added that the meat could be black or white. The most significant aspect of the strike was that black radicals had maintained a working alliance with white, mainly Polish, workers, something that had not occurred at Dodge Main in 1968, at Eldon in 1969-1970, or at the Chrysler Sterling stamping plant where white workers had rebelled in a week-long wildcat in 1969 over working-condition grievances similar to those voiced by DRUM and ELRUM. Doug Fraser put a bold face on his growing anxiety: "Radicals are creating a serious problem at Forge, but we don't feel it is unmanageable."

The day after Forge got back into production, Chrysler was hit at its Mack stamping plant with yet another work stoppage. This time,

William Gilbreth, a white member of the Progressive Labor Party, touched off the strike. Gilbreth had been fired for agitation to improve safety and health conditions the day before. He returned to the line at the Mack plant for his regular shift and sat down on the conveyer belt. When the plant protection people came to remove him, he struck a guard with a metal pipe. The plant shut down, as 200 workers in Gilbreth's department sat down with him. Soon Gilbreth was reading announcements to the press which emphasized the demands of the Workers Action Movement, a front organized by his party. Gilbreth stressed that he was an avowed communist and listed various party demands, including the generally popular call for a 30-hour work week. Only a few of the people who remained in the factory belonged to the Workers Action Movement, and many belonged to the International Socialist grouping and the United National Caucus, which were organizational rivals of WAM. Well-known militants, including Isaac Shorter, Larry Carter, Jerome Scott, Jordan Sims, John Taylor, and Pete Kelly, observed the action from outside the plant.

Fraser had said that "Chrysler lost its manhood" in the Shorter-Carter debacle, and what seemed like an unending plague of wildcats was not making the UAW look virile either. The newspapers spoke of "plant hijacking" and played up Gilbreth's overt radicalism. The police and the union sensed that it was a good opportunity for them to make a show of strength. Police Commissioner John Nichols, already a declared candidate for mayor, personally led a detachment of police into the Mack plant to arrest Gilbreth for striking the guard and to put an end to the sit-down. Fifteen workers, including Gilbreth, were arrested after some minor scuffling. The next morning, workers who wanted to keep the strike going were confronted at the plant gates by Doug Fraser, Irving Bluestone, Emil Mazey, and other top UAW executives backed up by a force of nearly 2,000 older or retired UAW loyalists. There was some fighting with local militants, but the sheer size of the union force guaranteed that the strike was over. It was a bitter day for many UAW members around town who remembered the fierce organizing drives of the 1930s. The old guard of the UAW had once led the same kind of flying squads to keep factories shut. Now, they had come full circle and saw the task of the union as seeing that the plants remained open. The inspector of the local police precinct thanked Doug

Fraser personally for his help and said it was great being on the same side. The daily media emphasized the role of radicals in each of the wildcats, and the *Detroit Free Press* went so far as to do an article on the various radical groups active in the factories. The sudden visibility of the groups was connected to a process that had been going on at least since the time of DRUM. As the radical white movement turned from a student orientation to a working-class orientation in the late 1960s, American radicals spoke of Detroit as being the Petrograd of the Second American Revolution. Virtually every Marxist group in the country sent some members to Detroit to organize workers in the auto factories. By and large, their methods were similar. Some members sold or gave away literature at the gate, while others entered the workforce inside and tried to take leadership roles in local struggles. By the summer of 1973, there were dozens of such groups in Detroit with hundreds of members in the factories.

True to their traditional viewpoints, the newspapers and union officials tried to blame the factory unrest on "outside agitators" rather than on the mammoth problems of safety, health, race, and alienation that faced the American industrial worker. Many of the workers remained confused about the causes of their problems; but some situations, such as the phenomenon of runaway factories, were clearly a result of the structure of American capitalism. Instead of renewing their capital investments in Detroit, the auto companies preferred to find safer surroundings. A few plants were set up in places like Lordstown in what was heralded as a decentralization program; but, far more frequently, new facilities were built in the South, where wages were lower and unionization lagged behind the rest of the country.

A typical example of a runaway plant was the Briggs Manufacturing Corporation. Once an independent giant in the auto parts industry whose owner also owned the Detroit baseball team and ran the ball park as a kind of civic duty, Briggs was purchased by Chrysler in 1953. Nineteen years later, Briggs workers learned that their factory was to be moved to Tennessee within a year. The workers were told that they were guaranteed a job if they moved to Tennessee, too, but their wages would be $2.40 an hour instead of the Detroit rate of $4.30. The stunned workers also learned that Tennessee had a "right-to-work" law which hampered union activity and that the state was granting Chrysler an interest-free loan of $6.5 million. The Detroit workers discovered that they would lose their pensions, group insurance benefits, job security, workman's compensation claims, and numerous other "fringe" benefits. The affected workers were not the "new" workers written about in scholarly journals, but people whose average age was 45 and who had an average of 20 years' seniority. Many of them came from white ethnic groups. One hundred and fifty of these workers organized to fight the company. The insurgents could get no action from the union, so they turned to radical labor attorneys John Taylor and Ron Glotta, who promptly took legal action to protect the workers' financial interests.

The workers' move to organize themselves and the link-up to the radicals finally drove the UAW to take action. It negotiated a "termination" agreement with the company. This agreement provided for deferred pensions to take effect at age 65 for employees with ten or more years' seniority and severance pay ranging from $450 for a worker with one year's seniority to $5,000 for a worker with 30 years' seniority. This represented a partial victory, but many of the Briggs workers were willing to take an all-or-nothing chance on going to court. The "termination" agreement negotiated by the UAW was approved only by a slim 39-vote margin, after a long and bitter debate. The courts then dismissed the workers' suit on the grounds that a judge could not interfere with a ratified collective-bargaining agreement between the company and the union.

On May 11, 1973, the Briggs workers voted out the Woodcock slate by a 2-1 margin in an election of local officers. On August 26, the rank and file voted unanimously to condemn the union leadership, particularly that of Local 212, for using a flying squad to break the strike at the Mack stamping plant. On September 5, the UAW's executive board voted to place the Briggs local in receivership, thus removing power from the newly elected shop committee. Forty Briggs workers appeared at Solidarity House, the national UAW headquarters, to back their stewards, but democracy did not prevail. It must have been a particularly sour day for Emil Mazey. Twenty-six years earlier, Mazey had personally led the most popular and forceful of all the union flying squads, the men of Briggs Local 212. Time had wrought many changes. As Gary Kapanowski, a spokesman for the workers whose father had also been a Briggs worker, observed to MCLL news reporters in November, "We at Briggs have received our master's degree in union-company collusion and right-wing politics. We will carry that knowledge with us in our new workplaces."

Wildcat summer and the agitation over the Briggs closing were indications that Chrysler workers were in a fighting mood. The UAW was not. It approached the 1973 contract negotiations determined to hold the line on all the accepted formulas. Once again, the union was more concerned about retirement benefits and other long-term gains than about improving current conditions or dissociating wage increases from higher productivity. Woodcock went so far as to say that a strike most likely would not be necessary. He was only partially correct. The UAW went through a token three-day walkout in late September before the leadership presented Chrysler workers with a contract that represented a fresh step backward with respect to control of the shop floor.

A hundred years after the massive nationwide drive for a 40-hour week, the UAW's major gain was a guaranteed 54-hour week! Legitimating once more the company's insatiable drive for higher production, the UAW agreed that its workers could *only* be scheduled to work nine hours a day, six days a week, with a qualified right to have every third Saturday off, and the absolute right to refuse work on Sunday. Relinquishing the struggle for the 40-hour week for another three years was bad enough, but the contract had numerous loopholes that made even those guarantees the union had obtained meaningless. A "critical plants" clause allowed the company to exempt key plants unilaterally, from the voluntary overtime rules for as long as three months. The company also won the right to suspend the voluntary overtime provisions for an entire plant for two weeks if any group of workers disrupted production by refusing overtime. Another clause required a worker to give notice of not wanting to work on a Saturday considerably in advance, and no worker who was absent on Mondays or Fridays was eligible to refuse such work. Thus, the contract actually served the company by helping it to hold down Monday and Friday absenteeism, a growing problem that often significantly reduced production in certain plants. Closely linked to the whole overtime question was the minuscule wage increase of 3 percent a year for the life of the contract. This was considerably less than the constantly rising rate of inflation and meant that workers would need to volunteer for more overtime than they had done in the past just to maintain their existing standards of living.

The UAW boasted that the 1973 contract contained the "30 and out" clause sought by older workers. According to the contract, a worker with 30 years' seniority could retire with a pension of $550 a month, a figure which would rise to $700 a month for workers retiring after 1978. This long-term retirement benefit, which did nothing to help active workers, was paid for by virtually no action on health, safety, and speed-up problems. The company did agree to more union representatives on the shop floor and to a revised grievance procedure. For the first time, there was formal recognition of Section 502 of the Labor Management Relations Act of 1947, which allowed workers to strike if a job were unsafe. It was this provision that the Eldon Safety Committee had cited to justify its work stoppages in May 1970. None of the men fired in that action were rehired, however; and it seemed unlikely that Chrysler's interpretation of Section 502 would coincide with that of wildcat strikers. The gain was more academic than substantial until tested in court by workers willing to risk their jobs in a confrontation with the company and the union. A major "hidden" defeat involved new workers. To begin with, these workers were to be paid 45 cents less an hour than other workers on the same job. The newcomers could still be fired at any time during the first 90 days, and only after they had worked for six months could they apply for the additional 45 cents an hour, which would he granted as a back-pay bonus. Since more than one-third of new workers were generally fired in the first 90 days, the "bonus" was, in fact, a pay cut for thousands of workers, a pay cut negotiated by the UAW, which still collected its initial fee and three months' dues directly from the workers' paychecks.

The established pattern in the auto industry for decades had been that agreements arrived at in one contract were more or less matched in the others. This proved to be the case in 1973, with the General Motors and Ford pacts following the Chrysler pattern. Each agreement was approved by the UAW's general membership, but there was a significant number of "no" votes. Dodge Main ratified the new contract 613-528. At the Jefferson Assembly plant and Eldon, a 33 percent "no" vote was recorded. The ratified national contract was backed up by local pacts dealing with individual plant grievances. The effectiveness of these local agreements depended upon the strength and militancy of the local union leadership. The overall pattern was unmistakable. Overtime amid deteriorating conditions and falling real wages remained the norm, as the union pursued a policy of helping older and retired workers at the expense of younger and active workers. Wage gains remained tied to increases in productivity, which, in effect, meant speed-up. The UAW had not gone so far as to volunteer a non-strike pact, but that seemed just around the corner.

The new contract, the election for mayor, and the murder rate were prime coffee-break topics in the fall of 1973 when Detroit workers got an unexpected boost from black Judge Damon Keith sitting in the Federal District Court. Judge Keith ruled that Detroit Edison had been guilty of discriminating against blacks. He punished the company by ordering it to pay more than $4 million and to change its employment practices at once. The payments ordered included payments to blacks who might have applied for work, as well as to those who actually had sought jobs. Detroit Edison took months to rally its forces. While moving to hire and upgrade black workers as fast as possible, the company retained William Rogers, formerly Richard Nixon's first secretary of state, to represent the utility in the court of appeals and in what seemed an inevitable Supreme Court test. The Keith decision opened the door to attacks on all companies systematically discriminating against any particular group. Just the threat of legal action and fines was sufficient in and of itself to make employers go easy on the "divide the races and rule" strategy that dominated so many American industries.

Auto workers were less excited by the Keith decision than radical activists were. The auto workers were most concerned about conditions in the plants, and the most typical reaction of an angry worker was direct action. At Ford Local 600, a militant union official shot at a skilled tradesman protesting the contract, and, a few months later, another Detroit foreman was killed by an irate worker in an incident reminiscent of the James Johnson case. The frustration over working conditions and overtime was suddenly augmented late in the year by even greater frustration over the prospect of having no work at all. The energy crisis, which struck the nation so unexpectedly, highlighted the economic dinosaurism of the auto industry. Consumers worried about the shortage of gasoline quit buying large, low-mileage cars like Pontiacs and Oldsmobiles. Sales of those lines fell by more than 50 percent, and Detroit auto makers began to retool to produce smaller, more economical cars. GM's announcement that it would produce a mini-Cadillac was the clearest sign that the industry was serious about decreasing car size. The auto industry had long depended on high-priced accessories, more powerful engines, and sheer size to maximize profits. Its new tactic was to make money on expensive safety features and anti-pollution devices, using the energy crisis and concern for ecology to keep attention away from prices. The long-term effects of the new emphasis on small cars seemed unlikely to include any basic change in industry profit patterns. The immediate effect on auto workers, however, was disastrous. During most of 1974, official unemployment in Michigan ran to more than 10 percent. In towns like Flint and Pontiac, where large-car production dominated, the unemployment rate was considerably higher and the hardship greater. Unemployment benefits alleviated some economic suffering; but galloping inflation, the prospect of being permanently without work, and the fact that thousands of workers were not eligible for various benefits cast a cloud of gloom over auto workers. Speed-up and the 54-hour week remained the order of the day, in spite of the cut-backs. More profits could still be made by working fewer and fewer workers harder and longer than by any other method.

2

Physically, Detroit has acquired freshness and vitality. Acres of slums have been razed, and steel-and-glass apartments—angular and lonely in the vacated landscape—have sprung up in their place. In the central business district, hard by the Detroit River, severely rectangular skyscrapers—none of them more than five years old—jostle uncomfortably with the gilded behemoths of another age.

—*National Observer*, July 15, 1963

Detroit had not changed much since the Great Rebellion. Wildcat summer had brought together white and black workers, the skilled and the unskilled, communists and anti-communists, but the mayoral election, street violence, and job insecurity had fed the old antagonisms with fresh fuel. The bleak Detroit winter hit with its usual cacophony of whining engines as the city ended 1973 by establishing several all-time records. Homicides reached a historic peak; car production reached a historic peak; and the earnings of General Motors reached a historic peak. Workers worried about wholesale layoffs just as the prices of fuel, food, and other necessities also reached all-time peaks. The Cotillion Club, an organization of Detroit's black elite, gave its 1973 awards to Judge George Crockett, Attorney Kenneth Cockrel, and Judge Damon Keith; yet all the basic problems facing black America festered as lethally as ever.

Carefully picking its way through the Detroit reality, the *U.S. News & World Report* of December 10 was enraptured by the latest plans for building a new Detroit, plans which, like the old plans for a new Detroit, concentrated on buildings, professional classes, and a narrow strip of waterfront. The heart of the new program was a $350 million Renaissance Center with hotels, luxury apartments, office buildings, and quality entertainment facilities to be built on the riverfront, directly to the east of Woodward Avenue. The showpiece of the center was to be a 70-story glass-encased hotel with 1,500 rooms. Four 30-story office towers with banks as major ground-floor tenants would share the complex with the hotel. Contributions for the center included $6 million from Ford, $6 million from GM, $1.5 million from Chrysler, $500,000 from American Motors, and smaller contributions from more than 30 Detroit firms. The hotel, offices, and projected apartment dwellings were to be serviced by a variety of shops, restaurants, and retail stores. Robert Hastings, a leading city architect, spoke of "recycling" American cities and was quoted in the magazine article as saying: "Detroit has always been thought of as a vibrant, can-do place. If you want to get something done, take this marvelous collection of technical people this city has. . . . Take the people and point them. The problem is to point them. This is what Henry Ford has done."

The enthusiasm of men like Hastings was similar to the enthusiasm that swept most American cities during the days of the New Frontier. In 1964, three years before the Great Rebellion, the Detroit Community Action Program had announced a total assault on poverty: "The overall objective in Detroit is to develop programs which will assist people in becoming self-sufficient and socially responsible citizens, generate participation in community life and the problems of others, and build into the lives of the impoverished the skills and aspirations necessary for useful and rewarding lives."

3

*. . . the grayness and the grit, the dirty funky, hardheavy city, home of
greasecake hands and the baddest right hook you've ever seen.*

detroit.

—b.p. Flanigan, "Freeway Series/1"

At 12:01 a.m., January 1, 1974, Detroit recorded its first homicide
of the year. Gerald H. Johnson, 46, was killed while standing on a corner by a bullet fired by someone celebrating the New Year with the Detroit custom of firing a gun. Two more homicides were recorded before
the sun came up. Karl Bestman, 73, was shot and killed by robbers as
he wiped snow off the windshield of his car. The body of the third victim, Johnnie Harper, 25, was found in an east-side apartment after her
neighbors reported hearing gunfire.

Along the darkened streets of the city, the squad cars of the Detroit Police Department passed the 2,500 abandoned homes and 5,000
empty houses taken over by the Federal Housing Administration,
whose program to halt urban decay and abandonment had become
mired in corruption and discredited by questionable decision-making.
The squad cars passed supermarkets whose huge glass windows had
been bricked over ever since the Great Rebellion and whose entrances
had been sealed off by metal posts to prevent people from stealing
shopping carts. The Goodyear sign by the Ford-Chrysler interchange
had already begun to crank out the new year's car production.

During their lunch break the next day, many Detroit workers discussed a new, black-owned professional football team to be called the
Detroit Wheels. It was to replace the Detroit Lions, which had moved
to Pontiac to be nearer the suburban audience. Later that afternoon,
there was an accident at the Eldon Avenue Gear and Axle plant.

A week later, Mayor Coleman Young made a glittering populist de-
but at an inaugural ball attended by 15,000 people. Diana Ross came
back home from Hollywood to be the featured entertainer, and the national media spotlighted Mayor Young as he said, "I issue a warning
now to all dope pushers, ripoff artists, and muggers. It is time to leave
Detroit. Hit the road!" A photo in the *New York Times* showed a con-

cerned mayor listening to Leonard Woodcock, president of the UAW, whisper in his ear as a beaming Henry Ford II spoke from a micro-phone-studded podium about Renaissance Center.

The rebels and revolutionaries you have read about in this book were not involved in the inaugural. Most of them were now in their late twenties and early thirties. They continued to pursue their own vision of a new Detroit.

Chapter 11

Thirty Years Later

The founders of the League of Revolutionary Black Workers came of age in the manufacturing center of the world's greatest industrial power. By the mid-1960s, they understood that the industrialists and financiers who had reshaped America in the early twentieth century had begun to abandon the regions and the populations that had made them so wealthy and powerful. The era of chronic underemployment, factory relocations, and deteriorating work conditions had begun. Hit hardest was the African-American working class, which had begun to score significant gains in the 1940s and 1950s but was still denied the benefits, status, and opportunities of other workers.

The League sought assistance from the traditional sword and shield of labor, the trade union movement and the government. They discovered that the United Auto Workers had purged itself of the radicals who had made the UAW such a dynamic force in the 1930s and 1940s. The UAW was now largely in a defensive posture, preoccupied with preserving the gains already won rather than seeking new advances. Verbal and financial support was given to the civil rights movement, but the UAW had done very little to empower African Americans in its own ranks.

City government, which had been so vital to the gains of labor and immigrants in the past, was increasingly characterized by law-and-order rhetoric that often seemed little more than camouflaged racism. In similar fashion, state government, which had occasionally been responsive to organized labor, had embarked on policies that would economically isolate the city of Detroit from the rest of the state. The same pattern was in place nationally. While allocating endless millions of dollars to prosecute the war in Vietnam, national government skimped on funding for desperately needed assistance to the nation's industrial base.

Like the counter-culture rebels of the time, who were mainly white college students, the League founders understood the role played by mass media and other organs of the dominant culture. These institutions posed political issues in terms that guaranteed the only logical outcomes must be negative for working people, black or white. One of the League founders was only half-joking when he counseled, "Read the *New York Times*, and then assume the opposite is true until otherwise proven."

With an analysis of work, class, and culture in place, the League embarked on the organizing initiatives we have chronicled in the preceding pages. The League's multifaceted approach, while often criticized as overly ambitious, was an attempt to create the foundation required for significant change to be possible. This perspective remains accurate 30 years later. What should disturb all Americans is that the analysis the League's founders offered regarding the future of the auto industry, the UAW, the city of Detroit, and African Americans now applies increasing to the nation as a whole.

At the time the League was formed, auto executives made approximately 25 times the salary of the average auto worker. By the 1980s, they made 45 times as much—and, by 1996, 145 times as much. What was true for auto executives was true for corporate executives as a class. This enormous economic chasm between workers and employers was a new phenomenon in the United States and unique in advanced industrial societies, being four to five times greater than the ratios found in Germany and Japan, our two major economic rivals. In the same 30-year period that executive pay exploded, the buying power of the average worker declined by some 20 percent. In 1996, John Sweeney, the new president of the AFL-CIO, launched an America Needs A Raise campaign, rightly noting that real wages had not increased since the 1960s. Perhaps that explains why executives have been so well rewarded.

In fact, economic power in the United States is now concentrated as never before in our history. The wealthiest 1 percent of all Americans owns 40 percent of the national wealth; the next wealthiest 19 percent owns another 40 percent. Thus, 20 percent of all Americans own 80 percent of the national wealth. In addition, the wealthiest 20 percent also pockets 55 percent of the nation's annual after-tax income. Further aggravating economic unfairness is the fact that payroll taxes, property taxes, sales taxes, and other taxes borne by the average American have risen dramatically, while the corporate share of taxes and the taxes paid by the richest Americans have declined dramatically. Consequently, for the first time in American history, parents are beginning to realize that their children will likely have a lower standard of living than they have enjoyed. More often than not, both adults in a household must work to maintain the quality of life that formally could be provided by one wage-earner. Increasingly, more students graduate from college to begin their earning years encumbered with huge loans, while retired Americans afflicted with a chronic disease have to impoverish themselves in order to secure government aid. For ethnic groups who face discrimination, conditions are even grimmer.

This is indeed a new world order. When pundits speak of biting the bullet or tightening the belt, it is the average American who ends up being bitten and squeezed. The problem is not that the capitalist system has ceased to function effectively, but that it has worked all too well in the interests of those at the very top. They have served their own interests with considerable skill, maximizing profits by lowering their financial commitment to workers, their obligations to the environment, and even their commitment to "national interests." The sequences the League used to dramatize this reality in the film *Finally Got the News* remain valid.

The AFL-CIO had its first contested election for national officers in 1995. The victorious New Voice slate soon announced that it was determined to put an end to the 40-year decline in its membership and power. A key change would be to vigorously confront racism in the union movement. African Americans and other ethnic groups systematically excluded from key policy positions in the past would be brought into the leadership. Not least of the reasons advanced for these changes was the understanding that the gender and ethnic composition of the working class had changed significantly since the successful organizing of the New Deal era, but that change was not reflected in the composition of the leadership. Thirty years earlier, the League had offered the same analysis and similar proposals for inclusion. Whether genuine reform will indeed take place remains to be seen. If another 30 years are lost, the trade union movement, as we have known it, may cease to exist.

Nevertheless, American trade unions, with all their shortcomings, remain the most powerful democratic force with a national presence and a national agenda. American trade unions show every sign of wanting to regain their lost dynamism. What is not clear is whether or not that movement remembers what it takes to win. The long newspaper strike in Detroit is emblematic of the crisis at hand. Here was a strike in one of the most pro-union and liberal cities in America. The striking unions were militant and reasonably well organized. Other unions were genuinely interested in a victory and gave significant financial support. The corporate foe was a national newspaper, not a mighty transnational. But two years into the struggle, workers felt compelled to accept the terms they had originally struck against, only to have the publishers respond that not all the strikers would be rehired. This humiliating scenario occurred in the home city of the UAW! If such treatment could be meted out in Detroit, what hope was there for success in less militant cities?

The Detroit labor movement had lost touch with the tactics that had brought victory over General Motors in Flint in 1938 and over Ford at River Rouge in 1939, the tactics the League had revived at Dodge Main and Eldon Avenue Gear and Axle. But future struggles will require even more daring, inventiveness, and grit. Transnational corporations now possess war chests, mobility, media power, and political clout even the first generation of Rockefellers, Fords, and Vanderbilts would have envied. Factories can now be moved across international borders; and international agreements can be subverted by corporations in the way factories were once moved across state lines and local law was subverted. Trade unions will need to devise a comparable international strategy. This was a reality the League had understood in the late 1960s when it met with representatives of Italian auto workers based in Turin to exchange organizational lore and consider possible joint projects.

Strategies for reforming even local government have also become more complex. Despite occasional victories and achievements, if one compares Detroit of the 1960s with Detroit of the 1990s, the city has deteriorated. Where once white neighborhoods at the city's rim surrounded a mainly black inner city, primarily white suburbs now surround a primarily black metropolis. The Renaissance Center, widely heralded in the 1970s as the engine for revitalizing the city, has proven a disaster. A few short blocks from Ren Cen, the J.L. Hudson Department Store, occupying a full square block and once the crown jewel of downtown commerce, remains a deserted shell surrounded by block after block of boarded buildings. From the onset, Ren Cen had remained viable on paper only because considerable staff from Ford headquarters in Dearborn had been transferred to fill its office space. Built at the cost of $350 million in the 1970s, Ren Cen was sold in 1996 to the General Motors Corporation for $73 million. GMC planned to move its staff from its midtown headquarters, while Ford's staff would return to Dearborn, resulting in an immediate net loss of Detroit jobs. The viability of the midtown business district around the historic GMC Building being vacated was another concern for local politicians.

The failure of Detroit to revive and rebuild after the Great Rebellion in 1967 is often attributed to the mercurial mayoralty of Coleman Young or some lacking in the city's 80 percent black population. The explanation, however, lies elsewhere. For decades now, we have seen the conscious abandonment of cities by state and federal government. This malign neglect is visible throughout the nation. The quixotic and illusory pursuit of lower taxes has masked the gutting of the industrial heartland and the sacrificing of the needs of millions of Americans to corporate greed. The latest evolution of this scenario is the calculated assault on public education, with teachers and their unions targeted as the major causes for the deterioration of a system that was once the pride of American democracy.

The role of dominant media in how we remember the past or project plans for the future is critical. In the 1990s, the corporate media is more shameless than ever in its lowering of national expectations and destructive framing of critical issues. When French workers took to the streets in 1996 to defend long vacations, livable pensions, and early retirement, Americans were informed by the media that the French had lost their senses. The implication was that sensible workers should demand shorter vacations, smaller pensions, and delayed retirement.

Every national issue is presented in a manner that makes all possible options unfavorable for working Americans. We are told Social Security is in trouble because soon there will be too few active workers to support retired workers. Left unexamined is why Social Security has to be funded by a payroll tax at all. A few pennies of tax on the millions of shares traded hourly in the stock markets or a small percentage increase in corporate taxes would easily take care of any shortfall and could actually lower the share now being paid by workers. No national pundits observe that since the Social Security funds have been used to fund other parts of the government, reversing the process would be fair and logical if Social Security is in financial trouble. Instead, the discussion is framed to foster generational conflict from which images of greedy old geezers and callous youngsters soon emerge. Rather than suggesting we might consider economic security in old age an inalienable right that government ought to promote, the media speaks scornfully of entitlements. Means testing is then advocated as a just method of dispersing government aid, further dividing wage sectors, creating yet another bureaucracy, and confusing human rights with charity.

The continuing dynamic of race relations encapsulates the economic, political, and cultural mindset of a society based on a model of economic scarcity. Rather than discuss the necessity of equal opportunity in any society that considers itself democratic, attention is diverted to mechanisms which by their very nature are divisive: affirmative action, privatized mass education, special electoral districts, user fees, means testing, and the like. Rare is the option offered that would lift all Americans. In the matter of higher education, for example, rather than promote divisive schemes to allocate limited slots in what must always artificially privilege one or another sector of the population, enough slots should be funded for all who qualify, a prudent investment in the most precious of all national resources.

In our view, the nation is being herded in exactly the wrong direction. We need more socializing of resources rather than more privatizing, a more rigorous progressive income tax rather than regressive flat taxes or payroll taxes, increased health and Social Security coverage rather than restrictions enforced by higher fees and means testing. The new technology at hand needs to be utilized on behalf of workers rather than against them. Appropriate goals would include reducing the hours of labor, slowing the volume and pace of production, and increasing disposable income. We need less of the economic chaos generated by speculative markets and more of the stability offered by democratic planning. The nation desperately needs a new vision and a new kind of leadership.

In the 1960s, the League of Revolutionary Black Workers was part of a massive political movement that took up that challenge. The League put its finger on all the hot buttons and had the courage to push them. Many of the strategies advanced by the League remain viable or could be adapted to address current conditions. It understood that mistreated groups must organize independently to get redress for their grievances. The League did not exist long enough to shape the means to realize those needs within the broader class context they also advocated. That organizational task remains. But the League understood that problems would not be solved until their root causes were defined. It further understood that any direct challenge to the economic elites must be accompanied by an assault on the cultural institutions that promote their interests.

The League of Revolutionary Black Workers asked black workers what they were prepared to do when they finally understood how their dues were really being used. We echo that query by asking what the average working American is prepared to do when he or she finally comprehends how our resources, taxes, and goodwill are being used. Americans are being offered nineteenth-century solutions to third-millennium problems, solutions which have always had disastrous consequences.

Soon, Detroit will be celebrating its 300th birthday, an event that is generating considerable enthusiasm in the city and even some hope that real renewal might at last be at hand. Detroit has served as a metaphor for much that is wrong in America during the second half of the twentieth century, just as it once served as a metaphor for much that was positive in America. But Detroit is much more than a metaphor. Detroit is a real place where real people live. Throughout this nation, Americans living in numerous cities and regions are facing the same problems that have beset Detroit. Like the Detroiters we have written about, these Americans do not mind working, but they definitely do mind dying.

Chapter 12

The Legacy of DRUM: Four Histories

Sheila Murphy Cockrel

To this day, the League's role in opening up the United Auto Workers' leadership to people of color and focusing the UAW on racial issues remains unheralded. The League leaders were visionary, and I don't mean just my husband. I mean all of them. They understood that if the UAW and craft unions did not genuinely open up their organizations, other opportunities to advance would not follow either for those unions or for African Americans.

When conventional politicians, historians, and unionists talk about seminal groups of that time, they don't acknowledge the League. Coleman Young's autobiography doesn't mention them once. I think that's a testimony to how much they feared the League and the movement the League represented.

Ignoring Ken's particular contributions hasn't been so easy. Ken is still vivid in the memories of people who are 40 and older. That age group remains aware of what he and those associated with him did to change the local legal system. I still go to meetings where people will come up afterwards to tell me how Ken helped them in one way or another, and they will say, "We were cheated. He should have become our mayor." Well, that was not to be. Nonetheless, a decade after his death, people still feel his presence in the political culture of this city. Ken Cockrel is remembered as a leader who stood up for justice in all its dimensions. I think the League is remembered in the same way.

What the state legislature wants is to undo some of the gains we made. Right now, they are seeking to integrate Recorder's Court into a circuit court that will take in all of Wayne County. That would include Dearborn, the Grosse Pointe communities, Romulus, and other cities whose racial and class composition is different than Detroit's. Judges would have to run countywide. More significant would be the change in the composition of juries. Right now, we have predominantly black juries that routinely give guilty verdicts followed by incredibly tough sentences to criminals who commit crimes in and against their communities. These same verdicts and sentences by racially mixed or predominantly white juries could send a different message and will almost surely inflame racial sentiments regarding crime. I think this is a very treacherous road. Ken had foreseen this before he died. He predicted there would be an effort to terminate the independent status of Recorder's Court and make it part of a circuit as in the rest of the state, as if Detroit is like the rest of the state.

President Clinton has called for "a national dialogue on race." On the surface, that's a positive and needed initiative. But this is not an issue to be played with. You can't pretend. You can't do politics with it. Racism is a core issue for America. I face it every day in my personal and political life. My ethnic background is Irish and my experience in Detroit has been that Irish people are either very progressive on race issues or to the right of Attila the Hun. I've been reading about Irish immigration and the process by which a people who were opposed to slavery have become "white" and taken on the standard "white" prejudices. My own parents were grounded in a different ethical tradition. They were the Catholic Worker movement here in Detroit. I was brought up in that perspective. What I see now is that everything I do and say on the political scene is viewed through a racial lens, whatever the race, gender, or ethnicity of the person with whom I am in contact. That's a reality.

I am a mother of a child of mixed racial heritage. She tells me, "Mom, I love you very much, but I feel more African American." That's perfectly fine with me. My responsibility to her is to make both of her heritages available to her and let her choose whatever she wants of each to shape and create her personality. Those choices are hers.

What disturbs me to the core of my being is that so many children don't get to make any real choices about the course of their lives. We've had two to three generations of children growing up in a world where they were afraid, unsafe, and at war. That's unacceptable to me. I find it unacceptable that we cannot create jobs for everyone who wants to work. I find it unacceptable that we cannot properly prepare people for work. I find it unacceptable that we still have homeless people. My parents took in and fed the homeless. They would be appalled at the scale the homeless problem has attained.

I am disheartened by what some people at the local level define as political activism. They will go to a meeting to complain and to blame: "I am being victimized. I'm not getting this or that." The blame is on "you people," with "you people" always being some other racial group. I'm all for voicing grievances, but that's only a beginning. Without a vision of how to make change and without a vision of what should replace the existing system, grievances largely go unaddressed or are treated with Band-Aids. The movements that began in the mid-1950s and extended into the 1970s provided that kind of vision, and I think that is why we were perceived as truly radical. We went to the root of our problems.

My personal core of values has not changed very much. They were the foundation of my life with Ken and of my life since. I still want a world where economic health is defined as meeting the needs of people, not corporations. I still demand a world where color doesn't matter and where people have access to opportunity. I'm for all those things that were associated with the League and its allies. The main changes in my thinking are that I have less patience for those who only talk about problems and more patience for those who want to do something positive, even if what they want to do differs from what I prefer. For decades, I've listened to ivory-tower, pie-in-the-sky purists who end up doing nothing to help this city and its people. I think progressives have got to step up to the plate and offer some answers for here and now and not wait for some distant perfect revolutionary moment.

So, I am a socialist who supports a new way of organizing public housing, a new way of running the Detroit Institute of Arts, the introduction of casino gambling, and a new sports complex. For some of my critics, this means I've given up on the old visions. What I see are imperfect solutions to a desperate situation. Let's take public housing. Purists want the same massive public housing as in the past. But how in the hell can we honestly argue that what we have now ought to be maintained? Public housing has gotten worse and worse, and the daily life of people in that housing has deteriorated. So, I support the concept of public housing on a smaller physical scale with greatly reduced density. These urban villages could provide a climate in which families could function and even prosper. I have colleagues who say, "no, no, no." They believe we are selling out the New Deal and the Great Society. But those programs only went so far, and part of what they were about doesn't work. So, we've got to adjust our thinking. We've got to get out of those old boxes, even righteous lefty boxes. Often I find the Left vigorously defending some liberal compromise or even some grotesque entity the Right has made out of what began as a radical concept, as if the current mess is what the reforms were about in the first place.

We are struggling to maintain the Detroit Institute of Arts, which is often cited as being the fifth most important art collection in the United States. We've fashioned a new governing body that includes suburbanites who want to support the institution in every way possible, including financial support. Some critics deride this as privatization. What I see is that the city is going to save a lot of money while the DIA is refurbished physically and its collection enhanced. The city of Detroit, a city with an 80 percent African-American population, will remain the total and only owner of the collection, the building, and the land. The city is also legally guaranteed that residents of Detroit will make up 33 percent of the board of directors, 25 percent of the executive board, and 58 percent of the staff. This arrangement allows us to maintain a prime city asset, a destination asset if you will, while having more money to keep the lights on in the neighborhood. Those who say this is not good asset management need to give us an alternative. Do we let the building and collection continue to decay due to lack of funds? Or do we let the city decay while we preserve the museum?

Rhetoric will not solve problems. Nostalgia for the good old days, whenever they were supposed to have been, won't do either. Capital raped and pillaged the industrial centers of our nation for decades and now it has walked away, abandoning the cities and the structures and the workers that sustained it. Economic decisions are being made in a global context in which the interests of even a nation-state as powerful as America are not the prime concern. As the century ends, we see a profound redefinition of work, a total rearrangement of communications, and the addition of generational tension to the evil old brews of race, gender, and class division. Any plan for revitalizing a city or creating new jobs and industries has to be put in that context. Tough as the task is, we can have an effect at the local level. We can act so that as few people as possible are hurt or left out of this new economic reality. The greater representation and involvement of women and minorities is one way to realize the goal of thinking globally but acting locally. We have to put our hands on some levers of power and show people that we can affect daily life in a positive fashion.

These issues come into play when we turn to the revitalization of Detroit. We need to create a downtown Detroit that is a destination. Northwest Airlines will soon offer non-stop flights from Asia. Given the linkage of Asians to the automobile industry, why can't Detroit be a place where they relax, as well as do business? Why should they take a Lear jet to Las Vegas or cross the river to gamble in Windsor? To tear down unrehabilitatable housing in Detroit, housing that is a cancer on our development, we need $23 million. Where is that money going to come from? We see $1 million a day go to Windsor, which offers state-sponsored gambling. I'd like to have that money stay on this side of the river, even if it goes to private enterprise. The tax revenue, jobs, and hotel traffic would be of enormous assistance. I think a sports complex is another aspect of that same entertainment picture.

I am perfectly willing to admit these are not elegant or traditional answers to economic problems. I believe all of us must understand that we don't have the only set of answers and that we will make mistakes. But we can't sit on the sidelines and grouse. We have to offer realistic solutions and immediate relief to the working people of the city of Detroit.

I think we would have better answers and more systematic answers if we could return to some of the better organizational models of the late 1960s and early 1970s. Nothing can replace a core group with a shared view of the world, a shared commitment to political action, a shared sense of urgency, and a shared assurance that each and every member will do whatever is politically necessary. A shared agenda or a shared response to a personality is the not same as shared convictions.

As critics of how this society is structured, we must understand that, more often than not, we are going to be on the margins. In one way or another, even if we are occasionally in the spotlight, we are going to be outsiders. To survive, we have to hold on to our core values, find ways to pass those values on to others, and struggle to realize them to the degree possible in this time and in this place.

Herb Boyd

My memories of the League are part of a somewhat misty but halcyon past, a time when I was coming of age in the city and attending Wayne State University, a time when we waged struggles on the cultural and political fronts to eradicate the widespread injustice and racism that constricted our lives. I recall the efforts to rid the city of STRESS (Stop the Robberies, Enjoy Safe Streets), the police decoy unit that wrecked havoc in Detroit's inner city, exterminating young black lives with a ruthless disregard for human life. I recall DRUM, the Dodge Revolutionary Union Movement, which for a moment was a wellspring of hope for thousands of downtrodden workers. I remember James Johnson, a factory worker defended by Kenny Cockrel after the pressures of the job drove him to murder a plant foreman. I remember how Judge Justin Ravitz would preside with his cowboy boots peeping out from underneath his judicial robes. But there is little need to ruminate on the virtues and value of that time. The book you have in your hands deals with those issues. What is of more importance is to reflect on the lessons that can be drawn from those times and from our lives since those times.

Ironically, when I was approached to contribute an essay to this new edition of *Detroit: I Do Mind Dying*, I had recently returned from a meeting in Chicago at which a number of black radicals had convened to see what could be done to revive the "Left." You might call it the 45 club, since that was about the total attendance and the median age. Most exciting for me was to see activists at the meeting who were publicly antagonistic, a few so ideologically at odds that one waited for the fireworks; but those fireworks did not materialize. It was also encouraging to have the opportunity to renew some old acquaintances, both among the nationalists and the Marxists, many of them advocates of political positions so bitterly opposed in the early 1970s that it disrupted the remnants of the black liberation movement, thereby ending any possibility of operational unity. As one participant put it, "The narrow nationalists met the mechanical Marxists and suddenly the internal contradictions outweighed the external ones."

Consequently, it came as little surprise when we assembled in smaller units at the conference that the agenda included discussion of a few problems that had derailed us in the past. In several ways, this planning session envisioning a future summit was but a larger version of the study group I had joined a year or so earlier. We had examined these topics to the point of boredom, but here were some new voices. I was curious to know how they would grapple with such issues as whether socialism has any relevance to the economic and social realities of contemporary America, or if the Marxist theory of class analysis effectively accounted for race and gender issues. Moreover, and perhaps the burning question for the gathering, was it possible for a group from very distinctive political backgrounds—democratic socialists, revolutionary nationalists, radical feminists, and leftist trade union and labor activists—to constructively revive the old principle of "unity without uniformity" and find strengths in their differences?

The fact that such a disparate gaggle of radical intellectuals, artists, and activists could sit still long enough to consider their collective plight was itself a step in the right direction and was so perceived by all present. Delegates to the conference, such as the members of my study group in New York City, had a mutual interest in curtailing the increasing influence of conservative black leaders and jackleg demagogues who mislead people with their opportunistic rhetoric. Consensus also emerged about the recent elections and the rightward drift of the Democratic Party. People were particularly disturbed by attacks on affirmative action, proposals for a "zero immigration" policy, and Draconian welfare reform measures, making the so-called safety net about as reliable as having a rabbit deliver lettuce.

The general assault on the poor, high unemployment, the lack of decent housing, and the rampant spread of police brutality were not only critical topics at the Chicago conference, but examples of the social and political malaise that is gradually creating the conditions that make organized resistance inevitable. Beyond the conference and the study group, I am encouraged by the number of organizations taking to the streets protesting against a racist criminal justice system and the "prison-industrial complex," angered by politicians who make big promises and then disappear until reelection time, and tired of an inefficient educational system, corrupt cops, and deteriorating urban centers. In this age, when so many people are seeking communities, whether in the marketplace or cyberspace, it is good to know the veterans of the Civil Rights Movement and the activists who came of age in the fight against apartheid are not mired in the cynicism that was so prevalent just a decade ago.

Signs of renewed optimism and a desire to struggle against injustice and social abuses are everywhere. More and more interest is being given to international events. People are concerned once again about the situation in Asia, Latin America, and Africa, especially in the central part of the continent that is enduring a horrific refugee tragedy in the wake of the decline and fall of the dictatorship in Zaire (now Congo). Dialogue has intensified around immigration issues. The turmoil in Haiti and Cuba is being addressed by humanitarian groups that have reported on the crippling effects on the Cuban people of the embargo against the Castro government.

New political formations are popping up all over the place, many of them demanding alternatives to the traditional political parties. Activity in the unions is much more hopeful than it was in the 1980s when Reagan smashed the air traffic controller's union. The emergence of a more active rank and file in the Teamsters, UAW, and numerous AFL-CIO unions is further indication that the take-it-for-granted stagnation of organized labor will no longer be tolerated. Even airline pilots and well-paid athletes are galvanized, demanding higher salaries and better contracts.

In an article in *New Politics*, the noted African-American scholar Robin Kelley has noted:

> During the past couple of years at least, we've witnessed an intensification of class-based opposition to inequality, falling wages, and the overall erosion of working-class life in the United States. Of course, we're far from the intense labor struggles of say 1877 or 1935 or 1946, but there are incredibly hopeful signs of movement—from the resurrection of the old AFL-CIO under John Sweeney, Linda Chavez-Thompson, and Richard Trumka, the response to union summer, to the founding of the Labor Party, the New Party, and other progressive

third party formations. In fact, even the language of populism now permeating much of American political discourse shows flashes of class analysis, if not outright embrace of class struggle: it's "us against them"; time to end "corporate welfare as we know it"; we are engaged in nothing less than a "class war."

All of this indicates that while many of the goals and objectives of the League of Revolutionary Black Workers may have been undeveloped and much too audacious for the times, many of them are now vital components in groups and organizations far less radical than the League. Consider the number of flourishing book clubs hosting authors and helping to mold a more literate society. The League's achievements in that area are a model. That the League used book projects partly as study groups and partly as organizing tools that successfully attracted white liberals distinguishes it from most of today's book and reading clubs and indicates a path activists might wish to follow.

The League recognized the importance of using the media, a lesson learned by hundreds of activist journalists weaned at the *Inner City Voice* and the *South End*. Helping to edit the *Voice* and writing for the *South End* was one connection, albeit indirect, that I had with the League. A more direct association came through the interaction I had with students when I was a Black Studies instructor at Wayne State University. Many of the students were members of the League. There were even a few with whom I'd worked during my short tenure at Dodge Main auto plant. The students, with their working-class outlook and analysis, helped hone the curriculum and enliven the discussions. Education was stressed by the League and the students were "all fired up" to learn.

My task was made easier one year when Gloria House, David Rambeau, and Ernie Mkalimoto (now Allen) team-taught a course with me. Ernie was also director of political education for the League, and I gained a deeper insight on black history working by his side. His summary of the rise and fall of the League can be found in *They Should Have Served That Cup of Coffee*, a collection of essays by 1960s activists edited by Dick Cluster. That essay remains one of the best dialectical assessments of the League.

Culture—the visual arts, music, theater, literature, and film—was the realm where I felt most useful and this area, too, was something the League promoted, both individually and collectively. Young filmmakers today, especially those interested in documentary, can learn about the craft from viewing *Finally Got the News*, a film produced and edited by the League with the assistance of a mainly white production staff. The film, widely circulated in the movement and shown in several European countries, became a primer for organizations and individuals engaged in political activity who sought to discover how working-class theory and practice could be applied to an emergent revolutionary situation in black America.

Another tangible aspect of the League's impact can be gauged in the continuing political work of General Baker and Marian Kramer. Both were League stalwarts, and they remain as committed as ever to a life free of racism and oppression. Similar to the advocacy of the Coalition of Black Trade Unionists and Black Workers for Justice, Baker and Kramer of the Communist Labor Party have been unstinting in their push for full employment and their opposition to the nefarious welfare reform bill.

The League's attempt to stimulate a mass reaction to race and class oppression was only minimally achieved. What may be its most practical and visible legacy was realized through electoral politics, primarily the successful candidacies of Justin Ravitz for judge and Ken Cockrel for a seat on the Common Council, which followed the League's success in leading the fight against STRESS. Cockrel was in a good position to win the mayoralty before his sudden death from a heart attack at age 51.

To some extent, the spirit of the League, particularly its direct challenge to the status quo, can be seen in the massive rallies in support of Mumia Abu-Jamal, the defiant journalist who has been on death row for more than 15 years on what many believe are trumped-up charges and after what was certainly an unfair trial. The Million Man March, despite its narrow focus on atonement, also captured some of the League's "in-your-face" bravado. But these events are fraught with the same problems that plagued the League—the failure to create a larger political agenda that would have impact and meaning beyond the immediate objective. There is a critical need today to have a full and open dialogue of a kind that did not occur in the past. Otherwise, differences metastasize and debilitate a movement or activity. An inability to give voice to its contradictions hampered the League's growth and development. In an interview published in Bob Mast's *De-*

troit Lives, Mike Hamlin observed, "The leadership never wanted a full airing of all of the issues. I'm not saying that I'm any less guilty than anybody else. But at no time in any of these splits do I recall a situation where people wanted to have a battle of ideas in front of the membership and let the membership decide."

Even so, the League of Revolutionary Black Workers looms as a metaphor in my life, a promising political moment that was part of the era's belief that a revolution was right around the corner. We were young men and women then, full of hope and convinced of our power to change things, to remove the wretched conditions that often made life a living Hell. We did not succeed, but, to the degree that we have learned from some of our follies, we did not fail. Frantz Fanon once hypothesized, "Each generation, out of relative obscurity, is doomed to either fulfill its mission or betray it." I believe we neither fulfilled our mission nor betrayed it. We are still giving it our best shot.

Edna Ewell Watson

My association with the League profoundly affected my subsequent political activities in ever-changing ways. For purposes of economic and political survival, after all the splits were completed and the dust settled, I leaned toward marginalizing and minimizing my League years. I had been terrified at the levels of surveillance we experienced. We were followed, our phones were tapped, our mail was intercepted, our passports were stolen. There were visits by the FBI, particularly during the filming of *Finally Got the News*. Until then, I had, like most of the comrades, evinced a rather cavalier attitude about how far the government would go to stop us. The casualness of the FBI and the FBI's animosity was similar to that of the Klan. Their visits and interrogations were intimidating and chilling. I decided that protecting all the world's children, starting with mine, was equal in importance to protecting the revolution.

As a hospital nurse, I had developed many contacts with doctors and nurses involved in the Medical Committee for Human Rights. I had spent time in the spring of 1970 with Angela Davis and the hospital-employee members of the Che-Lumumba Collective in Los Angeles. I was more politically interactive with health professionals than with my immediate comrades in the League. My house was one of the home bases for the movement and that suited my personality. By housing hungry and traveling comrades, I had the luxury of contributing to the struggle while fulfilling my goal of having children. But increasingly I identified with the women's movement. I understood that gender issues needed articulation with my spouse if we were to remain together and gender issues needed articulation within the League if it was to achieve its agenda of liberation.

The League influenced many of those who served as the backbone and linchpin of Coleman Young's administration. While many of us disagreed with some things Coleman did, in 1973 we had come together as the League to support his campaign. He had mentored some of us through his endeavors in the Freedom Now Party and thus represented a continuum of left-based struggles for black liberation. Most of us continued to support him until he decided he no longer wanted to hold those positions of public leadership.

By the mid-1970s, radical black feminism was already a major factor in my political thinking. I had become a single parent with four children and had little contact with my old comrades. My immediate need was to get a permanent home and a modicum of economic independence. I saw Ken Cockrel regularly between 1978 and 1981 because I lived next door to his son. I focused on preparing my children for survival in a hostile society and trying to protect my sons from an America determined to cast all black men as the designated suspect. Unfortunately, I lost my son Che to violence and racism in 1990.

In 1976, I became the superviser of Communities United for Action (CUFA), one of the last of the local CETA-funded organizations. We were based in Highland Park, whose urban blight had begun to surpass Detroit's. Most of my work was with seniors and the unemployed. I also worked nights as a vocational nurse at Harper Hospital, but there were no longer any radical doctors or nurses with whom to organize. I began to realize what a force the League had been. With all its flaws, the League represented the closest America ever came to having a unified and functional black left cadre organization.

In 1977, CUFA sponsored a program with American Black Artists to showcase the works of black painters, sculptors, musicians, and dancers. Representative John Conyers had been successful in getting funds through the National Endowment for the Arts. Many of the artists coalesced to form the Consortium of Black Artists. To my surprise, I was selected chair. Our goal was to build political support for continued public support of the arts. By then I considered myself to be a doctrinaire Marxist-Leninist who was also a worker, a black feminist, a recovering Christian, and a recovering anarchist. I became involved in study groups that discussed Malcolm, interracial marriages, the Venceremos Brigades, and the role of women in society.

Later, I was the administrator of the Pioneer Jazz Orchestra and worked with Dan Aldridge, Sam Sanders, Oscar Brown, Jr., and Marcus Belgrave to develop the first blending of spirituals and jazz in Detroit. We put together benefits, including one for the National Conference of Black Lawyers. I also worked on the board that placed the first metal sculpture by an African American in the Renaissance Center. I was active in arts publications, the Detroit Jazz Center, and the People's Creative Ensemble. At this time, I came to share a home with Ivy Riley, a single mother who was a member of the Glotta law firm and the Communist Labor Party. While sharing this home, our children were nannied by Peter Wenger, a red-diaper baby and jazz musician from New York. Peter, who has since become an M.D., talked to me about the wider radical community's view of the League activities as awesome at times but also somewhat reckless and doctrinaire.

In the 1980s, I finally obtained a B.A. in Journalism, Marketing, and Public Relations and then an M.A. in Library Science. In 1988, I became a professor at Eastern Michigan University. Like Trotsky had been, I am a librarian. After one too many conversations that included "you people/those people" rhetoric, I decided to obtain a second M.A. in Women's Studies, raising hell about sexism and racism all the way. For a time, I was elected to the Faculty Council. I became involved in mentoring students and junior faculty struggling with the bureaucracy. I have assisted minority students and mostly white welfare recipients in staying in school and fighting as a group. I like to practice civil disobedience whenever I can. One time, when Gloria Steinem was speaking on campus, they refused to let some 200 or so students and faculty in to see her. I snuck in through the back doors of the auditorium and flung them open. The frustrated crowd surged in and sat on the floor, defying the campus police.

During a sabbatical in 1995, I began a study of Mary McLeod Bethune. I think she is a personality who is poorly understood by activ-

ists. I want to write about her extensively at some point. My studies of
Bethune and others have grounded me in the historic and often ignored strategies of black women who have struggled in ways no one
else could. Slave women historically struggled to keep their children, to
maintain relationships, and to minimize the tyranny of forced labor.
No other American group was systematically purchased as livestock
and repeatedly raped to breed humans for profit. No one's chastity,
morality, intelligence, and value has been as routinely maligned as the
black woman's. No single group of children of wealthy and poor white
men has had their paternity denied, then been as abandoned and
abused as the children of black women in America. This informs our
discourse. I think the wonderful and timely battlecry that emanated
from the Negro female club movement, "Lifting as we serve," meets today's black feminist goals as well. I always reintroduce students to the
spaces occupied and the processes and the endeavors of black women
in American life. Citing the example of the nurture that black women
gave to white children as domestics, I exhort students to be fair and
kind to each other, to always look for the class-interest elements in any
given situation or problem.

The role of women in the League was traditionalist in terms of
black patriarchal ideology and political priorities. Women were posi-
tioned and constructed to be supportive of the male leadership. My
own relationship was always centered and focused on John's goals,
needs, and wants. My own goals, desires, and aspirations beyond the
collective were not of interest. I was an important part of what in a
field struggle would have been called the home base or a semi-safe
house. That's why we had our dogs. The feds and locals were not going
to sneak up on us unannounced, and they were not going to ransack
the place when we were out. The dogs gave us a modicum of privacy.
We thought of ourselves as self-designated and self-assembled cadre
acting out what we perceived to be a historic mission derived from a
collective consciousness of our collective oppression. As in traditional
patriarchal cultures, women were seen as limited by their biology. Mo-
nogamy for females in dyads was assumed to be a value and much the
norm, if not required. But womanizing among the males was acceptable. Women who wanted to be sexually expressive or experimental
were labeled as "loose," "easy," or "whorish." Many of the male leaders
acted as if women were sexual commodities, mindless, emotionally un-

stable, or invisible. A paired woman in a cadre organization was viewed with suspicion, and if it was known she was intimate with another man in that organization, she was ostracized. The same behavior was acceptable for males. There was no lack of roles for women in the League as long as they accepted subordination and invisibility. Homophobia, of course, was rampant.

This invisibility and subordination of women was not confined to the League or to black organizations. The women's movement of the 1970s came to understand that the traditional role of women in most societies has been to service the reproductive needs of men and society. We saw that white men continued to have sexual access to black women, but few white men would commit to those women through marriage. White males who were in the movement understood they were still members of the most privileged caste in society, despite their politics. If they fathered black children, their integrity might be compromised in the eyes of whites they were trying to influence; and, if you want to be cynical, having black children would make it much harder to renounce their radicalism later in life. Outmarriage was more prevalent among black men, but that represented a different paradigm.

Perhaps a different handling of gender issues might have made the League more viable, but history was against us. Black working-class women were just emerging from 300 years of rape, exclusion, terrorism, beatings, poverty, hard work, and illiteracy. We were just stepping into the realm of employment that went beyond the traditional domestic jobs. Most of us were not going to join a cadre organization, however perfect it might be. Most wanted to have children. Most wanted faithful husbands and stable families. Prior to the Civil Rights Movement, the most successful organizing of black women had come from the endeavors of women organizing clubs that focused on issues of health, child care, stability, and spirituality. Leaders such as Ida Wells-Barnett, Mary Church Terrell, and Mary McLeod Bethune not only represented the working class, they were able to successfully organize black women on a mass basis across intraracial class lines. Their structure was not unlike that of a cadre organization, but it did not include men.

In joint sessions with the Motor City Labor League, the League of Revolutionary Black Workers agreed that in order to oppose liberal compromises and build a radical, revolutionary movement we needed to be a cadre organization built on democratic centralism. But we didn't have much of a collective clue on how to best implement that perspective. Our hearts and minds were in the right place, but we lacked the training, the money, and the will to build cadre. *We* faded away instead of the state.

My personal experiences have affected my ability to totally trust a radical political man again. Trust is a terrible thing to lose. But as comrades we trusted each other and much residual trust remains. Lately, I have begun to re-evaluate my position to see if I have healed and matured enough to trust this particular set of comrades again. I think I have. We came together to mourn as a collective when Che died, when Charles Wooten died, when Ken died, when Jim Boggs passed, and just recently when John's son Tariq died. We planned a collective memorial when Robert Williams became gravely ill. This goes all the way back to when we supported Glanton Dowdell and his family. From a familial perspective, I have remained and shall remain cadre, sister, and friend to the League alumni. The pain and hurt remain, but the compulsion for struggle is stronger. I find myself wanting to get back into the trenches and start some shit. I now seek political contacts.

The downside is that the government will spy on you. Considering the nefariousness of the intelligence community, that so many of us survived is amazing. I shall always suspect that any IRS audit has been inspired by the government, and I will never trust the FBI. I am still an activist. I know you have to go to the grassroots. I also know the terrain has changed. The grassroots will kill you now if you fuck with them. I live in the hood, the ghetto. I respect the limitations. I also move in a mostly white academic world. Sometimes I get my codes crossed. I don't talk to college boys like I do the bloods in the hood. You cannot go into the streets of Highland Park and organize without taking into account the presence of criminal elements who are very turf conscious, most likely armed, definitely dangerous, and always on the lookout for a mark.

The League had the audacity to proclaim itself a cadre formation, but the League's communication style made us appear overbearing and self-righteous. We can learn something from the conservative movement. Racist, sexist, and dangerous as it is, that movement knows how to appear reasonable. They know how to do public relations effectively. They are friendly fascists; and I believe we must learn how to be friendly revolutionaries. But that friendliness must be genuine. We must understand that our success is dependent upon collective actions and collective decisions and that means genuinely involving everyone.

Any movement that has any chance of success must deal with gender as a social construct. From the onset, women and homosexuals must be validated as normal human beings who belong in the leadership. An important step toward that understanding is to ground ourselves in historical research that includes personal familial histories. Everyone of the working-class majority has a story to tell and contemplate. Reclaiming those histories and sites of memory produces a different consciousness of what society is, what we wish to preserve, and what we must change.

Michael Hamlin

What distinguished the League of Revolutionary Black Workers was that we were able to engage masses of black workers at a time when people didn't know how to approach or mobilize them. We learned to speak plainly in a language workers understood, but we did not talk down to them. We understood you had to speak with passion. You had to feel that passion. You had to have the courage to expose yourself as a person with revolutionary ideas and be willing to face the consequences.

The League was very good at building a broad coalition of forces. In spite of the problems and some of the contradictions in our message, we went across race and class lines. We were able to organize a group of middle-class white supporters. We had a book club. We had study groups. We had units in colleges and in local high schools. We had built a complex of forces that represented our society.

Some of the best and brightest people in our community were attracted to the League. We had high-energy talent; we had brilliant legal minds; and we had some of the best in-plant organizers this city has ever produced. Courageous people, young and old, joined us. We did not reject street people who came to us, but our focus was on organizing workers and their families.

The League leaders spoke from personal experience. Some of us had been in study groups and had a theoretical understanding, but we were not driven by abstractions. I can't emphasize this enough: we personally felt the desperate times. Our personal situations were desperate. Like so many others who took different roads, we felt that it didn't matter if we lived or died. The one sure thing was that we were not going to continue living under the existing conditions any longer. When we said we were willing to die for the people, we actually meant it. That wasn't rhetoric.

I was not an exception to this rule. I came to politics out of my personal experiences of injustice and even atrocities. I was aware that this was a general experience of black people in this country and not some fault of mine or an experience limited to me. As the years have gone by, my understanding about injustice in this country and throughout the world has deepened. I can't shut out people who are suffering. I've always felt a person needs a commitment to bettering the lives of people. Without that perspective, you won't last very long. You have to hold a high moral ground.

I can't account for how others respond to injustice. I can only account for myself. The people who I'm closest to, the people who I most love and most respect, are people who have, year-in and year-out, tried to make a difference. At a certain point, you get the idea that you see farther than the average person. You want to take command of the situation. What are the best tools for that? To find and fashion and put into practice the best tools for liberation is what we tried to do in the League. And you must have some victories to sustain you for the long haul. I know that from bitter experiences. When the movement faltered, I had friends who committed suicide or went back to drugs.

People often ask me what the League's major weakness was, and they are usually surprised by my response. At first glance, it seems to go against what I've just written about needing victories. But, at a certain point, the League had dizzying success. That caused us to lose sight of the limitations and capacities of the forces we had in place. We felt the sky was the limit. I don't mean we were conceited. We simply felt that nothing could stop us. Our historic moment had arrived. The League was the kind of organization we had always needed. We felt we could now engage in any kind of struggle, at any level, in any arena.

But, at a certain point, I realized we were in deep water. We needed to shore up our forces. Our solution was to reach outside of Detroit and bring in talents that were needed and to reach out to other groups on the national scene with whom we had the most in common.

I'm still not sure if bringing in outsiders when we did was a good or a bad move. I don't mean the personalities involved but the situation and the process. We had a lot of undisciplined people in our ranks at a time when the government was coming down hard in the form of the FBI and IRS. We recruited people like Michelle Russell and Ernie Mkalimoto to help us with our publishing enterprises. We reached out to James Forman to make a connection with the black power movement. We didn't realize that Stokely Carmichael and H. "Rap" Brown, the best-known leaders of the Student Nonviolent Coordinating Committee, were going in different directions. We sought to synchronize the movement. We thought we were all saying pretty much the same thing. We had accomplished a lot in Detroit. To the degree that we could show that accomplishment to people elsewhere and have it duplicated in other cities, we would all be stronger and safer. Some local people didn't like the outsiders coming aboard. Bourgeois ideology in America is a marvel. To see it work out, even when it is working against you, is awesome.

Another of the problems that we had to contend with was morality. The kind of cadre organization we were trying to build meant appealing to young people. That brings problems that any revolutionary organization anywhere in the world must face. The recruiters must be genuine. They must be moral. You are approaching the sons and daughters, brothers and sisters, nieces and nephews of workers. You don't recruit them to exploit them. You have to be absolutely honest with them. You have to be driven. You don't necessarily have to be an intellectual, but you have to study and to learn. You have to learn quickly. Only the quick learners will survive. We had people who didn't like other people. They were very talented people, but with those social attitudes, they could not endure for the long haul.

This, too, may sound odd to some, but one of my role models for this work was my mother. In ways that became more apparent to me later in my life, my mother, my aunt, and the neighborhood women I grew up with in Mississippi and Detroit shaped me. They were damn near saints. They were all-giving. My mother was only 15 years older than I was, and I saw her year-in and year-out always deferring, always self-effacing, always taking less than she needed. She did that to help others. So, I was molded in a culture where good people helped others. I think that accounts for the tremendous attachment men of my generation have for their mothers. I don't think that's been much written about. I haven't written anything about it before. People of my background don't generally write much anyhow. But I am from that culture. Although I've come a distance from it, I honor it.

I'm encouraged by the new direction of the AFL-CIO. But if labor is going to be anything dynamic again, there has got to be a lot of internal housekeeping. I've been teaching at labor schools for 14 years now, and I've been doing crisis management and conflict resolution in workshops and in plants. I'm the person they call in when there has been some violence at a factory: a shooting, a knifing, threats that neither management nor the union can deal with. I may have seen more of this kind of strife than anyone else in the country.

Technically, as we see a move away from Taylorism, there is a big reaction in the skilled trades, where arrogance, hostility, and racism remain rampant. They still hold that old idea of American exceptionalism and don't think they have anything in common with workers in Japan or Europe and very little in common with African Americans. When I'm called in and explain what has to be done, I tell the truth, even though that may mean I won't be called again. I don't have any patience for placating people with bullshit that I know won't work. I take the same approach in my classes. One result is that my student evaluations are usually only 85 percent positive. The rest say I'm not fair or they didn't come to school to hear this anti-racist stuff. I take those comments as compliments, that I'm saying what needs to be said.

The heart of the matter is that labor cannot forge ahead until it changes its own culture. There should be a major fight in the UAW over racism, sexism, and other discrimination. You can't go ahead divided. I've been called in when there is a problem. We've analyzed the situation, come up with a plan, but then, when they get back to me, the union has backed down for fear of the response of its membership. That's just suicidal. As I've already noted, I think it's most acute in the skilled trades. They don't see any commonality with other workers. To a certain degree, they negatively influence other workers. They vote the most frequently and they vote in a decisive manner. They determine who gets elected and sets policy.

My experience is that union leaders have not taken these problems seriously. They do little to promote a class perspective. So, you can have the leadership endorse a slate of fairly decent and progressive politicians and then watch a lot of their members march off in another direction. The Reagan Democrats were wooed by old ideas of racism, that the women's movement was doing this and that to them, that immigrants were taking their jobs, that homosexuals were corrupting their children. All that anti- stuff. Labor is not going to move until its membership, as well as its better leaders, embrace movements for social change rather than opposing them.

Unions were most effective when they were social movements themselves and their leaders took chances. Then the unions became entrenched in the system, squashed internal democracy, and lost passion. You would see Walter Reuther in a civil rights march, but he wasn't leading the rank and file. He wasn't leading at all. That won't wash anymore. If unions are to survive, they must teach their members what it means to be a trade unionist. They have to show their members why it is in their own self-interest to have solidarity with other workers. Trade unions were built on slogans of class struggle, but today, they don't speak about class, they don't discuss who's in that class with you, why you need to struggle as one force.

When black workers ask me for advice, I tell them to organize a caucus and march right toward the leadership. They must hold the leadership's feet to the fire of these principles. You have lots of corruption and incompetence in the unions. There are lots of shenanigans. Black workers today are naturally concerned about discrimination, but they are also heavily focused on democracy. They want to get the entrenched bureaucrats out. This isn't about affirmative action; it's just old-fashioned democracy. If dues are a kind of union tax, then blacks largely suffer taxation without representation.

My classes attract stewards, committee members, and officers of locals, as well as the rank and file. They all tell me the same thing: I came to this class mainly to learn how to be a trade unionist, because our leadership at the local, state, or national level ain't doing anything. I emphasize to them that unions are the single best instrument for the defense of workers, black and white. I exhort black workers to take the lead, but to lead *all* the workers. They will not succeed if they get pigeonholed into dealing only with obvious racial issues. They need to take the lead on wages, quality of work, benefits, the whole package. I know very well that most members don't want to come to meetings and I know that most unions are happy with that. I know that if you go to meetings, they will use all kinds of parliamentary procedures against you. We faced all that with the League. But that's the least of the problems you will face. If you are white or black, you have to fight—or you can be sure the companies are going to downsize you, run away from your cities, strip you of benefits, and try to strip you of whatever union protection you have.

Let me tell those who are serious about change that even though it's the 1990s and the climate seems much different than the 1960s, if you intend to raise revolutionary options, probably even if you only want to do serious struggle, you are risking your life. The Board Room has not forgotten how to fight. Retaliation doesn't usually come in the public arena. They work behind the scenes. First, of course, they try to buy you off. Some of us get pretty substantial jobs. As soon as you get such a job, even though no one tells you, you understand that if you keep saying the same risky things you used to say, you might lose that job. I am personally in that position. But I think I have kept the faith. I say things at professional meetings that are very controversial. I say things people don't always want to hear. I usually end with a majority because I'm talking reality. I'm personally not comfortable working any other way.

Despite all the problems we face, I feel good about the developments I see beginning to take shape. I think my generation has given a lot. We are still in the fight, but we don't have the same energy we had when we were younger. We are looking for younger people to pick up the banner. Never before have there been so many Americans who ought to be natural political allies. This is a great time to be a revolutionary.

Further Reading

The sources listed below are not meant to serve as a formal bibliography on the complex issues raised throughout this book. They were selected for their usefulness in understanding the historical and ideological background to the League and some of its longer-term impact. The authors have deposited various documents, posters, correspondence, printed materials, and other primary sources generated by the League and organizations closed related to it in the Reuther Library of Wayne State University in Detroit, Michigan. Collections deposited by various Detroit radicals at the same library also contain materials related to the League experience.

Allen, Ernest. "Dying from the Inside: The Decline of the League of Revolutionary Black Workers," in *They Should Have Served That Cup of Coffee*, edited by Dick Cluster. Boston: South End Press, 1979. Excellent insider account of problems that led to the League's collapse.

Arnow, Harriette. *The Dollmaker*. New York: Macmillan, 1954. A novel about Appalachian workers in Detroit that was widely read in the Detroit movement.

Babson, Steve, with Ron Alpern, Dave Elsila, and John Revitte. *Working Detroit: The Making of a Union Town*. New York: Adama Books, 1984. Combines historic photographs with hard-hitting vignettes of key historic moments in a decidedly militant tone.

Boggs, James. *The American Revolution: Pages from a Negro Worker's Notebook*. New York: Monthly Review Press, 1963. Boggs had a major impact on the early political development of many of the League founders. This particular book was extremely popular in the Detroit Left and a must-read for African-American radicals.

Boyd, Herb, and Robert Allen. *Brotherman: The Odyssey of Black Men in America*. New York: One World, 1995. Anthology recording the experiences of black men in America. Boyd was a student associated with the League and Allen is the editor of *Black Scholar*.

Boyle, Kevin, and Victoria Getis. *Muddy Boots and Ragged Aprons: Images of Working-Class Detroit, 1900-1930*. Detroit: Wayne State University Press, 1997. Photographs of everyday working-class life and work. Particularly strong on the interior of homes and workplaces.

Detroit Under Stress. Detroit: From The Ground Up, 1973. A pamphlet indicting the Detroit Police Department for brutality. Dramatic graphic design by b.p. Flanigan. Available at the Reuther Library, Wayne State University.

Denby, Charles. *The Indignant Heart.* New York: New Books, 1952. Later republished in 1978 by South End Press and 1989 by Wayne State University Press. An autobiographical account by a black worker from the South of his radicalization in Detroit's factories. Originally published by the group led by Raya Dunayevskaya, it was well known in Detroit radical circles and was part of the long tradition of independent publishing by African Americans and political radicals residing in Detroit.

Flanigan, b.p., Dan Georgakas, and Lenny Rubenstein. *Three Red Stars.* New York: Smyrna Press, 1975. Only existing anthology which includes Flanigan's poetry.

Forman, James. *The Making of Black Revolutionaries.* New York: Macmillan, 1972. Reprinted by the University of Washington Press in 1997. This organizing perspective appealed to the League leaders who wanted to work with Forman.

Forman, James. *The Political Thought of James Forman.* Detroit: Black Star Publishing, 1970. Issued by the publishing arm of the League, this volume was intended to be the first of many volumes designed to offer ideological and philosophical leadership to the black liberation movement. Available at the Reuther Library, Wayne State University.

Geschwender, James. *Class, Race, and Worker Insurgency: The League of Revolutionary Black Workers.* Cambridge: Cambridge University Press, 1977. The only other full-scale account of the League. It is recounted from a perspective that puts considerably more emphasis on the impact of the Great Rebellion as a radicalizing force than do the authors of this volume.

Glaberman, Martin. *Wartime Strikes: The Struggle Against the No Strike Pledge in the UAW During World War II.* Detroit: Bewick Editions, 1980. Although written after the demise of the League, the perspective on rank-and-file militancy expressed by Glaberman was well known to a number of the League's founders.

Glaberman, Martin. Symposium on the film *Blue Collar. Cineaste* 8.4 (Summer 1978). *Blue Collar,* written and directed by Michigan-born Paul Schrader, focused on black and white auto workers at war with the company, the union, and, finally, each other.

Gould, William B. *Black Workers in White Unions.* Ithaca: Cornell University Press, 1977. Offers considerable data on job discrimination based on race, with an extensive index citing specific cases.

Haywood, Harry. *Black Bolshevik: Autobiography of an Afro-American Communist.* Chicago: Lake View Press, 1978. Haywood lived for a time in the Watson household where he reputedly began the writing of this nearly 700-page work. He was highly respected by all factions in the League leadership and widely read in the Maoist movement of the 1970s.

Hersey, John. *The Algiers Motel Incident.* New York: Knopf, 1968. This exposé of police brutality during the Great Rebellion was widely cited in political agitation regarding a police force that African Americans and others considered out of control.

James, C.L.R. *Black Jacobins: Toussaint L'Ouverture and the San Domingo Revolution*. New York: Dial Press, 1938. Reprinted by Vintage Books in 1963 and 1989. James' ideas were well known to League activists, and *Black Jacobins* was the work which struck the deepest cord.

Joyce, Frank. Symposium on the film *Blue Collar. Cineaste* 8.4 (Summer 1978). In subsequent years, Joyce became the editor of the national publication of the UAW.

Lenin, Vladimir. "Where To Begin" (1901), in *Collected Works*, volume 5. Moscow: Progress Publishers, 1973. Also available in various collections. This essay on the role a newspaper plays in a revolutionary organization was studied formally by a group of African-American Detroiters who were among the founders of the League. This is was the one classic Marxist text which had a direct influence on the genesis of the League.

Mast, Robert H., editor and compiler. *Detroit Lives*. Philadelphia, Temple University Press, 1994. Foreword by Dan Georgakas. Mast offers more than 70 oral histories of Detroit activists in a work that uses the League period as a touchstone for moving backward and forward in time. Among those interviewed are Ishmael Ahmed, Herb Boyd, Gloria House, Mike Hamlin, George Crockett, Sheila Murphy Cockrel, Pete Kelly, Ron Aronson, Jim Jacobs, Frank Joyce, Ron Glotta, Dan Georgakas, Chuck Wilbur, Marian Kramer, and General Baker.

Meier, August, and Elliott Rudwick. *Black Detroit and the Rise of the UAW*. New York: Oxford University Press, 1979. Offers background on the relationship between African Americans and organized labor from the time of the New Deal through to the post-war period. Ends with the problem of image and reality that set the stage for the 1960s.

Russell, Michelle. Symposium on the film *Blue Collar. Cineaste* 8.4 (Summer 1978). Russell was one of the out-of-towners who the League brought to Detroit to aid them in education and outreach efforts.

Schrader, Paul. Interview with Gary Crowdus and Dan Georgakas, anthologized in *The Cineaste Interviews*. Edited by Dan Georgakas and Leonard Rubenstein. Chicago: Lake View Press, 1983. Writer/director Schrader discusses the making of *Blue Collar* with references to *Finally Got the News* and other radical influences. He also speaks about the controversy which resulted in a credit for Sidney A. Glass, the son of a black auto worker in Detroit who claimed major elements of the film had been stolen from him after a story conference with Schrader.

Serrin, William. *The Company and the Union: The "Civilized Relationship" of the General Motors Corporation and the United Automobile Workers*. New York: Knopf, 1973. Serrin's critical view of the cozy relationship between the auto companies and trade unions was shared by the League.

Sinclair, John, *Guitar Army: Street Writings/Prison Writings*. New York: Douglass Book Corporation, 1972. Sinclair's vision of a White Panther Party clashed with the League's view of desirable white allies, but Sinclair was never an opponent of the League. He was easily the most visible representative of hippie-style counter-culturism at the time the League was prominent.

The Spark (editors). Symposium on the film *Blue Collar*. *Cineaste* 8.4 (Summer 1978). The group called Spark was active in the Detroit factories throughout the period discussed in this book.

Widick, B.J. *Detroit: City of Race and Class Violence*. Chicago: Quadrangle Books, 1972. Offers a reformist perspective on the issues faced by the League. Note date of publication.

Wylie-Kellarman, Jeanie. *Poletown: Community Betrayed*. Champaign-Urbana: University of Illinois Press, 1989. Strong account of the destruction of the failed attempt by radicals and reformers to save an ethnic community in Detroit and Hamtramck from being bulldozed to make room for a new General Motors factory.

Young, Coleman. *Hard Stuff*. New York: Viking, 1994. An extremely uneven autobiography that manages to describe the late 1960s without one word about the League. Young and ghostwriter Lonnie Wheeler do a better job of discussing black radicalism and the Communist Party during the New Deal and World War II eras.

Filmography

The Black Unicorn. A 54-minute color film exploring the life of Dudley Randall, Detroit's Poet Laureate. Excellent visual and oral history segments on growing up black and working class in Detroit. Available through National Black Programming Consortium. 761 Oak Street, Suite A, Columbus, Ohio, 43206. Phone: (614) 229-4399

Finally Got the News. Described at length in this book. Available from the Cinema Guild, 1697 Broadway, Suite 506, New York City, New York, 10019-5904. Phone: (800) 723-5522. Fax: (212) 246-5525

Poletown Lives! Examines the destruction of a viable, mostly Polish area of Detroit and Hamtramck that was demolished in 1981 to make room for a General Motors plant. For more than a year, a vigorous community movement, sometimes involving radicals with League connections, fought to preserve the neighborhood. Available from the Information Factory, 3512 Courville, Detroit, Michigan, 48224. Phone: (313) 885-4685.

Taking Back Detroit. Blue Ribbon Winner at 1981 American Film Festival. An account of the electoral work of Justin Ravitz, Sheila Murphy, and Ken Cockrel. Weak on analysis but admirable reportage. Available from First Run Features/Icarus Films. Phone: (800) 229-8575.

Tales From Arab Detroit. A 54-minute color film that explores cultural differences in different generations of Detroit's Arab community. Available from Olive Branch Productions, 1511 Sawtelle Boulevard, Suite 265, Los Angeles, California, 90025. Phone: (310) 842-7010

Index

251

Republic of New Africa (RNA), 10,
54-55
Resist, 142
Reuther, Walter, 2, 32, 35, 43, 99,
100, 231
Revitte, John, 235
Revolutionary Action Movement
(RAM), 14, 19, 132
Revolutionary Union, 101
Richardson, Elroy, 92, 95, 99
"Right-to-work" law, 193-95
Riley, Ivy, 223
Rivera, Diego, 111, 180
Rizzo, Frank, 173
Roche, James, 2, 23
Rochester Street Massacre, 169-70,
171, 180
Rogers, William, 197
Roselyn, 108
Ross, Diana, 108, 200
Ross, Doc, 108
Rothschild, Emma, 105
Rubenstein, Leonard, 236, 237
Rubin, Jerry, 125
Rudwick, Elliott, 237
RUMs (Revolutionary Union Move-
ments), 41, 69-72, 76, 82, 102,
131, 132-33, 144; arts and, 109;
Communist League and, 148; in
the South, 140. *See also specific
RUMs*
Russell, Jack, 127
Russell, Michelle (Michele Gibbs),
127, 142, 145, 229, 237

S

Safety and health, 11, 26, 27, 98-99,
116, 190-93, 196; violations of, 85-
88, 92, 94. *See also* Working condi-
tions
Salt of the Earth, 123
Sams, George, 166
Sanchez, Sonia, 111
Sanders, Sam, 223

Saroyan, William, 110
Schrader, Paul, 237
Scott, Jerome, 191, 192
Scott, John, 93
Scott–Ashlock Incident, 93, 94, 95
SDS (Students for a Democratic Soci-
ety), 32, 44, 82, 125, 128, 146
Seale, Bobby, 166
Senak, David, 151
Seniority, 196
Serrin, William, 23, 25-26, 33, 237
Shachtman, Max, 178
Sheffield, Horace, 34
Sheik, The, 113
Sherman, Jannette, 27, 88
Shorter, Isaac, 189-90, 192
Sims, Jordan, 36, 89, 93, 101, 147,
192; Eldon Safety Committee and,
94, 99; ELRUM and, 95, 97, 102,
103; Taylor and, 91, 92
Sinclair, John, 75, 129, 178, 237
Sirhan, Sirhan, 64
Sitdown '37, 110
Slavery, 152-53
Smith Act, 57
SNCC (Student Nonviolent Coordi-
nating Committee), 14, 16, 17, 32,
186, 229; Forman and, 79, 136,
137
Social Security, 207-8
Socialism, 49-50, 78, 110, 185, 208,
217; Baker and, 21; BWC and,
132; Murphy and, 213
Socialist Workers Party, 16, 101, 185
Solidarity, 66
Solidarity Committee (Sweden), 121
Solidarity House, 11, 33, 39, 101, 194
Something Else Yearbook 1974, 60
Sostre, Martin, 121
South End, 41, 43, 44-54, 56-62, 109,
157, 165, 219
South End Revolutionary Union Move-
ment, 61-62
Southfield Sun, 48
Spark, 30-31, 238

About Haymarket Books

Haymarket Books is a nonprofit, progressive book distributor and publisher, a project of the Center for Economic Research and Social Change. We believe that activists need to take ideas, history, and politics into the many struggles for social justice today. Learning the lessons of past victories, as well as defeats, can arm a new generation of fighters for a better world. As Karl Marx said, "The philosophers have merely interpreted the world; the point, however, is to change it."

We take inspiration and courage from our namesakes, the Haymarket Martyrs, who gave their lives fighting for a better world. Their 1886 struggle for the eight-hour day reminds workers around the world that ordinary people can organize and struggle for their own liberation.

For more information and to shop our complete catalog of titles, visit us online at www.haymarketbooks.org.

Also from Haymarket Books

Black Liberation and Socialism
Ahmed Shawki

Autoworkers Under the Gun
A Shop-Floor View of the End of the American Dream
Gregg Shotwell

Boycott, Divestment, Sanctions
The Global Struggle for Palestinian Rights
Omar Barghouti

The Democrats
A Critical History (updated edition)
Lance Selfa

The Labor Wars
From the Molly Maguires to the Sit Downs
Sidney Lens

My People Are Rising
Memoir of a Black Panther Party Captain
Aaron Dixon

Printed in the USA
CPSIA information can be obtained
at www.ICGtesting.com
JSHW022009081023
49669JS00006B/7